The Future

of

Family Care

for

Older People

Edited by
Isobel Allen
and
Elizabeth Perkins

London : HMSO

CONTENTS

LIST OF TABLES & FIGURES

THE CONTRIBUTORS

Isobel Allen
Senior Fellow, Head of Social Care and Health Studies, Policy Studies Institute

Professor Sally Baldwin
Social Policy Research Unit, University of York

Lynda Clarke
Lecturer in Demography, Centre for Population Studies

Professor Janet Finch
Pro-Vice Chancellor and Department of Applied Social Science, Lancaster University

Reuben Ford
Research Fellow, Policy Studies Institute

Dulcie Groves
Honorary Lecturer, Department of Social Policy, University of Lancaster

Emily Grundy
Reader in Social Gerontology, Age Concern Institute of Gerontology, King's College, London

Professor Chris Hamnett
Department of Human Geography, King's College, London

Professor Heather Joshi
Social Statistics Research Unit, City University

Elizabeth Perkins
Research Fellow, Policy Studies Institute

Professor Anthea Tinker
Director of Age Concern Institute of Gerontology, King's College, London

Professor Alan Walker
Department of Sociological Studies, University of Sheffield

Professor Anthony Warnes
Department of Health Care for Elderly People, University of Sheffield

ACKNOWLEDGEMENTS

The writing of this book was funded by the Department of Health. The editors are grateful to the members of staff at the Department of Health and Department of Social Security who participated in the advisory group and provided information and comments at various stages in the preparation of this volume.

Karin Erskine of Policy Studies Institute prepared the text for desktop publishing and Rita Goldberg assisted in the standardisation of the references.

INTRODUCTION
ISOBEL ALLEN AND
ELIZABETH PERKINS

This is a book about the family care of older people. It reviews family change from a variety of different perspectives and examines the future of family care for older people in the context of a changing population structure. Much social policy is based on the assumption that the family is available and willing to provide care for its members at different stages of their lives. This book poses questions about the implications of an increase in demand for care from a group deemed to have substantial support needs when the demand is coupled with major changes in the pattern of family organisation. The book challenges some of the assumptions about the ability of younger generations to meet the needs of older people. It points to the need for new policy solutions to support the family in its caring role.

The authors of the chapters in this book were asked to review trends in areas in which they had particular expertise, and to draw upon the evidence to speculate about its implications for the future supply of family care. The point of departure was to examine and review what was known about the social and economic factors affecting the supply of family care for older people, but it was obviously necessary to place this in the context of the future demand for care by older people from whichever source it was available.

The evidence reviewed is subject to inaccuracies and contradictory interpretations. The further ahead forecasts are made, the greater the room for inaccuracy. The authors of the chapters mostly found it difficult to take advantage of the invitation to speculate about the future, and those who rose to the challenge often found themselves hedging their predictions with qualifications and provisos. We asked them to draw out the policy implications of the trends they described but, again, most of the authors were reluctant to go too far. Perhaps futurology is best left to the futurologists most of whose predictions are forgotten within a very short time.

The main value of this book lies in its detailed and comprehensive compilation of so much evidence on family care for older people and its analysis of what is known about past, present and future trends. Each chapter provides an extensive set of references, and in many cases presents new material not previously published.

The first two chapters in the book review the demographic changes as they affect the current and future generations of elderly people. In Chapter 1, Emily Grundy considers changes in the size and demographic composition of the current elderly population and the reasons for those changes. She then examines those changes which are relevant to the supply of care, such as living arrangements and availability of children, and finally reviews the evidence on the health status and patterns of service use of elderly people.

In Chapter 2, Lynda Clarke examines some of the implications of these demographic changes for future generations of older people and in particular the impact of an increase in the number of three or four generation families. She assesses the effect of changing patterns of marriage, divorce, cohabitation and childbearing on an ageing population.

In Chapter 3, Janet Finch examines the basis for family caring. She explores the meaning of concepts like 'responsibility' and 'obligation', as they are put into practice within contemporary families. She suggests that a 'commitments' model of family responsibilities provides a way of understanding how people negotiate a caring relationship with each other.

Chapter 4, by Tony Warnes and Reuben Ford, begins with a brief account of migration in later life. It reviews differential migration by age, marital status, household type, housing tenure and recent personal events (notably widowhood), and the relative propensities to make moves of different types and over various distances, for example, from large cities to remote rural areas or from suburb to suburb. They examine the relationship between a person's migration history and their current residential situation, including the distribution and proximity of family members and social networks and the nature of visiting and interactions.

In Chapter 5, Heather Joshi explores the significance of paid work and the potential conflict between work and caring for family members. She considers the structure and trends in the labour market as a whole as a background to the specific questions of whether caring and paid work conflict or combine. She highlights the continuing high degree of occupational segregation of paid work, the reliance of wives on their husbands' pensions in old age and the consequences for wives who divorce. This theme is picked up later by Dulcie Groves.

In Chapter 6, Sally Baldwin assesses whether the supply of family care for older people will match the need for it over the next twenty years and whether the financial penalties of caring will act as a disincentive to begin, or continue, caring for an older relative. She poses a set of questions about the influences on decisions about caregiving, and makes proposals for how public policy should sustain the supply of family caregivers.

In Chapter 7, Dulcie Groves examines the extent to which older people have the resources to pay for or contribute towards their care needs. She highlights the fact that most pensioners are far from affluent, although a substantial and increasing number own their own homes. Many pensioners are income poor and among the poorest are very elderly non-married women, who form a large majority among the age group aged 75 or more who are most at risk of physical and/or mental disabilities.

Chapter 8, by Chris Hamnett, takes up the theme of housing as a potential source of income in old age. The rise of home ownership has both widened the distribution of wealth and fostered the view that housing inheritance is of growing importance. Little attention has been paid to the role of equity extraction from the owner occupied housing market before death and its impact both on housing inheritance and the ability of older people to pay for care.

The theme of housing is continued in Chapter 9, in which Anthea Tinker examines the role that housing plays in the lives of older people, with specific reference to family links and the provision of family care. She looks in detail at technological advance in helping to maintain older people in their own homes.

In Chapter 10, Alan Walker looks at the possible impact of the changes inherent in a 'mixed economy of care' on the provision of support to older people by their families. This chapter examines the changing relationships between families and health and personal social services. He argues that policy is important in determining the context in which family care takes place and assesses the assumptions made, implicitly or explicitly, about the availability and supply of such care. He concludes by discussing the changes necessary over the next decade in order to support family care more effectively by ensuring that care is shared between the family and other providers.

In the final chapter, the editors of this review, Isobel Allen and Elizabeth Perkins, bring together the main findings of the preceding chapters and draw together some of the possible consequences of the trends identified by the authors.

Chapter 1
DEMOGRAPHIC INFLUENCES ON THE FUTURE OF FAMILY CARE

EMILY GRUNDY

Introduction

In 1901 those aged 65 or over comprised fewer than five per cent of the population of England and Wales, and those aged 85 or more only 0.2 per cent. The most recent official projections (OPCS, 1993) suggest that by 2001, 16 per cent of the total population will be aged 65 or more and 2 per cent will be aged at least 85. Increases in the absolute number of elderly people over the course of the century are even more striking. In 2001 it is expected that the size of the elderly (65+) population will be six times greater than in 1901, while the numbers aged 85 and over will have increased twenty-five fold. This substantial increase in the relative and absolute size of a population group deemed to have substantial support needs, coupled with recent changes in patterns of family organisation, has provoked serious concern about the ability of younger generations to meet the needs of the old. In this chapter we are concerned with documenting trends relevant to both sides of this equation. Firstly, we consider changes in the size and demographic composition of the elderly population and the reasons for those changes; secondly, we examine changes relevant to the supply of care, such as living arrangements and availability of children; and thirdly, we review evidence on the health status and service use patterns of elderly people, and possible changes in both. In the final sections we try to draw some conclusions relevant to both the short and longer term future; these need to be considered in conjunction with the findings presented elsewhere in this volume.

Trends in the number of elderly people

The absolute number of elderly people today is a function of the numbers born 65 years or more earlier and their subsequent survival (with an addition or subtraction to allow for net migration). Past fluctuations in the numbers of births in England and Wales have been considerable. In the first decade of this century they exceeded 900,000 per year compared with some 500,000 a year in the period 1841–45, 600,000 a year in the 1930s and eight and a half thousand a year in the early 1960s (OPCS, 1989a). These past fluctuations in births are reflected in fluctuations in the number of people in elderly age groups. During the 1990s the numbers of 'young' elderly people are expected to decline slightly, reflecting the passage to old age of the small cohorts born in the late 1920s and 1930s. This will be followed by renewed increase when the larger cohorts born during the post-war 'baby boom' attain the age of 65. As the number of births depends on the number of women of childbearing age, as well as on the rate of fertility, these fluctuations also have 'echo' effects evident in succeeding generations.

1

The chances of survival to old age have also changed dramatically. The cohort born in 1986–1900 was the first in which half reached the age of 65; current mortality rates (if they remain unchanged) imply survival to age 65 for three quarters of male and 86 per cent of female infants born in the late 1980s (OPCS, 1989b). Survival beyond the age of 65 to extreme old age has also become more usual. Between 1970–72 and 1985–87 the probability of a 65 year old woman reaching the age of 85 increased from 0.33 to 0.45 and female expectation of life at age 75 increased from 9.5 to 10.6 years (OPCS, 1979; OPCS, 1989b). Gonnot (1992) has estimated that between 1950 and 1980 the number of elderly women aged 80–84 increased by some 9 per cent and that of males of the same age by 5 per cent per decade as a result of changes in mortality.

These changes in numbers of births and in survival to (and beyond) the age of 65, account for the substantial increase in the absolute numbers of elderly people shown in Table 1 and illustrated further in Table 2. In Table 2, which includes projections of the size of the elderly population to 2026, the numbers in elderly age groups, and in the total population, are shown as a percentage of numbers in 1961. In the past three decades (1961–1991) the total population of England and Wales has increased by 10 per cent, the numbers of elderly people aged 65 and over have grown by some 50 per cent, while the size of the very old group aged 85 or more was in 1991 over two and a half times as great as in 1961. By 2026 projections suggest that those aged 65 and over will be twice as numerous as in 1961, while the size of the population aged 85 and over will have increased by more than five-fold.

Population projections are of course subject to error and the possibility of greater, or lesser, changes in the size of elderly age groups should be recognized. Rates of mortality are much higher at older ages, so under or over-estimating future mortality has a much greater effect on projections of the elderly population than on projections of younger age groups (Murphy, 1990). Mortality forecasts in the past have consistently underestimated declines in death rates at older ages (Murphy, 1990). The size of today's (1991) population aged 85 and over is 30 per cent greater than projected in 1976 (OPCS, 1976; OPCS, 1993) and the most recent projection of the population aged 75 and over in 2029 is 18 per cent higher than suggested in 1989-based projections (OPCS, 1991). This degree of uncertainty clearly makes planning difficult and indicates the need for policies which are flexible.

Trends in the relative size of the elderly population

These changes in the absolute number of elderly people, and particularly the increase in the number of very old, are clearly important in terms of planning services, especially health services. However, for many purposes it is the relative size (per cent of total population) of the elderly population which is most important as this will influence the priority attached to elderly people by policy makers and the capacity of a population to provide for the needs of its older members.

As shown in Table 1, the relative size of the elderly population has increased more than three-fold since the start of this century, while the past three decades alone have seen the proportion of very old people aged 85 and over more than double.

TABLE 1
The population aged 65 and over, England and Wales, 1901–2026

Year	Population ('000s) aged:			% of total population aged:		
	65–74	75–84	85+	65+	75+	85+
1901	992	340	44	4.7	1.3	0.2
1921	1645	573	76	6.1	1.7	0.2
1941	2751	981	131	10.0	2.9	0.3
1961	3526	1678	309	11.9	4.3	0.7
1981	4619	2389	541	15.2	5.9	1.1
1991	4515	2787	812	15.9	7.1	1.6
2001	4311	2922	1087	15.7	7.6	2.1
2011	4814	2935	1304	16.7	7.8	2.4
2021	5704	3494	1459	19.3	9.0	2.6
[2026	5759	4090	1627	20.7	10.3	2.9]

Sources: Census estimates; OPCS population estimates and 1991-based population projections.

TABLE 2
Changes in the numbers in elderly age groups, and in the total population, England and Wales 1961–2026 (1961 = 100)

Year	Total population	Population aged:			
		65–74	75–84	85+	65+
1961 No. ('000s)	46196	3525	1678	310	5513
=	100	100	100	100	100
1971	106	119	113	139	118
1981	107	131	142	175	137
1991	110	128	166	262	147
2001	114	123	174	351	151
2011	118	137	175	421	164
2021	119	162	208	471	193
2026	120	163	244	525	208

Sources: Derived from OPCS population estimates and 1991-based projections.

Causes of population ageing

The demographic determinants of population age structure are long-term trends in fertility, mortality and migration, and of these fertility is potentially of by far the greatest importance. (This is because every birth involves an addition both to the current generation of children and, assuming survival to reproduction, an augmentation in the size of succeeding generations.) As has repeatedly been demonstrated, the impetus for population ageing (a shift from a relatively young to an older age structure) is a transition from relatively high to low fertility rates (Notestein, 1954; Carrier, 1962). In England and Wales this transition was set in motion in the last quarter of the nineteenth century. The increasing spread of deliberate birth control in this period resulted in the Total Period Fertility Rate (TPFR) falling from 4.8 in 1871–75 to 3.5 in 1901–05 (OPCS, 1989a). There have been substantial fluctuations since then but, as the term transition denotes, no return to the 19th century or pre-industrial levels. (At the height of the post-war baby boom in 1964 the TPFR reached 2.9; since 1973 fertility rates have been below the level required for the long-term replacement of the population.)

The historical shift from relatively high to low mortality, also initiated towards the end of the last century, far from contributing to population ageing, in fact served to partially offset it. This was because the young, particularly infants and children, benefited more than the old from this decline in death rates. Declines in mortality among those with reproductive potentially naturally contribute to future increases in births, so falling mortality at young ages contributes both directly and indirectly to population rejuvenation.

While the historical mortality transition was not the initiator of what may be termed primary population ageing, more recent changes in mortality patterns have had a major influence on further population ageing, particularly the ageing of the elderly population itself. In England and Wales today fertility and mortality are both low, survival to the end of the reproductive span is near universal and the bulk of deaths occur after the age of 65. In these circumstances changes in mortality at older ages result in further population ageing; such changes have been shown to be the most important cause of population ageing in a number of developed countries with already old age structures (Preston, Hines & Eggers, 1989). Changes and differentials in death rates at old ages now also make an increasingly important contribution to overall mortality patterns. Half of the increase of 2.55 years in female expectation of life at birth between 1970–72 and 1985–87 was due to falls in death rates among those aged 75 and over.

Projections of the relative size of the elderly population involve making assumptions about future births, as well as deaths, and become increasingly uncertain the further into the future they are carried. The most recent (1991-based) projections assume a completed family size of 1.9 for women born in 1965 or later (this is in line with what is known about the fertility to date of women born in the 1960s and contrasts with the 1989-based projections which assumed a slight increase in fertility.) As Table 1 shows, these 1991-based projections indicate stability in the relative size of the whole elderly population in the current decade, followed by further growth as the large post-war birth cohorts reach the age of 65. By 2026 those over 75 are projected to account for some 10 per cent, and those over 85 for some 3 per cent, of the total population.

Demographic characteristics of the elderly population

Currently a major policy issue is the ageing of the elderly population itself; in 1961 those over 75 accounted for 36 per cent (and those over 85 for 6 per cent) of the whole elderly population, compared with 44 per cent and 10 per cent respectively in 1991. In the early decades of the twenty-first century the numbers of young (65–74) elderly people will increase, largely offsetting continued growth in the number of older old; even so, by 2026 those aged 85 or over are projected to account for 14 per cent of the total elderly population.

Apart from its changing age structure, one of the most distinctive demographic features of the elderly population is the preponderance of women. As Table 3 shows, women comprise 60 per cent of the whole elderly population, and 74 per cent of those aged 85 and over. Falls in mortality during the twentieth century benefited women more than men, leading to a widening of the sex differential in death rates. This pattern is a general feature observed in all populations experiencing the transition from relatively high to low mortality (Preston, 1976) and the reasons for it are still not fully understood. Waldron (1985), in a review, has pointed to declines in causes of death specifically or primarily affecting women (such as maternal mortality and respiratory tuber-culosis), gender differences in health-related behaviour and exposure to occu-pational hazards, and possibly the greater susceptibility of men to stresses associated with socio-economic change. Only recently in England and Wales, and some other developed countries, are there indications that this differential may be narrowing again (UN, 1988). This is illustrated in Table 4 which shows expectations of life at birth and at age 65 1901–10 to 1985–87. Specific historical events and circumstances, such as war-related mortality and excess male emigration earlier in this century, have also had a continuing impact on the balance of the sexes of the generations affected.

As a result of these changes in sex differentials in death rates and the effect of historical events, the elderly population has, until recently, become more female dominated, while the reverse is the case in young adulthood. Table 5 shows that between 1921 and 1981 the ratio of women to men in the 80–84 year old age group increased considerably. The past decade saw a reduction in this ratio and projections into the next decade suggest a considerable reversal of the twentieth century trend. At ages 20–24, by contrast, women now slightly outnumber men, while the reverse was true earlier in the century. This gender imbalance early in the life of those cohorts who now comprise the very old female population partly accounts for the higher proportion of very old women, compared with very old men, who have never married.

Marital status

The marital status composition of the elderly population is extremely important in the context of family support for older people. The currently married have a

TABLE 3

Percentage of women in the elderly population by age group, England and Wales 1991

Age	% Female
65–69	54
70–74	57
75–79	61
80–84	66
85+	74
65+	60

Source: OPCS (1993).

TABLE 4

Expectation of life at birth and at age 65 among men and women, England and Wales, 1901–10 to 1988–90

Period	Expectation of Life (years)					
	Male	At birth Female	Difference	Male	At age 65 Female	Difference
1901–10	48.5	52.4	3.9	10.8	12.0	1.2
1930–32	58.7	62.9	4.2	11.3	13.1	1.8
1960–62	68.1	74.0	5.9	12.0	15.3	3.3
1970–72	69.0	75.3	6.3	12.2	16.1	3.9
1983–85	71.8	77.7	5.9	13.4	17.5	4.1
1988–90	73.0	78.5	5.5	14.0	17.8	3.8

Sources: OPCS data reported in Grundy (1991); OPCS (1992).

TABLE 5

Number of females per 100 males in age groups 20–24 and 80–84, England and Wales, 1921–2021

Year	Age group	
	20–24	80–84
1921	118	169
1951	105	170
1981	97	231
1991	96	203
2001	96	176
2011	95	153
2021	95	135

Sources: Census data and OPCS population estimates reported in Coleman and Salt (1992); OPCS (1993).

TABLE 6

Projected distribution (%) of the elderly (65+) population by marital status, England and Wales, 1985–2000

Marital Status	Males 1985	1990	2000	Females 1985	1990	2000
Single	7	8	8	11	9	7
Married	73	72	69	37	38	39
Widowed	18	18	18	50	50	49
Divorced	2	3	5	3	3	6
ALL	100	100	100	100	100	100

Source: Haskey (1988).

spouse available as a potential source of practical help and emotional support, while the never married (among current generations of elderly people) are very unlikely to have the potential support of children. Marital status has a major effect on living arrangements which in turn influence service use (OPCS, 1989c) and, particularly among men, reported well-being and other indicators of health (Huppert *et al.*, 1987).

The major feature of the marital status of older age groups is the preponderance of widows; a reflection of sex differences in mortality and the common pattern of women marrying men older than themselves. In 1981 widows comprised half the female population at the age of 75 and increasing proportions in older age groups. Widowers, by contrast, formed a minority of the male population until the age of 87 (Grundy, 1989). However, as we have seen, sex differentials in mortality show signs of narrowing and this trend is projected to continue. As a result, despite the ageing of the elderly population, projections of the population by marital status (Table 6) show no increase in the prevalence of widowhood (or widowerhood) between 1985 and 2000.

Another positive feature, in terms of potential family support, of the trends shown in Table 6, is the decline in the proportion of never married women. This is a reflection of changes in marriage behaviour in the middle decades of the twentieth century which involved, among other things, a decline in the extent of permanent celibacy. Against this must be set the increase in the proportions of divorced elderly people projected to reach 5 per cent by the year 2000. In the longer term (as discussed in Chapter Two) divorce will have a greater direct impact on the elderly population. In the short-term, however, the most important effect of trends in divorce on the elderly population in England and Wales will probably be an indirect one: the largely unknown effects of divorce and remarriage among younger age groups on inter-generational relationships.

Availability of children

In terms of availability of children, the short-term future also appears encouraging. The cohorts born in the early decades of this century, as well as including relatively high proportions of never married women, also had higher rates of childless marriage than the later cohorts who married in the 1940s and early

TABLE 7

Distribution (%) of elderly people (65+) by number of surviving children, 1962, 1977 and 1986

Number of sur-viving children	Britain 1962	Four urban areas 1977	Britain 1986
0	23	30	17
1	25	32	27
2	26	34	35
3	18	18	21
4+	30	16	17
N	2500	1646	214

Sources:
1962: Shanas *et al.* (1968) 1977; Abrams (1978).
1986: British Social Attitudes Survey data analysed by Jarvis (1993)

1950s. Data from three surveys undertaken in 1962, 1977 and 1986 (Table 7) show a decrease in the proportion of childless elderly people, similar trends have been documented in the United States (Crimmins & Ingegneri, 1990). Timaeus (1986) has estimated that while 26 per cent of women who attained the age of 60 in 1971–76 would have no surviving children at the age of 85, among women reaching 60 during the period 1991–96 the proportion childless at age 85 would be only 16 per cent.

While the proportion with large families also decreased between 1962 and 1986, evidence at least on the effect of availability of children on living arrangements, suggests that the difference between having, for example, 4 as opposed to 3 or 2 children, is minimal compared with the difference between no and 1 or 2 children (Grundy, 1992a).

These trends suggest that in terms of demographic supply of potential close family supporters (spouses and children) the elderly population now and in the next decade will have some advantages over preceding cohorts. Against this must be set the longer term implications of the recent changes in marriage and family formation documented in Chapter Two. Furthermore, other changes may influence the willingness (and ability) of younger generations to provide (or of old generations to receive) family care. Changes in the living arrangements of elderly people, for example, have been substantial. These are considered in the following section.

Living arrangements of elderly people

In England and Wales marriage has been associated with the establishment of a new household since at least pre-industrial times (Smith, 1981). At times some 'doubling up' of newly married couples with their parents has been a common response to housing shortages (Holmans, 1981) but co-residence between elderly married couples and their married children seems always to have been unusual (Wall, 1990). What has changed, however, is the extent of co-residence between, for example, elderly widows and married children and elderly married

TABLE 8
Elderly people living alone (%), Britain, 1851–1985

Year	% living alone		
	Male	Female	Total
1851	5	9	7
1945	6	16	12
1962	11	30	22
1985	20	48	36

Sources: Wall, 1990; Shanas *et al*, 1968; General Household Survey (OPCS, 1989c)

TABLE 9
Elderly people living alone and living with a spouse (%), by age and sex, Britain, 1985

Age	% living alone		% living with spouse	
	Male	Female	Male	Female
65–69	13	33	65	50
70–74	21	45	65	39
75–79	21	55	65	28
80–84	34	62	50	13
85+	37	61	38	8

Source: General Household Survey, OPCS (1989c)

couples and unmarried adult offspring. Much of this change has occurred in the recent, rather than the more distant, past (Wall, 1984). In 1962, for example, 42 per cent of elderly people lived with a child compared with 14 per cent in 1986 (Shanas *et al.*, 1968; Jarvis, 1993). This change forms part of a broader post war shift towards smaller, simpler households which has been observed in much of the western world (Kobrin, 1976; Pampel, 1983; Keilman, 1987). As Table 8 shows, the proportion of elderly people living alone in Britain has increased considerably since the Second World War and now half of all elderly women live alone.

Marital status is obviously an important determinant of living arrangements in later life and gender and age differences in the extent of widow(er)hood largely account for the marked age and gender differences in the extent of solitary living shown in Table 9.

Living arrangements are important because they are associated with differentials in the use of services, including institutional care. Gender differences in marital status and living arrangements largely account for the higher use made by women of institutional care (Grundy, 1992b). The OPCS disability surveys (Martin *et al.*, 1988) showed that 45 per cent of women aged 75 or more in the most seriously disabled groups were living in institutions, compared with only 30 per cent of men of the same age and level of disability.

While this trend towards greater residential independence among elderly people has implications for the providers and planners of services, it cannot be taken to indicate an abandonment of elderly people by their younger relatives.

All the available evidence suggests that elderly people in Britain and other Western countries prefer to maintain their own households wherever possible (Louis Harris, 1982; Thompson and West, 1984) and that increases in residential independence largely reflect increases in incomes which have enabled more to exercise this preference (Michael et al., 1980; Ermisch, 1985). Moreover, among the very old, co-residence with younger relatives is still far from unusual. in 1981 over a fifth of women aged 85 or over lived with friends or relatives other than a spouse (Grundy, 1987). Among elderly people living in independent households in 1971, the proportion who ten years later were living with relatives or friends was slightly higher than the proportion who had moved to institutions (Grundy, 1993). Nor should it be assumed that trends such as the increases in divorce or in the proportion of married women in employment will necessarily result in a further decrease in inter-generational co-residence. Analyses of data from the OPCS Longitudinal Study (Grundy and Harrop, 1992) showed that rates of co-residence between adult children and their elderly parents were higher among the divorced than the currently married and varied little according to the employment status of married women. Analyses of data on carers from the 1985 General Household Survey reported in the same study showed that among men the provision of care was significantly higher among the divorced than the married and provided little evidence to support the hypothesis that women working outside the home are less likely to provide care to an elderly parent.

Health status of the elderly population

Health status is obviously a very major influence on the need for care from relatives or formal agencies and this component in the support equation merits consideration.

As noted in earlier sections of this paper, rates of mortality at older ages have fallen (and expectation of life at age 65 risen) in recent decades. This might suggest that the health status of the elderly population is improving. However, the use of mortality as an indicator of health status in old age has been challenged (many of the most common diseases of later life, such as arthritis, are not directly life threatening) and the implications of recent mortality changes remain controversial.

Implications for demand in health services

All indicators of health, particularly those based on measures of functional ability or disability, show marked relationships with age. The recent OPCS disability surveys (which included the institutional population), reported a prevalence of the most serious levels of disability of 133 per 1,000 among those aged 80 and over compared with 3 per 1,000 among adults aged under 50 (Martin et al., 1988). Use of health services is of course also strongly age-related. Government estimates of per capita public health and personal social service expenditure in 1989/90 show costs for those over 85 to be 15 times as great as expenditure on those aged 15–64, and four and a half times as great as expenditure on 65–74 year olds (Robins and Wittenberg, 1992).

Future trends in morbidity

The most optimistic view of future morbidity trends is that advanced by Fries (1980) and rests on the concept of a fixed biological limit to the human life span. The chief difference between Fries and earlier proponents of this view lies in the precise predictions Fries made about mortality change and the inference drawn about mortality. Fries argued that, in the not too distant future, changes in health-related behaviour would mean that the onset of morbidity was delayed while age of death would remain the same, resulting in a compression of morbidity. As a result, the majority would enjoy a vigorous life until about the age of 85 and then die after a very short period of ill health. Fries's argument has been challenged on methodological and theoretical grounds (Bromley *et al.* 1982; Schneider & Brody, 1983; Grundy, 1984), and rests on a number of heroic assumptions (e.g. that death rates at older ages were not changing). Even so, his hypothesis has attracted considerable attention and has been useful in promoting research in this area. Important too in the context of health care planning for the elderly is the recognition that it is not just trends in health status at a given chronological age which are important, but also trends in the duration of disability before death and the balance between 'healthy' and 'unhealthy' life expectancy.

Other researchers, notably Gruenberg (1977) and Kramer (1980), have also suggested that the relationship between mortality and morbidity is changing, but their view of the future is rather more pessimistic. Gruenberg, for example, has argued that reductions in mortality at older ages have been achieved by medical interventions that postpone the lethal sequelae of chronic diseases, rather than by reducing the incidence or rate of progression of degenerative conditions. There is some evidence to support this view, certainly the survival of old people with dementia seems to have increased (Blessed & Wilson 1982). Observed increases in age-specific incidence rates of fractured neck of femur have also been associated with decreases in mortality, suggesting that the increased survival of frailer groups may be a contributing factor (although higher activity levels may also be partly responsible) (Finsen 1988). Riley (1990), in a review based on data from Britain, the United States, Japan and Hungary, concluded that relationships between morbidity and mortality might now be negative, rather than positive.

A third interpretation of current trends, sometimes termed the 'dynamic equilibrium' approach, has been advanced by Manton (1982). His analyses of US multi-cause coded death registration data led him to conclude that the prevalence of chronic conditions was increasing, but not because of the postponement of lethal sequelae. He suggested that the effect of medical interventions and other health-related changes had been to slow down the rate of progression of certain degenerative diseases. In short, elderly people might be suffering health impairments for longer than in the past, but the consequent disability was less serious.

Regrettably no consensus on these divergent views of actual and possible changes in 'real' health status exists, partly because of substantial data and interpretation problems. One important factor to take account of, for example, is the different health legacy of different cohorts. The fact that the very old represent a selected group of survivors further complicates understanding of the relationship between ageing and health.

However, evidence from a number of studies on trends in various indicators of health does not at first sight appear encouraging. Studies based on data from Britain, North America, France and the Netherlands point to increases in reported morbidity; Sweden seems exceptional in showing the opposite trend. Calculations of changes in 'active' and 'disabled' life expectancy based on these data tend to show that gains in disabled life have been greatest. However, most of these studies employ data on self-reported health problems, long-standing illnesses and restricted activity gathered in household surveys. Answers to these types of questions have been shown to vary considerably between groups and over time, and it may well be that changes in health expectations and illness awareness (partly resulting from earlier diagnosis), rather than any change in 'real' health status may account for these findings. In the United States, for example, self-reports show enormous increases in the prevalence of hypertension in elderly age groups not supported by evidence from studies based on physical measurements (Grundy, 1992c). However, as health expectations influence health service use, even this explanation suggests increased demand for health care.

Clearly research on the measurement of health and of trends in health status is needed. Until we have a better understanding of these trends, it would seem unwise to assume that improvements in the health status of the elderly population are likely to result in a reduced need for family support in the immediate future.

Conclusion

The elderly population of England and Wales is currently ageing and the substantial increase projected in both the absolute and relative size of the very old group has major implications for the purchasers and providers of health and other services. However, in terms of potential family support for elderly people short-term future prospects are relatively favourable. Slightly fewer will be never-married or childless and the ratio of later middle aged to the 75 and over age group will increase slightly. The recent narrowing of sex differentials in mortality also suggests a later average age of widowhood. The proportion of elderly people who are divorced is still low and as yet the evidence does not support some of the more alarmist predictions about the effects of divorce and women's employment in younger generations on family support for older people. However, complacency is not an appropriate response to the situation. Long-term prospects appear much more uncertain. In the twenty-first century the relative size of the elderly population will increase further, and as discussed in Chapter two, recent changes in patterns of marriage and family formation suggest some return to higher rates of childlessness and higher proportions of either never or not currently married elderly people. Moreover the possibility of attitudinal changes in both willingness to provide and willingness to receive family support should not be overlooked. Data from Norway show a substantial shift between 1967 and 1989 in elderly people's preference for public rather than family assistance (Daatland, 1990). All this suggests that the next decade should be viewed as a window of opportunity for strengthening appropriate services, both for elderly people and their family supporters.

References

Abrams, M. (1978) *Beyond three score years and ten: a first report on a survey of the elderly*. Age Concern England, Mitcham.

Benjamin, B. and Overton, E. (1981) 'Prospects for mortality decline in England and Wales'. *Population Trends* 23: 22–28.

Blessed, G. and Wilson, I. (1982) 'The contemporary natural history of mental disorder in old age'. *British Journal of Psychiatry* 141: 59–67.

Bromley, D., Isaacs, A. and Bytheway, B. (1982) Review symposium, ageing and the rectangular curve. *Ageing and Society* 2: 383–392.

Carrier, N. (1962) 'Demographic aspects of the aging of the population', in Welford, A. T. *et al* (eds) *Society, problems and methods of study*. Routledge and Kegan Paul, London.

Coleman, D. and Salt, J. (1992) *The British population*. Oxford University Press, Oxford.

Crimmins, E., Saito, Y. and Ingegneri, I. (1989) 'Changes in life expectancy and disability-free life expectancy in the United States'. *Population and Development Review* 15, 2: 235–267.

Daatland, S. (1990) 'What are families for? On family solidarity and preference for help'. *Ageing & Society* 10, 1–15.

Ermisch, J. (1985) *Economic implications of demographic change*. Centre for Economic Policy Research Discussion Paper 44, CEPR, London.

Dyson, T. (1991) 'On the demography of South Asian famines', Parts I and II. *Population Studies* 45: 5–25, 279–298.

Finsen, V. (1988) 'Improvements in general health among the elderly: a factor in the rising incidence of hip fractures?' *Journal of Epidemiology and Community Health* 42: 200–203.

Fries, J. (1980) 'Aging, natural death and the compression of morbidity'. *New England Journal of Medicine 303*: 130–135.

Gonnot, P. (1992) 'Some selected aspects of mortality in the ECE Region', in G. J. Stolnitz (ed) *Demographic causes and consequences of population ageing, Europe and North America*. United Nations, New York, pp 82–94.

Gruenberg, E. (1977) 'The failures of success'. *Milbanke Memorial Fund Q* 55: 3–24.

Grundy, E. (1983) 'Demography and Old Age'. *Journal of American Geriatrics Sociology* 31: 325–332.

Grundy, E. (1984) 'Mortality and morbidity among the old'. *British Medical Journal* 288: 663–664.

Grundy, E. (1987) 'Household change and migration among the elderly in England and Wales'. *Espace, Populations Societes* 1, 109–123.

Grundy, E. (1989) 'Longitudinal perspectives on the living arrangements of the elderly', in Jefferys M (ed) *Growing old in the twentieth century*. Routledge, London.

Grundy, E. (1991) 'Women and ageing: demographic aspects', in J. George and S. Ebrahim (1991) *Health care and older women*. Oxford University Press.

Grundy, E. (1992a) 'The living arrangements of elderly people'. *Reviews in Clinical Gerontology* 2, 353–361.

Grundy, E. (1992b) 'Socio-demographic change and the elderly population of England and Wales'. *International Journal of Geriatric Psychiatry* 7: (in press).

Grundy, E. (1992c) 'The epidemiology of aging', in Brocklehurst J C, Tallis R, Fillit, H. (eds) *Textbook of geriatric medicine and gerontology*. Churchill Livingstone, Edinburgh.

Grundy, E. (1993) 'Moves into supported private households among elderly people in England and Wales'. *Environment and Planning* A 25, 1467–1479.

Haskey, J. (1988) 'Mid 1985 based population projections by marital status'. *Population Trends* 52, 30–32.

Holmans, A. (1981) 'Housing careers of newly married couples'. *Population Trends 24*, 10–14.

Huppert, F., Roth, M. and Gore, M. (1987) 'Psychological factors', in Cox, B. D. *et al.*, *The health and lifestyle survey*. Health Promotion Research Trust, London.

Jarvis C (1993) *Family and friends in old age and the implications for informal support: evidence from the British Social Attitudes Survey of 1986.* ACIOG/ Joseph Rowntree Foundation Working Paper No.6, Age Concern Institute of Gerontology, London.

Katz *et al.*, (1983) 'Active life expectancy'. *New England Journal of Medicine* 309: 1218–1224.

Keilman, N. (1987) 'Recent trends in family and household composition in Europe'. *European Journal of Population* 3, 297–326.

Kobrin, F. (1976) 'The primary individual and the family:changes in living arrangements in the United States since 1940'. *Journal of Marriage and the Family* 38, 233–238.

Kramer, M. (1980) 'The rising pandemic of mental disorders and associated chronic diseases and disabilities'. *Acta Psychiatrica Scandinavia* 62, suppl. 285.

Louis Harris and Associates Inc. (1982) *Priorities and expectations for health and living circumstances a survey of the elderly in five English speaking countries*. Louis Harris and Associates Inc., New York

Manton, K., and Stallard, E. (1984) *Recent trends in mortality analysis*. Academic Press, New York.

Manton, K. G. (1982) 'Changing concepts of morbidity and mortality in the elderly population'. *Milbank Memorial Fund* Q 60: 133–224.

Martin, J., Meltzer, H. and Eliot, D. (1988) *OPCS Surveys of disability in Great Britain*, Report 1. HMSO, London.

Michael, R., Fuchs, V. and Scott, S. (1980) 'Changes in the propensity to live alone'. *Demography* 17, 39–53.

Murphy, M. (1990) 'Methods of forecasting mortality for population projections', in *Population projections, trends, methods and uses*. OPCS Occasional Paper 38, OPCS, London.

Myers, G. C. (1989) 'Mortality and health dynamics at older ages', in Ruzicka, L., G. Wunsch and P. Kane (eds) *Differential mortality, methodological issues and biosocial factors*. Clarendon Press, Oxford.

Notestein, F. (1954) 'Some demographic aspects of aging'. *Proceedings of the American Philosophical Society* 98: 229–233.

Office of Population Censuses and Surveys (OPCS) (1976) *Population Projections 1974–2014* , pp2, no. 5, HMSO, London.

OPCS (1979) *Life tables* 1970–72, series DS no. 2, HMSO, London.

OPCS (1989a) *Birth Statistics, Historical Series*, FM1 no. 13, HMSO, London.

OPCS (1989b) *Mortality statistics*, series DH1 no. 20, HMSO, London.

OPCS (1989c) *General Household Survey* 1986, HMSO, London.

OPCS (1991) *National population projections: mid 1989 based.* OPCS Monitor, PP2 91/1, London.

Pampel, F. (1983) 'Changes in the propensity to live alone: evidence from consecutive cross national surveys, 1960–1976'. *Demography* 20, 433–447.

Preston, S. H. (1976) *Mortality patterns in national populations.* Academic Press, New York.

Preston, S. H., Hines, C. and Eggers, M. (1989) 'Demographic conditions responsible for population aging.' *Demography* 26: 691–704.

Riley, J. (1990) 'The risk of being sick: morbidity trends in four countries'. *Population and Development Review* 3: 403–432.

Robins, A. and Wittenburg, R. (1992) 'The health of elderly people: economic aspects', in *The health of elderly people, an epidemiological overview: companion papers.* HMSO, London (in press).

Schneider, E. and Brody, J. (1983) 'Aging, natural death and the compression of morbidity: another view'. *New England Journal of Medicine* 309: 854–856.

Shanas, E. *et al.*, (1986) *Old people in three industrial societies.* Routledge and Kegan Paul, London.

Smith, R. (1981) 'Fertility, economy and household formation in England over three centuries'. *Population and Develoment Review* 7, 595–623.

Svanborg, A. (1988) 'The health of the elderly population: results from longitudinal studies with age-cohort comparisons', in Evered, D. and J Whelan (eds) *Research and the aging population.* Ciba Foundation Symposium 134, John Wiley, Chichester.

Thatcher, A. (1981) 'Centenarians in England and Wales'. *Population Trends* 25: 11–14.

Thompson, C. and West, P. (1984) The public appeal of sheltered housing. *Ageing and Society* 4, 305–326.

Timaeus, I. (1986) 'Families and households of the elderly population: prospects for those approaching old age'. *Ageing and Society* 6: 271–293.

United Nations Secretariat (1988) 'Sex differentials in life expectancy and mortality in developed countries: an analysis by age-groups and causes of death from recent historic data'. *Population Bulletin of the United Nations* 25, United Nations, New York.

Waldron, I. (1985) 'What do we know about causes of sex differences in mortality? A review of the literature'. *Population Bulletin of the United Nations* 18, United Nations, New York.

Wall, R. (1984) 'Residential isolation of the elderly: a comparison over time'. *Ageing and Society* 4, 483- 503.

Wall, R. (1990) 'Intergenerational relations in the European past'. Paper presented to the British Sociological Association Annual Conference, Guildford, April 2–5, 1990.

Vaupel, J., Manton, K. and Stallard, E. (1979) 'The impact of heterogeneity in individual frailty on the dynamics of mortality'. *Demography* 16:439–454.

Chapter 2
FAMILY CARE AND CHANGING FAMILY STRUCTURE: BAD NEWS FOR THE ELDERLY?

LYNDA CLARKE

Introduction

The importance of the role of informal carers of the elderly has been widely acknowledged in the last decade and has been endorsed by recent legislation (Henwood, 1990; DoH, 1989; NHS and Community Care Act, 1990). The government has viewed the family as the most natural and preferred source of care for elderly people (DHSS, 1981), which is one reason why recent changes in the structure and dynamics of British family life have aroused serious concern. The demography of the family has changed substantially since the beginning of the 1970s and looks likely to continue to do so. The nuclear family is undergoing extensive change. The ageing of the population has increased the number of three or four generation families, although they do not usually live together. Marriage and childbearing are increasingly being postponed and, perhaps, forgone. Childlessness appears to be increasing while the proportion of births outside marriage has risen dramatically. Cohabitation has become the norm before or between marriage, and unions outside marriage are increasing as the family unit for childbirth. Divorce rates have increased, and the breakdown of families in general is demonstrated by the rise in lone-parent families and step-families over the last two decades. In fact these changes in family life have been so dramatic that they have been termed by some as the 'Second Demographic Transition' (Van der Kaa, 1987; Lesthaeghe, 1991).

Demographic forces have produced a three-fold increase in the relative size of the elderly population so far this century. This has been particularly noticeable for the very old population, aged 85 and over, the proportion of which has more than doubled in the past three decades, as shown in the previous chapter. The proportion of elderly people will remain stable in the current decade but increase further in the twenty-first century. Also, the ratio of elderly dependants to potential younger carers will continue to move in the wrong direction, as demonstrated in the previous chapter. Given these facts, any reports of weakening family ties, if substantiated, could be worrying. Before we sound the alarm bells for the care of the elderly in the next century it would be sensible to examine the evidence. What has been happening to the family? What is likely to happen in the future? What are the implications for the future of family care for people in old age?

Who is caring for the elderly?

First it is important to establish exactly who does look after elderly people. Does the caring capacity of the community extend beyond the immediate family? Is the Government right in its assumptions that informal care is mainly provided by kin and that care by relatives is the preferred option to formal (state-financed) care? Also, if the common perception that carers are predominantly middle-aged women looking after elderly parents is correct, will these women be available and willing to take on these caring roles?

The care of elderly people and the policy of community care has been raised as a public issue in the last decade. In 1982 the Association of Carers was formed with this explicit objective (Dalley, 1993). The importance and size of carers as a group was first identified by feminist writers on the domestic labour of women arguing for the need for recognition of the value of unpaid work (see Arber and Ginn, 1991). The dominant concern in the literature on the care of the elderly to date has been with the burden faced by women caring for frail relatives (Biegel and Blum, 1990). This attitude presents a one-sided account of elderly people as a social problem to be 'cared for' and generates panic about the growth in the number and proportion of older people in the population. It is important to remember that care flows in two directions – from young to old and from old to young. Elderly people also *provide* care – for spouses, elderly parents, other elderly people and for grandchildren (Finch, 1989; Arber and Ginn, 1991). Also, by focusing on the burden of caring, the needs and wishes of care-recipients tend to have been overlooked in the discussion about who should provide care.

Caring is generally considered a woman's issue, even an older woman's issue, because more women than men are carers and more women than men are cared for, given their greater longevity and dependency at all ages (Arber and Ginn, 1991), and this situation is likely to continue to be the case for the foreseeable future (Dalley, 1993).

Identifying carers

The plethora of recent studies of care for the elderly reflects a growing awareness of the increasing size of the elderly population in the next century and concern about who will provide care for this growing group. The data on who cares and who is cared for are complex to assemble, due to different sub-groups of carers being surveyed, different questions being posed to identify a carer and the possibility of different interpretation of the questions by respondents. The OPCS survey of informal carers is the most comprehensive and most quoted source of information (Green, 1988; OPCS, 1992). It was conducted as an integral part of the General Household Survey in 1985, which was repeated in 1990, and has proved invaluable in providing a national context for the large number of surveys of local (e.g. Qureshi and Walker, 1989) or special interest groups (e.g. ethnic minorities: Bould, 1990; McCalman, 1990 quoted in Dalley 1993; Cameron *et al.*, 1989; and elderly people: Carers National Association, 1992; Whatmore and Mira-Smith, 1991) or qualitative studies (e.g. Hicks, 1988; Lewis and Meredith, 1988; Twigg and Atkin, 1991; Wright, 1986).

The latest estimate from the 1990 OPCS data is that there were 6.8 million carers in Great Britain and that a substantial proportion were men – 2.9 million men and 3.9 million women. More relevant is a comparison of the proportion of each sex who are carers because of the larger proportion of women in the general population: 13 per cent of men reported that they were carers compared with 17 per cent of women. It would appear from this, superficially at least, that caring is not solely a woman's issue.

The GHS data, however, deserve critical examination. There are three main points that need to be taken into consideration when interpreting the GHS data. First, the figures quoted above refer to *all* care recipients, regardless of age or disposition, and include occasional visiting as well as onerous personal care. Women, however, were more likely than men to take the main responsibility for caring than men (10 per cent of women and 6 per cent of men), and to devote more than 20 hours a week to caring (3 per cent of men and 4 per cent of women). Also, if only the more arduous tasks are considered, women appear to do relatively more (Dalley, 1993). In addition, if only the peak age-band for caring is considered (45–64), 27 per cent of women caring compares with 20 per cent of men, a contrast particularly great among single persons in this age group, 34 per cent of single women were carers compared with 21 per cent of single men.

Second, the accuracy or comparability of any information about people providing informal care depends on how they are identified. The GHS asked broad questions in an attempt to locate people who 'look after or give special help to' or 'provide some regular service or help for' someone who is sick, elderly or handicapped. It has been argued that the questions were too liberal in phrasing and that women and men respond differently to such a question (Evandrou, 1990; Arber and Ginn, 1991). Women regard caring as part of their 'normal' duties, whereas men see it as something extra and so would be more likely to respond positively to the screening question.

Third, there is an important distinction between informal care provided within the household (co-resident care) and care provided to an elderly person living in a separate household (extra-resident care). According to the GHS, the range of activities through which a person is identified as being a carer for someone in another household is more inclusive than for co-resident care, where 'normal' services are excluded. It is, therefore, not surprising that the estimates of carers are much higher than other studies (e.g. Parker, 1985; Martin *et al.*, 1989) as the figures reflect the extensive definition used for extra-household caring (Arber and Ginn, 1991).

Recent evidence on carers of the elderly

The published GHS tables analyse carers by the time spent on caring and the caring tasks undertaken. They do not give detailed analysis of these features of caring by the age and gender of the carer and dependant. Fortunately, some recent secondary analyses of the 1985 GHS survey have shed some light on these issues for the elderly (Arber and Ginn, 1991: Askham *et al*, 1992: Parker, 1992). Unpublished tables from the 1990 survey, show that in 1990, 14 per cent of women and 11 per cent of men provided informal care to people aged 65 or over, which is an increase of 2 per cent since 1985 for both women and men (Table 1). This increase was due entirely to a rise in the proportion of people caring for an elderly person who was not living with them. In fact the proportion of co-resident carers decreased from 20 per cent in 1985 to 17 per cent in 1990.

TABLE 1

Carers of the elderly: percentage by sex by age of dependant, 1990

Age of dependant	Carer's sex	
	Male	Female
65–74	26.9	27.8
74–84	47.2	46.5
85+	25.9	25.7
Total % by Sex	40.0	60.0
Base = all carers	852	1282
All elderly carers	10.5	13.6
Base = all people	8103	9432

Source: General Household Survey. 1990. Unpublished data.

The rise has occurred almost entirely among the 45–64 age group which is largely accounted for by the growth in the number of people caring for parents and parents-in-law (McGlone, 1993). About three-quarters of carers in this age group are looking after a parent or parent-in-law. Most carers are looking after elderly dependants and nearly half of these (47 per cent) are caring for an elderly person aged 75–84 (Table 1). Table 1 also confirms that more of these carers are women (60 per cent of carers).

All the above sources confirm the major role played by women aged between 45 and 65 years of age in the care of elderly people, which has been found in other studies that focus on elder care (Askham *et al.*, 1992; Carers National Association, 1992), but the significant contributions of both older women and men should not be overlooked.

One measure of the burden of care is the time spent caring. Women are more likely than men to take the main responsibility for caring and to devote long hours to caring. However, the time devoted to caring is mainly due to whether or not the elderly person lives in the same household as the recipient which, in turn, is related to the relationship between care provider and care recipient. There are marked differences in the time spent caring and the type of help given according to whether the carer is co-resident or not (Arber and Ginn, 1991; Parker and Lawton, 1992).

Most carers are family members. Parents and parents-in law represented about half of the elderly people cared for both in separate households (56 per cent) and in the same household (46 per cent) in 1990. Spouses were the majority of the remainder of elderly people being cared for in the same household (41 per cent of all co-resident carers), as shown in Figure 1. In 1985, women were more likely than men to provide care for both relatives and non-relatives, but the difference between the sexes in the care of a spouse was small (Parker, 1992a). This reflects the greater longevity of women, as more men than women have elderly spouses to care for.

The majority of carers in 1990 were not living with the elderly person (83 per cent, see Figure 2). This type of care is likely to increase in future given the growth in elderly people living on their own. The increase in the number of carers between 1985 and 1990 was mainly accounted for by an increase in the

Figure 1
Relationship of carer and elderly person by household of residence, 1990

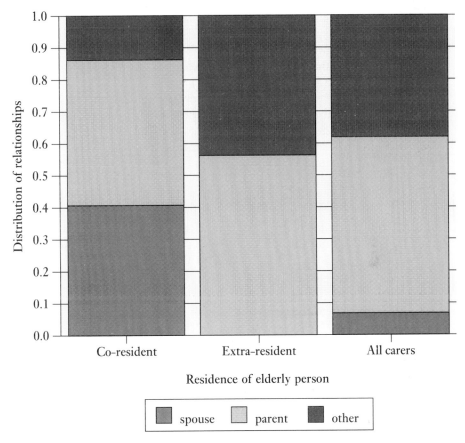

Note: Elderly person is main dependant of carer only
Source: 1990 General Household Survey. Unpublished data.

care of parents living in another household. Caring for an elderly person in another household involves many problems and worries which should not be underestimated (Allen *et al.*, 1992), but extra-resident carers are likely to spend much less time actually providing care than co-resident carers and less likely to provide personal or physical help, given the evidence to date (Parker, 1992). In 1985, co-resident carers spent on average 53 hours caring per week, almost six times greater than the average nine hours spent by those caring for a person in another household (Arber and Ginn, 1991).

Most time is spent by carers who support their elderly spouse, averaging 65 hours per week, with a negligible gender difference. In other relationships there is a consistent gender difference in both co-resident and extra-resident care, with women providing considerably more care (Arber and Ginn, 1991). Arber and Ginn have estimated that 61 per cent of the total time spent providing informal care for elderly people in 1985 was within the household, and 63 per cent of that was provided by women. Half of the total time was spent caring for parents and parents-in-law and 30 per cent for a spouse, while caring for a friend or neighbour represented only 7 per cent of the total volume of elder care (Arber and Ginn, 1991). Thus the bulk of informal care is provided by children to their parents (in-law) and by elderly people to their spouse. Informal care of the elderly is far from being 'community care', it is provided by the family and, for heavy caring commitment, especially within households.

There are important class differences in the provision of informal care which are rarely identified. Although informal carers as a whole are drawn equally from all classes, co-resident care – which we have seen places greater constraints on the carer's life, is more frequently provided by working class men and women than by the middle class (Arber and Ginn, 1992). Thus the working class bear the greatest burden of providing care, while at the same time possessing fewer resources with which to do so.

The popular conception of older people as non-contributing, highly-dependent recipients of informal care is challenged by the 1990 GHS, where 20 per cent of all carers of elderly people were aged 65 or over: 44 per cent of co-resident and 15 per cent of extra-resident carers (Figure 2). Elderly carers are the age group most likely to be co-resident carers because they are most likely to be caring for an elderly spouse (Figure 3). Previous analysis confirms that provision of care by elderly people themselves is considerable (Arber and Ginn, 1991; Parker, 1992). Arber and Ginn found that in 1985 elderly people provided 35 per cent of the total volume of informal care and almost half the co-resident care to people over 65, with little difference between men and women carers. The OPCS Disability Survey estimated that 40 per cent of the main carers for disabled adults were themselves over 65 (Martin *et al.*, 1989). Elderly people are less likely to be providing care to elderly people in another household (17 per cent according to Arber and Ginn, 1991).

The peak age range for caring is 45–64. In 1990 nearly half of all carers (46 per cent) were in this age group. This is the age at which one's parents are likely to need help, especially the very elderly – aged 75 or over (see Figure 4), which is the group of elderly people that is growing at the moment (see Chapter 1). The increase in the number of people aged 65 and over after the 2020s, when the 'baby boomers' of the 1960s cohorts reach these ages, may herald a greater

Figure 2
Age of carers by age of the elderly person and location of residence, 1990

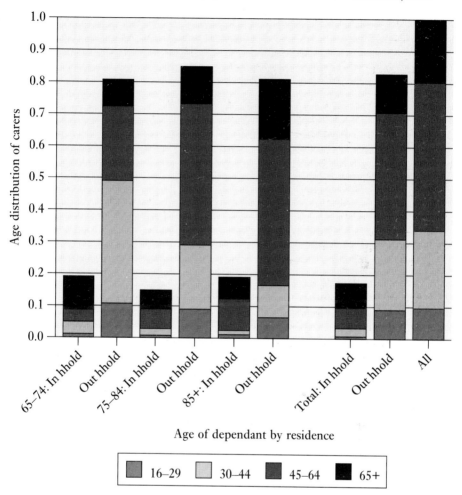

Note: Elderly person is main dependant of carer only.
Source: 1990 General Household Survey. Unpublished data.

Figure 3
Age of carers and residence to elderly person by relationship

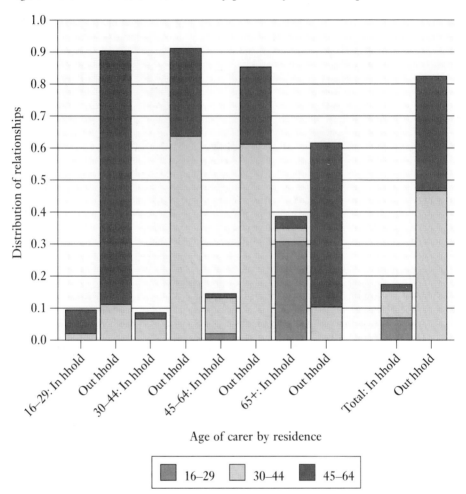

Note: Elderly person is main dependant of carer only.
Source: 1990 General Household Survey. Unpublished data.

Figure 4
Age of carers by the age of the elderly person and relationship, 1990

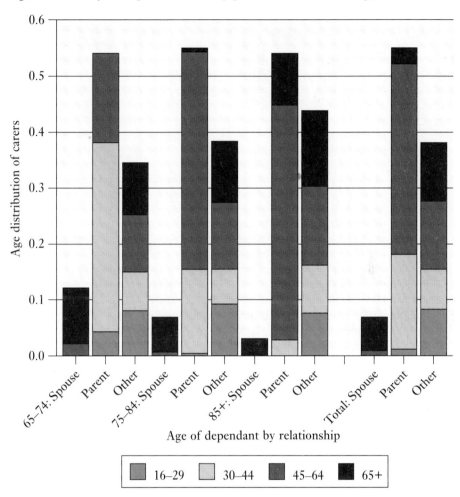

Note: Elderly person is main dependant of carer only.
Source: 1990 General Household Survey. Unpublished data.

TABLE 2
Births outside Marriage

Age of Mother						
Year	All ages	Under 20	20–24	25–29	30–34	35 and over
Percentage of births outside marriage						
1980	11.8	42.6	13.2	6.0	5.8	9.5
1985	19.2	64.8	24.6	10.6	9.0	11.8
1991	30.2	82.9	44.9	21.1	15.9	18.8
Jointly registered births as a percentage of all births outside marriage						
1980	57	46	57	66	71	70
1985	65	57	66	70	72	73
1991	74	65	75	78	79	80
Percentage of jointly registered births with parents at same usual address						
1985	72	56	71	79	81	80
1991	73	58	73	79	81	81

Source: Birth Statistics. Series FMI. OPCS.

reliance on children in their thirties and forties, especially if the average age at childbirth continues to increase, which will be examined later in this chapter.

The majority of middle-aged carers are women who are caring for parents or parents-in-law. In 1990 nearly three-quarters of carers aged 45–64 were children of the elderly person or the child's spouse (72 per cent: see Figure 4), with middle-aged women making the greatest contribution by providing 28 per cent of all informal care in 1985 in terms of time spent (Arber and Ginn, 1991). Thus, women provide the majority of informal care to elderly people, with middle-aged women making the greatest contribution, whereas elderly men provide more care than middle-aged men, with men under 45 contributing only 8 per cent of all care for elderly people (Arber and Ginn, 1991; Table 8.3).

Although the vast majority of carers of elderly people are married, 84 per cent in 1985 (Parker, 1992a, Table 2), single women aged 45–64 (34 per cent in 1990) and previously-married women aged 16–29 (18 per cent in 1990) are at particularly high risk of being a carer (OPCS, 1992). People caring for an elderly person in the same home were much more likely to be single than those with caring responsibilities elsewhere, and were also somewhat older (Parker, 1992a, Tables 2 & 3), suggesting that the demise of the 'domestic spinster' (or bachelor) is not as imminent as has been assumed (Parker, 1992a). In fact recent research carried out by the Social Policy Research Unit at York has shown that middle-aged, unmarried men and women have a much higher risk of becoming carers than any other group (Parker and Lawton, 1991). Men as a group are at much less risk of becoming carers (OPCS, 1992, Table 7), but, younger single men and older, ever-married men are as much at risk as their female peers (Parker, 1992). Co-residence is already known to be an important factor for men in assuming care responsibilities (Qureshi and Walker, 1989). That British men leave the parental home at a later age than women, or are less likely to leave at all, may go

TABLE 3
Projections of the Legal Marital Status of the Population, England and Wales 1989–2019*

| Year | Percentages | | | | Total = |
	Single	Married	Widowed	Divorced	100%
Ages 45–64					
Men					
1989	8	82	2	8	5373
1990	8	81	2	8	5408
2000	9	75	2	13	6083
2010	15	67	2	16	6904
2019	19	62	2	17	7129
Women					
1989	5	77	9	9	5479
1990	5	76	9	9	5505
2000	5	72	8	15	6180
2010	10	65	7	18	7050
2019	14	61	6	19	7212
Ages 65 and over					
Men					
1989	7	73	17	3	3203
1990	7	72	17	3	3225
2000	7	69	18	6	3411
2010	7	65	18	10	3718
219	8	61	17	14	4276
Women					
1989	9	38	49	3	4796
1990	9	38	49	3	4806
2000	7	38	49	6	4805
2010	5	37	48	10	4904
2019	5	35	45	15	5447

Source: Government Actuary's Department. Unpublished data.

some way to explaining their over-representation among those caring for parents in the same household. They become carers 'by default' because they have never left the parental home (Glendinning, 1992; Parker, 1992a).

The family type of carers illustrates some of the characteristics of carers (Green, 1988, Table 2.18). The majority of both co-resident (42 per cent) and extra-resident (45 per cent) carers in 1985 lived in a married couple family with children, as with the general population. One third of carers had dependent children, in most cases in addition to the person they were caring for. This highlights the issue of multiple caring, having both children and elderly dependants, as most dependants are elderly. The lower proportion of co-resident carers who had dependent children living with them probably reflects the older age structure of these carers. It is interesting that double the proportion of co-resident carers (13 per cent) were lone parents than extra-resident carers (7 per cent), possibly reflecting a greater tendency for these carers to live with their own parents.

In summary, the stereotype of carers being middle-aged women caring for parents or parents-in-law needs to be complemented by acknowledging the role played by spouses, most of whom are elderly themselves and about half of whom are men. Although the bulk of informal care is provided by the succeeding generation, a third of care is provided by elderly people themselves, mainly by spouses. Caring embraces a wide spectrum of tasks, time commitment and circumstances but the evidence to date is that the most burdensome caring is borne by co-resident family members, a spouse or child, who are providing help with personal/physical activities (Twigg, 1992). It is not so much a 'labour of love' as filial or conjugal obligation. Perhaps 'compulsory altruism' would be a better description. The caring capacity of the community depends on the availability and willingness of these family members to devote long hours to caring.

Is care by children or a spouse the preferred option?

The majority of elderly people may be cared for by family members but there is increasing evidence that is not wanted by many children or elderly people (McGlone, 1992). Instead most would prefer professional help, particularly when problems arise from disability or personal care (Phillipson, quoted in McGlone, 1992).

Arber and Ginn devised a hierarchy of care preferences of elderly people, which excluded state health or domiciliary services because these can be provided in any of the caring contexts. Care which is part of the marital relationship was most favoured, followed by care in the elderly persons home from relatives of the same generation, then care by children. Care by household members in the elderly person's home was preferred over extra-residential care but the least preferred option was care provided in the care-giver's home by a married child (Arber and Ginn, 1991). Arber and Ginn interpret these preferences as reflecting the perceived autonomy and independence possible in the different caring situations (Arber and Ginn, 1992a). It would appear that, although informal care by the family is the norm, this may not be the ideal situation for either the care provider or recipient. These preferences may not be new but their articulation probably reflects the increased choice available to individuals generally, given the overall increase in prosperity, including decisions about family life.

The availability and willingness of informal carers is ignored by present policy. Many elderly people do not have relatives to care for them (Abrams, 1978). Allen *et al.* found that 22 per cent of the elderly people in her study who were living in the community and a third of those living in residential homes either had either never borne children or had no living children (Allen *et al.*, 1992).

Finally, it should be remembered that the group requiring care in the immediate future are the very old, aged 85 and over, as shown in Chapter 1. These are most likely to be elderly women, who have a longer life expectancy than men but are disadvantaged when compared with men in terms both of disability and poor health in adult life (Arber and Ginn, 1991). In the longer term this gender difference may be less apparent with the increase of those aged 65–74 years in the 2020s. Elderly women are also more likely than men to be living alone and to be disadvantaged by having have lower financial resources as well as health problems (Arber and Ginn, 1991).

Family change

We can now turn to consider the changes in family life that have taken place in recent decades before assessing exactly how these changes will affect the future care of elderly people in Britain. Trends in family change that have become evident in the last thirty years show no sign of reaching a steady state. The nuclear family is undergoing extensive change and the ageing of the population has increased the number of three or four generation families living at the same time, if not necessarily at the same place. The main feature of household change is the move towards one-person, one-family households in contrast to the past diversity of family relationships (Clarke, 1989; Harrop and Plewis, 1993; OPCS, 1993). This has effects and implications for the housing circumstances and care of both elderly people and their extended family, which will be examined in a later chapter.

It is worth noting that the common perception that elderly people usually lived with children in the past is false and that it is has become even less likely in recent times. Only 10 per cent of households with an elderly person in 1980–1 contained an elderly person living with a child (Wall, 1989; Coleman and Salt, 1992). Research has demonstrated that the multi-generational household in the pre-industrial past is largely a myth (Laslett, 1972).

Many professionals involved with the care of people in old age are prone to believe that in the past there was an extended family system in this country in which the elderly person resided with their offspring who cared for them. They see the increasing number of very old people who live on their own and draw the incorrect conclusion that this is the result of weakening family ties, that family obligations are no longer recognised and old people are left to cope on their own or be cared for by professionals.

Family relationships are fundamentally social with the core unifying notion probably being the idea of obligation (Finch, 1989). Recent changes in family structure will have changed the obligations that kin impose on each other, but it has been argued by Wall (1992) that the obligation to care for elderly people within families has actually increased as the number being cared for way has grown. It could be argued also that kinship now involves greater obligations to the old than in the past as people now live longer and, as we shall see, have fewer descendants to share their care. It has been suggested that older people prefer not to share accommodation with their children in joint households if they cannot manage on their own (Arber and Ginn, 1991; Jefferys and Thane, 1992). It is the old people themselves who prefer to be independent and move to residential homes rather than those of their children.

The changes in family structure detailed below may indicate potential difficulties in managing the care of elderly people but they do not preclude this care. Demography can quantify changes in family life, but changes in attitudes and beliefs are equally important.

Marriage and cohabitation

The creation of a new family has traditionally been inextricably linked to marriage. However, this is an event in family life that has undergone major change, perhaps the most important change for families because of the ramifications it engenders for the care and welfare of dependants, including elderly people.

After the Second World War and up until the beginning of the 1970s, there was an increasing propensity to marry and for marriages to occur at increasingly younger ages and over a narrower range of ages (Kiernan, 1989). Since then, however, marriage has been delayed and for some couples forgone. First marriage rates have fallen, at least at younger ages (OPCS, 1992a) and there has been a sharp fall in marriage for both men and women born after the early 1950s (Haskey, 1993b). The proportion of both men and women ever-married by age 25 approximately halved between the 1950 and 1965 birth cohorts. Figure 5 demonstrates this sustained and substantial decline in first marriage for successive cohorts of men and women born since the 1950s. These sharp declines have either resulted from successive cohorts of women marrying at progressively older ages or from an increasing proportion of them never marrying. In fact it looks as though there is a combination of both postponement and rejection of marriage (for detailed analyses of marriage trends since 1950 see Kiernan and Eldridge, 1987; Eldridge and Kiernan, 1985). The increase in average age at first marriage which began in the early 1970s has continued into the 1990s. For both men and women it rose by about three years, reaching 27.5 and 25.5 respectively in 1991. Teenage marriages have declined significantly in recent years; 1 in 4 marriages in 1980 involved a teenage bride compared with nearly 1 in 13 in 1991.

Marriage at older ages partly reflects young people remaining in the parental home for longer than in the past and partly their living on their own or sharing with others. There is increased financial dependency of young adults on their parents, which is linked to recent changes in employment, education and training as well as social security legislation (Kiernan and Wicks, 1990). This trend may produce obvious constraints for the co-resident care of elderly people as well as a squeeze on finances for purchasing care.

Figure 5
Cumulative percentages, by age, of men and women who had ever-married for recent birth cohorts.
England and Wales

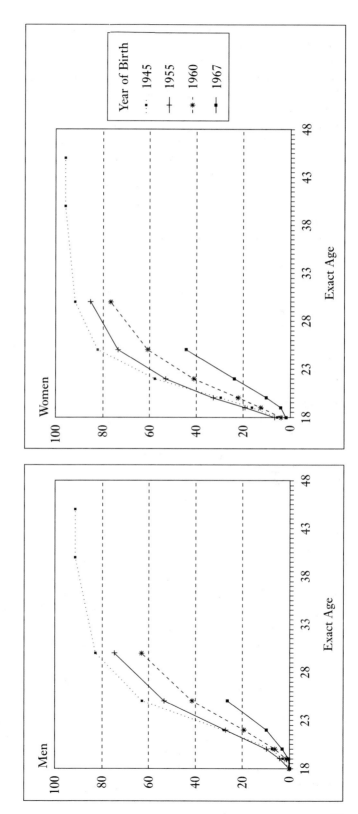

Marriage may be being rejected by a minority of individuals as well as being postponed by many others. There has been an increase in the proportion of single people in the population and, if present marriage rates continue, the expected proportions of men and women who will have married by age 50 will be 69 per cent for men and 75 per cent for women, compared with estimates of 93 and 96 per cent respectively in 1971 (OPCS, 1992a). The sharp fall in marriage rates since the 1970s have been accompanied by a dramatic rise in the proportions of young people cohabiting without legal marriage. It has been estimated that around a half of the reduction in the proportions of women ever-married at ages 20–24 and one third of the decline at ages 25–29 in the 1980s could be accounted for by the increased propensity to cohabit (Kiernan and Wicks, 1990). In 1990, nearly one fifth (19 per cent) of single women, over one quarter (27 per cent) of divorced women and 13 per cent of separated women aged 16–59 were cohabiting. Cohabitation is more likely if there is a dependent child in the household: for example, raising the proportion of single women cohabiting to over one third (34 per cent).

It is virtually normal practice to cohabit before marriage nowadays. Over half (51 per cent) of women and just under half (49 per cent) of men who married for the first time in 1985–89 had lived with their partner before marriage (OPCS, 1993). Certainly cohabiting between marriages is the norm and the length of time that divorced women have been cohabiting has increased: in 1979 the median duration of cohabitation was 28 months whilst in 1987 it was 34 months (Kiernan and Wicks, 1990). Not only have divorced people continued to cohabit extensively but they have been cohabiting for longer periods.

Relationships based on cohabitation share many of the features of legal marriage, especially for young never-married childless cohabitants and previously married people. But the relationship can be regarded as having similarities to a mutual contract, being based more on cooperation and perhaps lacking some of the formal obligations and ties of a marriage, which could be a crucial difference when considering the care of people in old age. Evidence from France indicates that consensual unions break down slightly more frequently than marriages (Leridon, 1990), in which case cohabitees may lack the care of a partner in later life if they do not find another partner. Differences in socio-economic circumstances have been detected for never-married couples with children, who tend to be more disadvantaged than their married counterparts (Kiernan and Estaugh, 1993; McRae, 1993).

Childbearing outside marriage

If cohabitation was a major feature of family change in the 1970s, then the separation of marriage and childbearing, which is not unrelated to developments in cohabitation, has been an important trend in the 1980s and is creating dramatic changes in family structure. The proportion of all births outside marriage has more than trebled from 9 per cent in 1976 to nearly 31 per cent in 1992.

The growth in extra-marital childbearing is partly a result of the older average age at marriage and the larger cohorts of the 'baby boom', born in the late 1950s and early 1960s, increasing the proportion of single women in the population (Ermisch, 1990). Marital childbearing has been postponed and somewhat depressed, which has tended to exaggerate the effect of childbearing outside marriage. Even taking these factors into account, the evidence points to a noticeable and increased propensity for women to have children outside marriage, a tendency which is by no means confined to teenagers (Kiernan and Wicks, 1990).

What is interesting is that a rising proportion of these births outside marriage are being registered by two parents and by parents living at the same address (see Table 2). The proportion of joint registrations has risen from 57 per cent of all births outside marriage in 1980 to 74 per cent in 1991. Moreover, of the joint registrations made in 1991, more than 7 out of 10 (74 per cent) were made by parents living at the same address. In other words, over a half (55 per cent) of all births outside marriage in 1990 were jointly registered by parents living at the same address. The older the mother the more likely the birth is to be jointly registered by co-resident parents. This suggests that there may be little difference in the family circumstances of many of the births outside marriage and those inside marriage. While cohabitation is considered generally to precede rather than substitute for marriage in this country, a growing proportion of couples are no longer marrying before the birth of their children. This accounts for some of the increase in extra-marital childbearing in recent years (Kiernan and Wicks, 1990). There is no reason to believe that such families will differ in their response to elderly care from families with married parents, unless there is a greater propensity for such partnerships to break down.

It should be remembered, however, that nearly 3 out of 10 births outside marriage are registered by the mother alone and nearly 3 out of 10 of the jointly registered births are by parents who do not live together. A significant proportion of these extra-marital births (45 per cent) are to mothers who, on the available evidence, would appear to be lacking the support of the child's father. Also, it has been shown that these are the families that are most likely to be suffering material hardship (Clarke and Eldridge, 1989; Kiernan and Estaugh 1993). The case of lone mothers and elderly people will be discussed later.

Childbearing within marriage

The majority of children are born to women in their first marriage but the proportion of such births is declining. Just under two-thirds (64 per cent) of all children born in 1991 were born to mothers in their first marriage, whereas the comparable proportion in 1980 was 82 per cent. The proportion of children born to mothers in their second or subsequent marriage has remained unchanged at 6 per cent throughout the 1980s until the present.

Birth rates fell after the baby boom of the 1960s. The decline in births observed in the 1970s has not been reversed substantially during the 1980s. Since 1974 the birth rate has remained below the level needed to replace the population, in common with many Western countries. The underlying causes of this low fertility are probably linked to those of the other developments in family formation. They include better prospects for women's education and employ-ment as well as higher aspirations and increased housing costs (Ermisch, 1990).

One major feature of recent fertility behaviour, apart from the increase in childbearing outside marriage, is the postponement of parenthood. Couples marrying since the late 1960s have been delaying starting their families. The average age at first birth among married women in 1981 was 25.4 years, but by 1991 this had increased to 27.5 years, being linked to the later age at marriage. The relative stability in the overall fertility rate (total period fertility rate [or the average family size predicted by period fertility]) in the last decade conceals considerable change in the age distribution of fertility. There has been a decrease in the fertility rates of women in their twenties and an increase in those of women in their thirties and forties, especially for first birth rates. Births to remarried women have contributed to this trend but the evidence is that more women are delaying childbirth, both in first marriages and outside marriage. Later childbirth and these increases in the fertility rates of the over-thirties are noticeable for women born since 1945 (Jones, 1992).

Later childbearing has not compensated for the shortfall of births at younger ages, at least not for women born between 1935 and 1950 who have completed their childbearing. Further declines in completed family size are projected for more recent cohorts of women; for example, women born in 1955 are projected to have on average 1.99 children, compared with the 2.19 already achieved by women born in 1945 and the 2.36 for women born in 1940 (Jones, 1992). There is growing conformity to the two-child family ideal, both in terms of actual family size and expectations about future numbers of children.

These trends reflect the increasing likelihood that recent generations of women nearing the end of their reproductive span will remain childless. A rising proportion of women born since 1945 are childless at each age (see Figure 6). Over one third of women born in 1960 reached the age of 30 without having at least one child, twice the equivalent proportion for women born in 1945. It can be seen that permanent childlessness has also risen, which in part explains the fall in average family size, and it is unlikely that later births will be widespread enough to reverse this trend (Jones, 1992).

This delayed childbearing, increased fertility for the over thirties and increase in childlessness have important ramifications for the care of elderly people in the future. There will inevitably be women 'caught in the middle', as Elaine Brody (1981) aptly termed the situation of women whose childcare and elderly care coincide. For women who have started a family late, like many women born since the mid 1940s, or for women who have had additional children in their thirties, there could be an overlap between caring for dependent children and caring for elderly parents. They could also be responsible for the care of an elderly spouse if they have married an older man. This will be a problem for the care of all elderly relatives, not only because it might be difficult to accommodate them in the same household as children, but also because women's time will be limited. The problem of opportunity cost and women's competing demands on their time, as shown for women's employment in Chapter 5, will be exacerbated in the future if women continue to return to paid work in increasing numbers at even shorter periods after having children or remain in the labour force throughout childbearing. If they have managed to combine childbearing and paid work they may be reluctant to abandon paid work to provide care for elderly relatives. It will make the additional pressure of caring for an older person extremely difficult to fit into their over-committed lives. The gravitation towards the two-child family and smaller family size

Figure 6
Percentage of women childless at successive ages

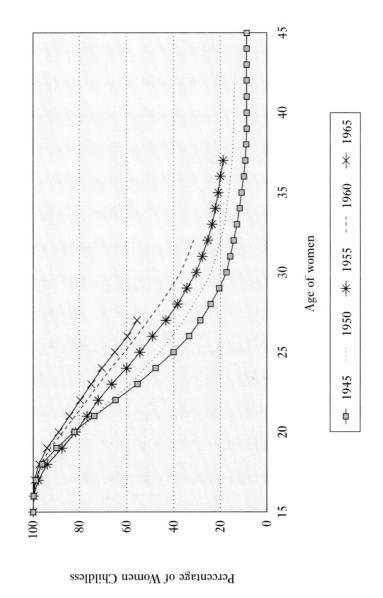

Source: Jones, C. Population Trends (no. 67; p11)

37

than in the past also means there will be fewer children to share the care of elderly parents.

The most important problem raised by these trends in fertility, however, is perhaps the increasing proportion and numbers of elderly people who will not have any children to assist with their care. These childless elderly people have been more likely to enter institutional care in the past (Grundy and Harrop, 1991; Allen *et al.*, 1992). What will happen to them in future given the changes in policy towards 'community care' is unclear.

Divorce

The family and marriage are also said to be under threat from the recent increase in divorce. Marital disruption among both elderly people and their children will cause discontinuity in the relationships between generations as well as between the divorcing partners themselves.

Britain has one of the highest divorce rates in Western Europe (Haskey, 1992b). Divorce rates doubled in the 1970s after the Divorce Reform Act came into force in 1971, from 6 per 1000 marriages to 12 per 1000 marriages, and has remained around 13 per 1000 marriages, during the 1980s. The rapid increase in the propensity to divorce can be seen by considering couples married in different years. Among couples married in 1961, 10 per cent had divorced by their 12th wedding anniversary, while 10 per cent of those married in 1971 had divorced by their 6th wedding anniversary and for those married in 1981, the same proportion had divorced within 4.5 years of marriage (Haskey, 1988). The highest proportion of marriage dissolution observed so far is 24 per cent of couples married in 1966 who were divorced within 20 years of marriage (Kiernan and Wicks, 1990). It is estimated that almost four in every ten marriages would end in divorce by 20 years of marriage if the divorce rates prevailing in the mid–1980s were to continue, compared with only 7 per cent of marriages contracted at the beginning of the 1950s (Haskey, 1989). It has also been estimated that 1 in 5 children will experience a divorce of their parents by the age of 16 (Haskey, 1983).

In order to examine how this increase in marital breakdown will affect people in the future it is essential to look at the divorce experience of people born in different years (birth cohorts). In general , there has been a tendency for the proportions of men and women ever-divorced to rise from one birth cohort to the next since the cohort of 1925 according to recent estimates (Haskey, 1993b). For example, 12 per cent of women born in 1925, had divorced by the age of 60, whereas this same proportion had been reached by women born in 1940 by the age of 37, and 14 per cent of women born in 1955 had been divorced by the age of 30. The highest levels have been experienced by the cohorts of the 1950s. Although the proportions divorced by the younger ages have fallen for the more recent cohorts, this does not mean that they will not ultimately experience lower proportions divorcing, since the decline reflects the change in the timing of marriage documented earlier. The experience of three birth cohorts of men and women are shown in Figure 7. The observed results for these cohorts are much lower than the projections of 4 in 10 marriages ending in divorce. This is because the projection relates to the future and the birth

Figure 7
Cumulative percentages, by age, of men and women who had ever divorced for selected birth cohorts.
England and Wales

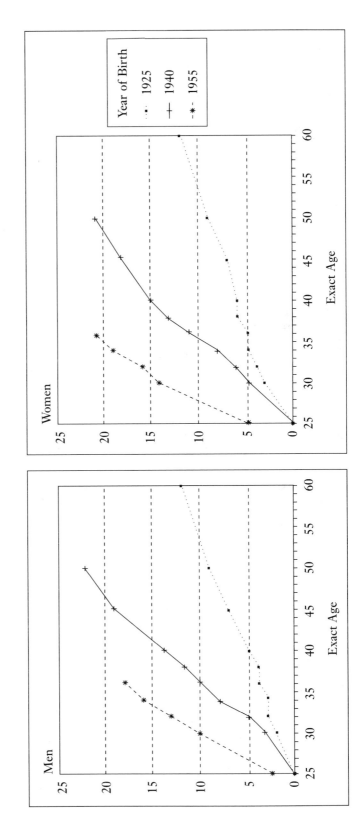

cohorts' experience to date relates to the past, which includes times when divorce rates were not as high as those of the mid-1980s which were used for the projection. Also, the projection is confined to married couples whereas the birth cohort results include all people born in that year, regardless of whether they are married.

Official projections of the future legal marital status of the population based on the 1989 population estimates are shown in Table 3. The most noticeable changes are the increases in the proportions of divorced men and women for both the middle-aged and elderly people. The proportion of divorced women aged 45–64 is projected to increase from 9 per cent in 1990 to 19 per cent in the year 2019, and the similar proportion of divorced elderly women from 3 per cent to 15 per cent of all elderly women. There is a consequent decline in the proportion of married women but for middle-aged women and men there is also an increase in the proportion of single people, reflecting the movement away from marriage discussed earlier.

Divorce among people in old age will become more widespread in the next century, which suggests that reliance on care from a spouse may be misplaced for some people now in their forties and fifties, who were born in the 1940s or before and will be aged 65 or older in the first quarter of the next century. This is also likely to be the situation for subsequent cohorts, although the movement away from marriage may mean that lower proportions divorce. It has been shown that people who cohabit before marriage are more likely to experience divorce than married couples who do not cohabit (Haskey, 1992a). However, the evidence is that the alternative – cohabiting unions – are likely to be even less stable. Thus, there may be even higher proportions of breakdowns in relationships among subsequent birth cohorts than observed to date.

Marital disruption will affect intergenerational contact not only in a negative way. It is frequently the stimulus for intergenerational assistance and increased contact, perhaps even co-residence (Bumpass and Sweet, 1991). With the breakdown of marriage women may return to the parental home and may in time provide care to their elderly parent but initially the care flows in the other direction, from the grandparent to the daughter (Twigg, 1992). There will be discontinuity in many relationships connected with marriage, for example, with the relatives of a spouse, or, for children, with the grandparents on the side of the absent parent. Even if contact is retained with grandchildren, the obligations between the ex-daughter-in-law and the ex-parents-in-law are unclear. It is difficult to generalise about this, as much depends on the personalities concerned, but it is unlikely to create clear pathways for caring responsibilities. It probably would not strengthen previously distant relationships nor go against the grain of the social forces that are tending to reduce intergenerational dependencies (Bumpass and Sweet, 1991).

Lone parent families

One effect of the divorce trend is growth in the number of lone-parent families. Currently about one in five families with dependent children is a lone parent family (Haskey, 1993a; Haskey, 1993c; OPCS, 1993). The United Kingdom has the highest proportion of lone parent families in the European Community (Roll, 1993). Nine out of ten of these parents is a lone mother, two-thirds of whom have previously been married. As mortality has declined so have the number of widows with dependent children, the increase in marital dissolution has been mainly responsible for the large increase in lone-parent families during the 1970s. In 1991, 6 per cent of all families with dependent children were headed by a divorced lone mother, 4 per cent by a separated lone mother and 1 per cent by a widowed lone mother (OPCS, 1993). There has been an increase in the proportion of lone mother families headed by never-married mothers in the 1980s, resulting from the growth in childbearing outside marriage noted earlier. These lone mothers are on average younger than other lone mothers. In 1991 the median age of never-married lone mothers was 25 years compared with 37 years for divorced lone mothers.

Lone parenthood may have little impact on elderly care because for the majority of women it is a transitory state which will not coincide with having elderly relatives requiring care. More never-married lone mothers leave the lone-parent status through marriage or cohabitation before their child (who was born outside marriage) reaches the age of 16 than other lone mothers. Mothers who had their children outside marriage are likely to leave lone motherhood at an earlier stage than lone mothers who had their children in a marriage that subsequently broke down (Ermisch and Wright, 1989; Clarke, 1992).

Any concern about the increase in lone parenthood is usually because there is a large differential in the economic well-being of two-parent families and female-headed, lone-parent families. In 1987 nearly 50 per cent of single parent families were living in poverty, (defined as living below 50 per cent of average income) (Oppenheim, 1990). The plight of so many lone mothers reflects the disadvantages they face in the labour market (Joshi, 1987) and the social security system (Bradshaw, 1989; Burghes, 1993). Women who remain in the lone-parent status and are unlucky enough to have elderly dependent parents will be at an economic disadvantage before they take on any extra caring roles. It may be that they will be living with their parent(s) already and, if not, they will probably have to resort to this solution, as suggested by the GHS carers survey results mentioned earlier.

Remarriage and reconstituted families

Lone parenthood is often not a permanent situation for many women and their children since it is often terminated by cohabitation and/or marriage, or children reaching adulthood. A substantial proportion of divorced people eventually remarry. An increasing proportion of marriages are remarriages for one or both partners; in 1990, 63 per cent of marriages were first marriages for both partners, 19 per cent were remarriages for one partner only, and 13 per cent were remarriages for both partners (OPCS, 1992a). Data from the General Household Survey in 1991 show that one third of women (33 per cent) who had divorced in the period 1983–1986 had remarried within 3 years of divorce and over half (56 per cent) of women divorced during the period 1979–1982 had remarried within 4 years of divorce (OPCS, 1993). Men are even more likely to remarry than women and more quickly; in 1991 nearly half (45 per cent) of men divorced during the period 1983–1986 had remarried within three years of divorce and nearly two-thirds (60 per cent) of those divorced during 1979–82 had remarried within four years of divorce (OPCS, 1993). Divorced men are also more likely to cohabit than divorced women; in 1991 38 per cent of all divorced men under 60 were cohabiting, compared with 25 per cent of divorced women of these ages (OPCS, 1993).

Men and women can remarry more than once, but the registration data do not distinguish second from subsequent marriages. The experience of remarriage for selected birth cohorts can be seen in Figure 8, but because of the way the data are collected these may count a small number of people more than once if they have remarried more than once. The three cohorts illustrate patterns of low, medium and high proportions of those ever-remarried. It must be remembered that these are the product not only of the proportion of a birth cohort remarrying but also of the proportion marrying and divorcing (Haskey, 1993b). The proportions of men and women who had ever remarried by age 30 started declining for cohorts after about 1955 (Haskey, 1992a, 1993b). Part of this decline has been due to falling first marriage rates and part is due to the growth in cohabitation before or instead of remarriage (Haskey, 1993b).

We know that remarriages are at greater risk than first marriages of breaking down (Haskey, 1988) but we do not know whether different types of reconstituted family have different risks of breaking up (Kiernan and Wicks, 1990). Evidence from the United States suggests that risks increase with the complexity of the reformed families (White and Booth, 1985). For example, couples where only one partner has been married before and there are no children have the lowest risk of breakdown, whereas couples where both partners have been married previously and have children from their previous marriages have the highest risk (Kiernan and Wicks, 1990).

The impact of recent trends in marriage, divorce and cohabitation on the circumstances of children have been shown to have resulted in an increase in lone parenthood since the beginning of the 1970s and an increase in reconstituted families during the 1980s (Clarke, 1992). The most recent General Household Survey in 1991 asked both men and women for the first time about the presence of stepchildren, producing the estimate that 8 per cent of families with dependent children were stepfamilies (OPCS, 1993). The survey also identified some differences between stepfamilies and other families with dependent children headed by a married couple, most notably that stepfamilies were more likely than other families to live in local authority housing, probably partly a result of their greater likelihood of having a weekly household income in the lowest category tabulated (£200 or less) (OPCS, 1993).

The increase in remarriage and cohabitation after the breakdown of a relationship and the resulting increase in reconstituted families are likely to have produced families with increasingly complex familial ties. It is likely that this complexity will grow with the passage of time if relationships continue to fail and be replaced with alternative liaisons. Obligations for elder care will be unclear in these complex situations and it is possible that many people will not be willing or able to take on time-consuming or co-resident care of elderly parents or 'parents-in-law'. Where the 'daughter-in-law' is younger than her partner she may well be reluctant to undertake the care of her partner's parents.

Figure 8
Cumulative percentages, by age, of men and women who had ever remarried for recent birth cohorts.
England and Wales

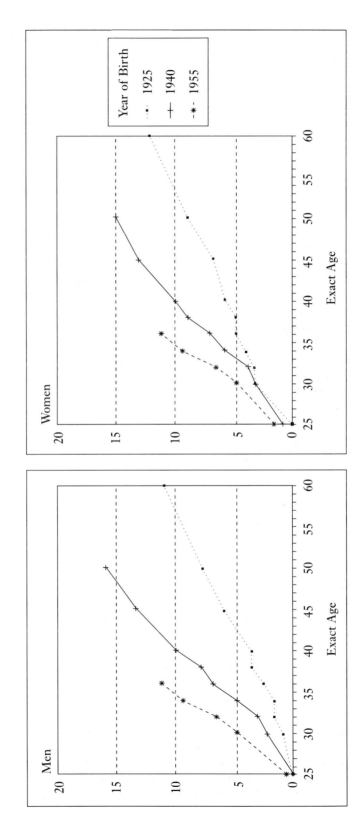

If stepfamilies are more likely to disadvantaged in terms of housing and income this alone will render the care of elderly parents more difficult, creating economic and housing constraints on co-residence or the purchase of alternative care. The care of spouses or cohabitees in these reconstituted families may not be viewed with the same commitment if the relationship is less stable and of shorter duration than first relationships. These trends are likely to affect men and women born since the early 1940s, with men being more likely to form further relationships than women.

Conclusions and implications for the future

We have seen how the nuclear family is undergoing extensive change and that this is likely to continue for some time into the future. The changes in family structure arise from fewer marriages, more cohabitation and births outside marriage, increases in divorce and remarriage, declining fertility and smaller families, and the rise of lone-parent and reconstituted families. While the conventional married couple family is still predominant at any one point in time, for many individuals it is often only one of several family types they experience during their lives.

The short-term prospects for family care of people in old age are not adversely affected by these recent changes in family structure. The present generations of carers have not suffered high rates of divorce nor have the current elderly generation experienced high levels of childlessness. In the longer term the situation is far less clear. The effects of divorce will become evident for elderly people themselves in the second decade of the next century, and higher rates of childlessness are evident so far for women born in the 1960s, who will reach their eighties in the fifth decade of the twenty-first century.

The most important changes for the future care of elderly people are those in marriage and fertility patterns. One result will be that informal family care will not be available for some elderly people, starting with those born after the mid-1950s. The changing nature of relationships and women's life decisions about whether to have children will mean that some men and women will not be able to expect care from a spouse. The majority probably will still marry, or at least form a 'marriage' type of relationship, but they may not have children. Childless elderly people are at a disadvantage in relation to informal care, especially if they do not have a partner because of death or separation. This will be more problematic for elderly women because of their greater longevity than men.

Divorce has more far-reaching implications for informal care. It has had an increasing effect for succeeding generations throughout this century, but the effect may become substantial for people born since the 1940s. The question of who will care for the divorced elderly is still to be answered. Will divorced elderly men maintain contact with their children and will these children provide care for elderly fathers if required? For many, the answer may not be encouraging. In the children's generation divorce may have removed daughters-in-law from caring for the current generation of elderly people, a situation which is likely to be exacerbated in the next decade. Remarriage or the creation of stepfamilies may either alleviate or complicate these issues. The familial obligations are complex and the elder care implications far from clear. The continuity of intergenerational reciprocity in support and services will be severely disrupted or, in the very least, hampered.

One other important aspect to consider is the change in the timing of childbirth. The trend towards later first birth and an increase in first birth rates for women over thirty is evident elsewhere in Europe and is particularly marked in the Netherlands (Haskey, 1992b). These women may find themselves with multiple dependants, both the young and the elderly. Will these women and/or their partners be free to devote time to the care of elderly parents and will they be willing to do so? The increasing participation rates of mothers in paid work militate against these multiple caring roles. Changes in attitudes should not be overlooked. People may not be willing to provide care given their other family and work commitments. This will be equally true for people in stepfamilies.

Social forces are also encouraging independence and autonomy for elderly people. There is evidence that the current generation of elderly people prefer care from independent sources rather than from the family. They want to maintain their autonomy and view co-residence with children as an unsatisfactory option. Finance will be crucial for determining the care of elderly people in the future; resources create choice.

The fundamental issue for public policy is the nature of the partnership between the family and the state that will enable the increasing number of elderly people to live their final years with autonomy and dignity. Care in the community will require substantial state support and intervention in the negotiation of the responsibility for care. Care of elderly people cannot be ignored as a family responsibility. The policies required to support elderly people and their families are more all-embracing than might be thought. The policy agenda should include finance (pensions, social security, housing, employment) as well as the more obvious statutory and voluntary health and personal social services. Only then will the caring capacity of families be supported rather than exploited.

Acknowledgements

Thanks are due to the General Household Survey at OPCS for supplying unpublished tables from the 1990/1 GHS survey on carers.

Footnote (The family is usually identified as the co-resident group linked by marriage, cohabitation or descent, but the extended family includes non-resident relatives. The family has shared and reciprocated duties.)

References

Allen, I., Hogg, D. and Peace, S. (1992) *Elderly People: Choice, Participation and Satisfaction*. Policy Studies Institute, London.

Abrams, M. (1976) *Beyond Three Score and Ten – A First Report on a Survey of the Elderly*. Age Concern, London.

Arber, S. and Ginn, J. (1991) *Gender and Later Life: A Sociological Analysis of Resources and Constraints*. London: Sage.

Arber, S. and Ginn, J. (1992) 'Class and Caring: A Forgotten Dimension'. *Sociology* 26, 4, pp 619–634.

Arber, S. and J. Ginn (1992a) '"In sickness and in health": care-giving, gender and the independence of elderly people', in (ed) Marsh, C. and Arber, S. *Families and Households: Divisions and Change* Macmillan, London.

Askham, J., Grundy, E. and Tinker, A. (1992) 'Caring: the importance of third age carers'. Research Paper Number 6. *The Carnegie Inquiry into the Third Age.* Carnegie United Kingdom Trust.

Bradshaw, J. (1989) *Lone parents: policy in the doldrums*. Family Policy Studies Centre: London.

Bould, M. (1990) 'Trapped within four walls'. *Community Care*, 19 (April), 17–19.

Bumpass, L. and Sweet, J. A. (1991) *The Effect of Marital Disruption on Intergenerational Relationships*. National Survey of Families and Households Working Paper 40. Centre for Demography and Ecology, University of Wisconsin-Madison. USA.

Burghes, L. (1993) *One-Parent Families – Policy Options for the 1990s*. Family Policy Studies Centre: London.

Cameron E., Evers, H., Badger, F. and Atkin, K. (1989) 'Black Old Women, Disability, and Health Carers', in (ed) Jefferys, M., *Growing Old in the Twentieth Century*. London: Routledge.

Carers National Association (1992) *Speak Up, Speak Out. Research among members of Carers National Association*. Carers National Association.

Clarke, L. (1992) 'Children's family circumstances: recent trends in Great Britain'. *European Journal of Population*, 8, 309–340.

Clarke, L. and Eldridge, S. (1989) *The structure and characteristics of families: A review of the circumstances of children in the 1980s*. CPS Research Paper 89–3, December 1989. London School of Hygiene and Tropical Medicine.

Coleman, D. and Salt, J. (1992) *The British Population: Patterns, Trends and Processes*. Oxford University Press.

Dalley, G. (1993) 'Caring: a legitimate interest of older women', in (ed) Bernard M. & Meade K. *Women Come of Age: Perspectives on the Lives of Older Women*. Edward Arnold.

Department of Health (1989) *Caring for People. Community Care in the Next Decade and Beyond*. Cm 849, London: HMSO.

DHSS (1981) *Growing Older*. Cmnd 8173, London: HMSO.

Eldridge, S. and Kiernan, K. (1985) 'Declining first marriage rates in England and Wales: a Change in timing or a rejection of marriage?' *European Journal of Population*. Vol. 1, No. 4 pp 327–345.

Ermisch, J. and Wright, R. (1989) *The duration of lone parenthood in Britain*. Discussion Paper 303. Centre for Economic and Policy Research: London.

Ermisch, J. (1990) *Fewer Babies, Longer Lives: Policy implications of current demographic trends*. Joseph Rowntree Foundation: York.

Evandrou, M. (1990) *Challenging the Invisibility of Carers: Mapping Informal Care Nationally*. Suntory-Toyota International Centre for Economics and Related Disciplines, London School of Economics, London.

Finch, J. (1989) *Family Obligations and Social Change*. Cambridge: Polity Press.

Henwood, M. (1990) *Community Care and Elderly People: Policy, Practice and Research Review*. London: Family Policy Studies Centre.

Glendinning, C. (1992) *The Costs of Informal Caring*. HMSO, London.

Green, H. (1988) *Informal Carers*. Series GHS No. 15. Supplement A. OPCS, London. HMSO.

Grundy, E. and Harrop, A. (1991) 'Co-residence between Adult Children and their Elderly Parents in England and Wales. *Journal of Social Policy*. 21, 3, pp325–348.

Harrop, A. and Plewis, I. (1993) *Two decades of Family Change: Secondary Analysis of Continuous Government Surveys*. Paper given to the Royal Society of Statisticians, Official Statistics Section, March 1992. (Submitted to the Journal of the Royal Statistical Society).

Haskey, J. (1983) 'Children in divorcing couples'. *Population Trends*. No. 31. Hmso: London.

Haskey, J. (1988) 'Trends in marriage and divorce, and cohort analyses of the proportions of marriages ending in divorce'. *Population Trends*. No. 54, 21–28. HMSO: London.

Haskey, J. (1989) 'Current prospects for the proportion of marriages ending in divorce'. *Population Trends* No. 55, 34–37. HMSO: London

Haskey, J. (1992a) 'Pre-marital cohabitation and the probability of subsequent divorce: analyses using new data from the General Household Survey'. *Population Trends* No. 68, pp 10–19. HMSO: London.

Haskey, J. (1992b) 'Patterns of marriage, divorce, and cohabitation in the different countries of Europe'. *Population Trends* No. 69, 27–36. Autumn 1992. HMSO: London.

Haskey, J. (1993a) 'Trends in the numbers of one-parent families in Great Britain'. *Population Trends*. No.71, 26–33.

Haskey, J. (1993b) 'First marriage, divorce, and remarriage: birth cohort analysis'. *Population Trends* No. 72, 24–33. Summer 1993. HMSO: London.

Haskey, J. (1993c) 'Lone parents and married parents with dependent children in Great Britain: a comparison of their occupations and social class profiles'. *Population Trends* No. 72, 34–44.

Hicks, C. (1988) *Who Cares? Looking After People at Home*. Virago Press, London.

Jefferys, M. and Thane, P. (1989) 'Introduction: An Ageing Society and Ageing People', in (ed) Jefferys, M. *Growing Old in the Twentieth Century.* pp 1–18. London: Routledge.

Jones, C. (1992) 'Fertility of the over thirties'. *Population Trends* 67. Spring 1992. pp10–16. HMSO: London.

Joshi, H. (1987) *Obstacles and Opportunities for Lone Parents as Breadwinners in Great Britain.* Paper 8. OECD Conference of National Experts on 'Lone Parents: the Economic Challenge of Changing Family Structures'. Paris, December.

Kiernan, K. (1989) 'The Family: Formation or Fission', in (ed) Joshi H. *The Changing Population of Britain.* Basil Blackwell, Oxford.

Kiernan, K. and Eldridge, S. (1987) 'Inter and intra cohort variation in the timing of first marriage'. *British Journal of Sociology* 38, 1. pp44–65.

Kiernan, K. and Estaugh, V. (1993) *Cohabitation, Extra-marital Childbearing and Social Policy.* Family Policy Studies Centre: London.

Kiernan, K. and Wicks, M. (1990) *Family Change and Future Policy.* Family Policy Studies Centre/Joseph Rowntree Memorial Trust, York.

Laslett, P. (1972) *The World We have Lost.* London: Methuen.

Leridon, H. (1990) 'Cohabitation, marrriage, separation: an analysis of life histories of French cohorts from 1968 to 1985'. *Population Studies* 44 pp. 127–144.

Lesthaeghe, R. (1991) *The second demographic transition in Western countries: an interpretation.* Interuniversity programme in deomography IPD – Working Paper 1991–2. Vrije Universiteit, Brussels.

Lewis, J. and Meredith, B. (1988) *Daughters Who Care.* Routledge, London.

Lewis, J. and Meredith, B. (1989) 'Contested territory in informal care', in (ed) M. Jefferys, *Growing Old In the Twentieth Century* London: Routledge.

McRae, S. (1993) *Cohabiting Mothers: Changing marriage and motherhood?* Policy Studies Institute, London.

Martin, J., White, A. and Meltzer, H. (1989) *Disabled Adults: Services, Transport and Employment.* OPCS Surveys of Disability, Report 4, London:HMSO.

McCalman, J. A. (1990) *The Forgotten People.* King's Fund Centre, London.

McGlone, F. (1992) *Disability and dependency a demographic and social audit.* Occasional Paper 14. Family Policy Studies Centre, London.

McGlone, F. (1993) 'A million more carers – but how many more to come?' in *Family Policy Bulletin*, June 1993. Family Policy Studies Centre, London.

OPCS (1992) *General Household Survey: Carers in 1990.* OPCS monitor SS 92/2. OPCS, London.

OPCS (1992a) *Marriage and Divorce Statistics, England and Wales, 1990.* OPCS Series FM2 No.18. HMSO, London.

OPCS (1993) *General Household Survey 1991.* Series GHS no.22. HMSO, London.

OPCS (1993a) *Birth Statistics.* Series FM1 no. 20. London: HMSO.

Oppenheim, C. (1990) *Poverty: The Facts.* Child Poverty Action Group, London.

Parker, G. (1992) 'Counting care: numbers and types of informal carers', in Twigg J. (ed) *Carers: Research and Practice*. London:HMSO.

Parker, G. (1992a) *Informal Care of the Older People in Great Britain: Evidence from the 1985 General Household Survey*. Paper for the European Conference on Informal Care, 23–35 September 1991. (Revised September 1992) Social Policy Research Unit, University of York.

Roll, J. (1993) *Lone Parent Families in Europe*. Family Policy Studies Centre: London.

Twigg, J. and Atkin, K. (1991) *Evaluating support for informal carers*. (Part II): Final Report. Social Policy Research Unit, University of York. Forthcoming as OUP publication.

Twigg, J. (ed) (1992) *Carers: Research and Practice*. London: HMSO.

Qureshi, H. and Walker, A. (1989) *The Caring Relationship: Elderly People and their Families*. Macmillan, Basingstoke.

van der Kaa, D.J. (1987) 'Europe's Second Demographic Transition'. *Population Bulletin* 41, 1. Population Reference Bureau, Washington DC.

Wall, R. (1989) 'Living alone and leaving home'. *Population Studies* 43:3, 369–390.

Wall, R. (1992) 'Relationships Between the Generations in British Families Past and Present', in (eds) Marsh, C. and Arber, S., *Families and Households in Modern Britain*. London: Macmillan.

Whatmore, K. and Mira-Smith, C. (1991) *Eldercare in the 1990s. A national survey on attitudes towards older people and caring for older people*. The National Carers Survey Research Team. London.

White, L. and Booth, A. (1985) 'The quality and stability of remarriages: the role of step-children'. *American Sociological Review* Vol 50, No. 5.

Wright, F. (1986) *Left to Care Alone*. Gower, London.

Chapter 3

RESPONSIBILITIES, OBLIGATIONS AND COMMITMENTS

JANET FINCH

Responsibilities for family care: definitions and concepts

This chapter examines the idea that informal, family caring rests on the foundation of family responsibilities. My aim is to discuss what that means in practice, to assess how this aspect of family life is likely to change in the future, and what such changes could mean for the future availability of family care for infirm elderly people.

In order to examine these important issues, we need to understand the meaning of concepts like 'responsibility' or 'obligation', not from a philosophical perspective, but as they are put into practice within contemporary families. Although probably they do not use these words, we might expect that most people recognise the idea that obligations or responsibilities are part of family life. But what does that actually mean to them?

The simplest starting point for this is to consider the concept of what I would call 'fixed obligations'. This implies that simply being related to someone else – through blood or through marriage – carries with it certain duties and obligations, which include the provision of personal care should this become necessary. It is assumed that such obligations flow simply from the fact of being related, and from the natural feelings associated especially with the closest family ties.

This idea that there are fixed obligations associated with family relationships is reflected in much contemporary debate about families, as indeed it has been for the past two centuries (Finch, 1989a). But is it a realistic picture of family responsibilities in practice? I shall argue that, once we look at the empirical evidence, we see that family life does not operate like this. In reality the responsibilities which people feel and acknowledge towards their relatives have more complex and more individual roots. For example, as Allan (1988) has pointed out, there has been a long-standing expectation in British family life that adult children should be able to live lives independent of their parents, and vice versa. Thus feelings of responsibility for the well-being of elderly parents must necessarily be tempered on both sides with a desire to retain mutual independence. In this chapter I shall propose an alternative model of family responsibilities which I shall call the 'commitments' model and which, I argue, offers a better way of understanding how family responsibilities operate in practice than does the concept of 'fixed obligations'.

Responsibilities in practice

What evidence is there about the nature of family responsibilities in practice, especially as they relate to the family care of older people? The short answer is, not a great deal. Although there have been many studies about informal care over the last decade, most have focused on documenting who provides care, the conditions under which they provide it, and the personal consequences of doing so (Ungerson, 1987; Lewis and Meredith, 1988; Qureshi and Walker, 1989; Parker, 1992). Seldom have these studies tried to study directly any underlying sense of obligation or responsibility, and to understand what this means.

It was in recognition of the lack of evidence about this issue specifically that the project on *Family Obligations*, in which I collaborated with Jennifer Mason, was established (1). As this remains the only recent British research which attempts directly to study the nature of obligations and responsibilities in families, I shall draw on it quite extensively in this chapter, although I shall also make reference to other studies. Its purpose was not to study informal care specifically, but to examine more broadly the nature and foundations of responsibilities between adult kin, covering all types of practical and financial assistance. Because of the particular focus of the research our data on responsibilities between parents and children are more extensive than those on spouse responsibilities, and therefore I shall have more to say about the former than the latter in this chapter.

Beginning with the 'fixed obligations' model we can reason that, if family responsibilities do work on this basis, then we should be able to identify among the British population some common agreements about what these responsibilities are. Our *Family Obligations* survey sought to identify any such areas of agreement, across a random sample of almost 1,000 adults, interviewed in 1985 and 1986 (2). The purpose of the survey was to tap publicly expressed norms about family obligations, to find out whether there is agreement about what people in general ought to do for their relatives in given circumstances, rather than to find out what respondents themselves actually did for members of their own families. Findings from this survey are reported in detail in Finch and Mason (1990a, 1991, 1992).

In general, the survey found that there are very few issues on which there is any clear agreement across the population. Looking at the position of elderly people particularly, we asked respondents to say whether they agreed or disagreed with the following statement:

Children have no obligation to look after their parents when they are old

57 per cent of our sample indicated that children *do* have an obligation to look after parents and 37 per cent said that they do *not*. It is also interesting to note that older people in the survey were less likely than younger respondents to say that children have a responsibility to care for their parents. The pattern of answers here is in line with findings from other similar studies (for example, West, 1984).

Other questions in our survey tend also to confirm that there is little agreement about the nature of children's responsibilities for parents. At the same time they indicate that, along with the marriage relationship, the parent-child link is regarded as being in a special category of relationships in adult life. This itself is linked to ideas about responsibilities. When given the choice between a range of different relatives who might provide help for an elderly person, most respondents identified clearly a child or children as having a responsibility to offer help beyond that of other kin (Finch and Mason, 1990a).

This is in line with earlier work on British kinship (Firth *et al*, 1970; Morgan, 1975) and is parallelled by findings from an American study of kinship obligations which was taking place at the same time as the British *Family Obligations* study (Rossi and Rossi, 1990).

Thus we have an apparent paradox. On the one hand, people clearly identify children as the people who should step forward first to offer assistance to a mother or father. On the other hand, there is nothing approaching clear agreement that children have a responsibility actually to look after their elderly parents. This paradox can, however, be resolved by some other findings from our survey. Essentially, it seems that there is broad agreement that children have a responsibility to do *something* to help elderly parents if this is needed. But there is little agreement at this public normative level about *what* they should do.

Survey findings on this issue are reported in detail elsewhere (Finch and Mason, 1991; 1992). In brief it seems that, when faced with clear evidence of parental need, our respondents indicated that there are different ways in which a child might legitimately respond. For example, in one question which postulated an hypothetical situation in which parents needed nursing care, a quarter of our respondents thought that the best way for children to respond was to give the parents money to purchase help, rather than become directly involved. Other answers in our survey suggest that people's judgment of *how* children's responsibilities should be fulfilled is influenced by what they know about the circumstances of the particular case. Certainly most people treat it as quite legitimate for adult children to consider the circumstances of their own lives – their own jobs, their spouse and children, other commitments – before deciding how to respond to parental need. In another survey question, about different options for where an infirm elderly person should live, we offered as one choice that the elderly person should move in with relatives, provided the circumstances were right. If respondents chose that option, we then asked them to say what the 'right' circumstances would be. Most of these answers emphasise the personal situation of the 'receiving' relatives. The message is that children should not take an elderly parent into their home unless they really want this, or unless they have enough space for it to be comfortable, or unless it will not impose on other aspects of their lives too much (Finch and Mason, 1991).

So the idea of 'fixed obligations' does not stand up to the evidence. There is really no agreement among the British population about what obligations are attached simply to being an adult child. Certainly there is no consensus that this should involve providing practical or nursing care. How can we reconcile this with the evidence that in practice family carers – some, though not all, of them – say that they do provide care out of a sense of obligation or responsibility towards the person being cared for? (Ungerson, 1987; Lewis and Meredith, 1988).

At this point, we need to turn to a different way of thinking about responsibilities, which I am calling the 'commitments' model. In the course of conducting the *Family Obligations* study, my collaborator and I became convinced that the idea of commitment is the key to understanding responsibilities of all types in families, at least those responsibilities which entail one adult giving help to another. We came to this view not only on the basis of the survey data, but also from our analysis of semi-structured interviews with 88 people about their own family experiences.

In this alternative model, we see responsibilities as commitments which are built up over time between specific individuals. They are built up (often over many years) through contact, through shared activities, and particularly, through each giving the other help as it is needed. This process of reciprocity – accepting help and then giving something in return – is the engine which drives the process of developing commitments. Although people do not work with a simplistic balance sheet, reciprocal help given and received over time is a crucial factor in understanding how family relationships operate (Allan, 1988; Finch and Mason, 1992). It means that each child will build a set of commitments with her parents which is different from each of her sisters' and brothers' commitments. When people talk about responsibilities to their relatives they mean responsibilities arrived at in this way, through the process of developing commitments over time and between real people, not obligations which flow simply from the genealogical link (Finch and Mason, 1992).

I have concentrated on the responsibilities of children for their parents because children are of much greater significance in the provision of care for elderly people than are any other group of relatives (Green, 1988). The only other significant group are spouses caring for a disabled or infirm partner. Does the 'commitments model' also apply to spouses? Or do the responsibilities which spouses feel for each other come closer to the 'fixed obligations' model? It is quite possible that they do, although there is no directly comparable research data, so this conclusion must necessarily be more speculative than my comments about parents and children.

There seem to be good reasons why spouse responsibilities might conform more closely to the model of fixed obligations than do others. Marriage is a relationship which differs from all other family relationships in ways relevant to this issue: it is based on a legal contract, it entails making promises about each caring for the other, it is the result of a deliberate step taken in adult life. In addition, it normally involves a shared household, which itself is of key significance in developing responsibilities for providing care (Qureshi and Walker, 1989). All these would suggest that responsibility to care for one's spouse may well be viewed as an intrinsic part of being married, not dependent upon the particular relationship which any individual has with a husband or wife. The evidence of who actually provides care tends to support this analysis, in that it indicates that both women and men are equally likely to be caring for a disabled spouse (Green, 1988; Qureshi and Walker, 1989). This suggests perhaps that there is rather little room for a spouse to decline to offer care, although there is certainly evidence that many find the experience of providing care for a spouse challenging and difficult (Oliver, 1983; Ungerson, 1987; Parker, 1992). Furthermore, evidence based on the International Social Survey Programme indicates that, by comparison with some other European countries especially, British respondents tend to say that their spouse is the first person to whom they would turn for help when they are ill. This suggests that there is a particular tendency in this country to emphasise support between spouses rather than other relatives or friends (Finch, 1989b).

So, in practice, the model of 'fixed obligations' may have some reality as the basis for responsibilities which spouses acknowledge towards each other. But for other family relationships, we need to see responsibilities (including the responsibility to provide personal care) as 'commitments' which build up over time between *certain* parents and *certain* children, rather than as obligations which flow simply from being an adult child.

The impact of social and demographic changes

What does the analysis which I have offered imply for thinking about the future of family care? Given that the responsibility to provide care is not (with the possible exception of spouses) a fixed inherent feature of family relationships, the key question is: are the conditions of family life changing in ways likely to foster or to impede the development of commitment to provide care to an elderly relative, especially a parent?

There are many ways in which this theme could be developed, since there are various ways in which family life is changing. I am going to focus upon one in particular: increased rates of divorce and remarriage. Perhaps more than any other factor in public debate this is often taken for a symbol of the fragmentation and disintegration of family life which many people predict and fear. Yet the full effects of present trends will only be seen in the next century. Rates of divorce and remarriage have risen significantly only over the past twenty years, which means that we have yet to see their full significance. In the future many more people will reach old age having been divorced, or having contracted more than one marriage. Many more will have children who themselves have 'reconstituted' families (Haskey, 1989; Elliott, 1991). Is this likely to have a long-term effect on family relationships, not only couple relationships? Are such changes relevant to responsibilities to provide care in old age? I shall consider this first in relation to parents and children, then spouses, and finally I shall discuss briefly some other social changes which may have a bearing on this analysis.

Divorce, remarriage and filial responsibilities

I have argued that filial responsibilities, the commitments between a particular child and his or her parent(s) develop by a complex process based fundamentally on reciprocity. One important reason why some children develop much stronger commitments to their parents than others is that their life circumstances have meant that they have had more need to call on their parents for assistance, and that their parents have been in a position to supply it (Finch and Mason, 1992). If we link increased rates of divorce and remarriage into this picture, the question becomes: where people have passed through several marriages, is this more or less likely to lead to parents and children developing highly committed relationships? Although our *Family Obligations* study did not examine this as a central focus, we do have data on the family relationships of people who have been divorced. These data point to the conclusion that the experience of divorce and remarriage is likely to make relationships with other kin stronger rather than weaker, especially to accentuate the significance of relationships within the family of origin, normally based on blood ties.

Our data suggest this in various ways, centred around the theme that the experience of divorce is frequently distressing in an emotional sense and creates some urgent practical needs (for financial assistance, for a temporary home, for help in caring for children, according to the particular circumstances of the case). Blood relatives are seen as the appropriate people to turn to for help in these circumstances. For example, in our survey we asked a question about the situation of a 19 year old who has a baby and has split up with her boyfriend. 79 per cent of our respondents thought that she should go back and live with her parents, rather than other possible options and a further 16 per cent thought that, although this was not necessarily their preferred option, the parents should certainly offer their daughter and grandchild a home. Although our respondents' judgments were undoubtedly influenced by their perception both of the genuineness of need and the deservingness of the characters – as some of our other survey questions show very clearly – (Finch and Mason, 1992), most people see it as very appropriate, in cases of genuine need following the break-up of a marriage or cohabiting relationship, that people should turn to their close kin for help.

This conclusion is certainly supported by our interview data, where people told us about a range of relevant experiences in their own families (3). 17 out of 88 interviewees spoke about emotional support given or received at the time of a divorce. These examples were given, not in response to specific questions about divorce, but in response to very open-ended questions asking the interviewee to give any example of support of any kind passing between members of his or her family. The fact that one fifth mentioned emotional support in the circumstances surrounding a divorce suggests that it is an important way in which people use their kin. Most of these examples are of emotional support offered by parents to children, or between siblings.

In several cases which we studied in detail it was clear that separated or divorced children had relied very heavily on their parents for practical help. In two particular cases a man, McNeil Jackson, and a woman, Sarah Allen, each had returned to their parents' home with a small child and had lived there for several years, relying on their parents for accommodation, financial help, assistance with the care of the child and emotional support. This set them off on a path of reciprocal commitments which was different from that of their siblings even though, in Sarah Allen's case, she had always found her mother difficult on a personal level (see Finch and Mason, 1992). In each case, some twenty years later and with parents now well into old age, it was clear that each of them felt a stronger commitment than their siblings to become involved in personal care when the need arose.

This is the kind of evidence which points to the conclusion that the experience of divorce may well strengthen the significance of the family of origin, and foster the kinds of relationships between parents and children which result in a clear commitment to provide informal care in old age. But of course divorce will not have this effect in all cases. As can be seen from the situations I have described, the dynamic was created by fact that the divorced child needed a home and other practical assistance, and that the parent was able to provide it. In other circumstances that would not be a practical possibility, for a whole range of reasons. Moreover there is evidence from elsewhere that some people see their parents as the last people to whom they would be prepared to turn when their marriage fails (Brannen and Collard, 1982).

However, despite this variety of experience, which it is vital to acknowledge, the underlying tendency in a situation of high divorce and remarriage rates is bound to be to accentuate the importance of relationships with one's family of origin, certainly not to undermine them. Where people are passing through several marriages and marriage-like relationships during an adult lifetime, ties to blood kin provide the single stable elements in an otherwise changing kin universe. And since, on our evidence at least, having a family to whom one 'belongs' is something which most people value highly (Finch and Mason, 1992: 29–33) this element of stability cannot but be significant. We can add to this the evidence that the actual process of divorcing itself may be conducive to developing commitments between parents and children, because it often creates urgent needs for practical or financial assistance.

The converse is that in-law relationships may be more tenuous than in a situation where each individual has only one set of in-laws during a life-time. This is interesting, given the evidence that daughters-in-law in particular rank quite high in the 'hierarchy' of likely informal carers (Qureshi and Walker, 1989). Will high rates of divorce have an impact on the responsibilities which in-laws feel towards each other? On the surface it seems likely that they will. If the responsibility to provide care is a commitment which builds up over time between two individuals, it seems inherently less likely that such a process will occur when someone has several different sets of in-laws over their life time.

Broadly that prediction is probably correct, but there are two factors which may pull in the opposite direction. First, existing literature on in-law relationships suggests that traditionally in English kinship husbands and wives have been seen as a unified entity who 'own' each other's kin (Wolfram, 1987). Thus although relationships between in-laws (especially parents-in-law and children-in-law) are seen conventionally as problematic, husbands share in the responsibilities which their wives feel for a parent, and vice versa (Finch, 1989: 49–51). Thus, a daughter-in-law who gets involved in providing care for an infirm parent-in-law is, in a sense, doing so as part of the responsibility which she feels to support her husband, as much as any direct commitment to his parents.

Second, there is an interesting question about whether divorce necessarily fractures the relationship between in-laws, in a way which would rule out any commitments between parent-in-law and child-in-law outliving the ending of the marriage. We considered this issue in our Family Obligations study and found that there are indeed some instances where a child-in-law continues a close and committed relationship with former parents-in-law. They seem to be few in number and probably grow out of a relatively unusual combination of circumstances – good, close relationships whilst the marriage was intact, a long history of reciprocal support, a divorce process which consolidates those particular relationships rather than undermines them, and the ability to successfully reconstitute these relationships on a different basis after the divorce has occurred (see Finch and Mason, 1990b for detailed discussion). Moreover in response to survey questions about post-divorce situations we found a high degree of public support for the view that, where relationships between former in-laws had outlasted the end of a marriage, it would be quite appropriate for commitments to continue. In an hypothetical case, where we postulated a continuing pattern of mutual support between a woman and her ex-mother-in-law, including some personal care for the latter, 77 per cent of our survey respondents said that it would be appropriate for this to continue even if the younger woman remarried. Thus it seems clear that continuing commitments between in-laws are not ruled out by the ending of a marriage, even though we should not expect to see this actually happen except in a minority of cases.

To recapitulate, I have argued that, although in-law commitments may normally be weakened, the experience of passing through several marriages during a lifetime is more likely to strengthen rather than to weaken relationships between parents and children in adult life. However, whether divorce really does consolidate commitments of this kind will depend on the way in which the relationship between a parent and a child does actually *develop* over time. My argument is that high divorce rates should not be seen as a factor which necessarily undermines responsibilities between parents and children. Indeed if it has any effect at all, it is more likely to strengthen them. In that sense we should not anticipate that high divorce rates will reduce the likelihood that adult children will feel a responsibility to care for their elderly parents.

Divorce, remarriage and spouse responsibilities

What is the relevance of increased rates of divorce and remarriage to responsibilities between spouses in the future? It is evident that future cohorts of elderly people will contain a much higher proportion who have been through two or more marriages. On the surface it looks as if marriage as a permanent arrangement, 'for better or for worse', will be confined to a minority. It would be easy to conclude that the likely effect on the availability of spouse care in old age is that many husbands or wives simply would not be sufficiently committed to a spouse to provide this, indeed that some might be ready to leave a marriage in order to avoid it.

That conclusion would be easy to draw – but it would probably be incorrect. Although there is no contemporary research which looks at this issue directly, there is no reason to suppose that the responsibilities which people do seem to associate with the married state are undermined simply because one reaches old age married to a different person from the spouse of one's younger years. Indeed, all the recent research on marriage suggests that people place high value upon, and have a high regard for, the idea that marriage is a committed relationship. The very fact that more people divorce and marry again can be seen as an indication of the high regard in which marriage is held and the high standards which are applied to it – people want a strong, committed relationship, and if they do not succeed in achieving this the first time, they try again with someone else (Mansfield and Collard, 1988; Clark and Haldane, 1990). Viewed in this light therefore, we can predict that the responsibility to provide care for a spouse would be relatively unaffected by the increasing likelihood that future generations of elderly people will have passed through several marriages.

In the future there may be some people who have made and broken several marriages during their lifetime, and who will therefore feel able to end another one in old age, perhaps influenced directly by the prospect of providing informal care for a spouse who has become disabled. Although this *could* occur, existing data on divorce and age give little hint that it is happening now in a way which might constitute a trend. The likelihood of divorcing drops dramatically in early middle age – so much so that the standard population statistics group together everyone over the age of 45. In this 45+ age group the proportion of married people who divorce drops to about one quarter of those divorcing in the 35–44 age group, for both women and men. Although the absolute number of divorces has risen, these age-related patterns have remained constant over the past thirty years (*Population Trends 69*, 1992:74).

Meanwhile the dominant way in which marriage is viewed suggests that most people would see the responsibility to provide care as an intrinsic part of this relationship, and that this would be so whether the marriage is the first or the fourth which an individual has contracted, whether it has lasted for five years or for fifty at the point when the need for care arises. The limited evidence available on spouse care would suggest that this is equally true of husbands and wives, although of course what providing care actually means may vary for men and women, as may the level of informal and formal support to the main carer (Green, 1988; Arber and Gilbert, 1989). If this analysis is correct, it suggests that spouse care will remain the most reliable form of informal care, in the sense that it will be offered most predictably, provided both spouses are still alive at the point when one of them begins to need personal or nursing care.

Therein lies a much bigger issue. It is well known that women's life expectancy on average is about five years longer than that of men and that, amongst the very elderly population where the need for care is most likely to arise, widows and other single women outnumber men by two to one (*Social Trends*, 1993: 14,97). Insofar as this is likely to continue, we can predict that those who reach an age where they are most likely to receive care are those least likely to have a spouse who can provide it, and the majority of these people will be women. Thus differential life expectancy rates are likely to have a much bigger impact on the availability of spouse care in the future than continuing high rates of divorce. The picture which emerges is one in which men are much more likely than women to continue to have available the most predictable form of family support, namely spouse care.

Interlocking social trends

In this discussion of the impact of social and demographic trends on responsibilities for family care, I have focused upon divorce and remarriage because they are factors which are changing significantly the shape of families, and where the effects of those changes will not be fully experienced until the next century. However, it is obvious that there are other predictable social and demographic changes which will interlock with the impact of divorce and remarriage, and which a fuller analysis should take into account. For example, in discussing the availability of spouse care in the future, I have suggested that differential survival rates may be much more important than any consequences flowing from the likelihood that increased numbers of elderly people in the future will have been through more than one marriage.

Looking specifically at the question of responsibilities to care, there are two other kinds of social change which seem particularly important to mention in this context. The first of these is inheritance. This used to be a significant matter only for a minority of wealthy families, but it is now becoming the concern of the majority, thanks to the spread of home ownership. Since two-thirds of households are now owner-occupied, this means that many more than in the past can expect to be a beneficiary or a testator in a bequest which involves substantial material assets. Little is known about how these matters are handled in families although work currently under way, in which I am involved, is designed to redress that (4). Preliminary findings certainly confirm earlier work on one point, namely that the great majority of bequests made through wills go either to spouses or to blood relatives. If people die without making a will (as about two-thirds still do) then intestacy laws also acknowledge the claims of kin with a blood tie (Mellows, 1983). Thus the increased importance of inheritance will, I would argue, have the effect of enhancing the significance of relationships within the family of origin and points in the same direction as my argument about divorce.

The second factor which needs to be integrated with this discussion is changes in the pattern of women's employment. This has particular relevance to the availability of daughters as carers for their elderly parents, although there will be a few cases where it may affect the availability of spouse care if a woman is married to a man much older than herself, or if her husband becomes incapacitated at a much younger than expected average age.

The basic question is: if a daughter is in employment, particularly full-time employment, at the time when the need for care arises does that mean that she will not be available as a carer? Alternatively, will the pressures be such that daughters will give up their jobs in order to become carers for their parents? In the context of this chapter, we need to look at this question from the perspective of responsibilities to provide care. In earlier sections I have shown that responsibilities, especially filial responsibilities are not fixed obligations, but are commitments which build up over time between individual parents and children. In the light of that we should expect that it will be only *certain* daughters for whom the issue of a conflict between employment and providing care will be a real one, namely those daughters who have developed the kind of commitments to their parents in which direct provision of care looks like a natural consequence. For the rest, it is unlikely that the issue will arise in that form. For them, the question is more likely to be how these daughters can provide some kind of help, which falls short of a direct involvement which they will see as inappropriate.

In those cases where commitments have been built up between daughter and parent(s) which move naturally in the direction of her becoming a carer, what is likely to happen if the need for care arises while she is in full-time employment? Will the responsibility to care over-ride all else, and lead her to give up her job? Here the existing evidence does not give us very clear pointers for the future. On the one hand, there are certainly individual cases reported in some research studies where daughters have indeed given up jobs in order to care for an infirm parent, and have felt that it was part of their responsibility to the parent to do so (Wright, 1983; Lewis and Meredith, 1988). However these individual cases do not really amount to a generalisable pattern, in the sense that they are drawn from small samples, and are not necessarily typical even of all cases within their respective studies.

Pointing in a somewhat different direction is the evidence from our Family Obligations study. In our survey we posed three questions about hypothetical cases in which a woman was faced with the possibility of giving up a job in order to care for an elderly relative. The responses depend somewhat on the circumstances of the case, but the proportions favouring the woman's giving up her job were 22 per cent, 29 per cent and 43 per cent respectively. The case which attracted 43 per cent in favour of the woman giving up her job was one where we had built in a history of significant mutual support between the two main characters. But even here, less than half our respondents favoured a woman's giving up her job, and in the other questions the proportions giving this answer were much smaller. We concluded that most people see it as legitimate for woman's employment to be put before the possibility of becoming a family carer. Our data from the interview study suggest that what most people endorse at the level of public norms also happens in practice. In cases where the dilemma of choosing between a full-time job and becoming a carer had been faced in reality, we found that women tried to retain their jobs, while seeking compromise strategies which enabled them to give some support to an elderly parent, falling short of becoming the main carer (see Finch and Mason, 1990c).

So this brief consideration of how other social trends which might interlock with the impact of divorce and remarriage on the development of commitments to provide care presents something of a mixed picture. On the one hand, trends in home ownership, feeding through to inheritance, seem to operate in the same direction as divorce in that it appears that they will tend to strengthen the significance of the family of origin for more people. To that extent these trends together may serve to enhance, rather than to undermine, the likelihood that children will develop the kinds of commitments to their parents which would result in the offer to provide care. On the other hand, trends in women's employment would seem to point in the other direction. The need to preserve women's employment status, and the legitimacy accorded to this, suggests that the more women who remain in full-time employment throughout their adult lives, the more limited will be the number of daughters who will be prepared to take on significant caring roles.

Conclusion

In discussing the nature of family responsibilities, and their likely significance in supporting the care of elderly people in their future, I have emphasised that they are based on individual 'commitments' rather than on 'fixed obligations' associated with a genealogical link. This certainly applies to filial responsibilities, although obligations between spouses may have a more fixed character. Thus it is in the nature of family responsibilities that they vary between one family and another, between one child and another. There is no reason to suppose that this basic picture will change in the foreseeable future.

From a social policy perspective, this means that filial responsibilities cannot be relied on as the basis for the provision of care. Whether a particular child feels that becoming a carer for her parent(s) is natural and reasonable is not predictable, without close knowledge of the history of the particular relationships in which such commitment to care does exist. The circumstances of the child's life at the point when the need for care arises (including employment status) has a direct bearing on the offer to provide personal care. This concept of family responsibilities as variable and personal is apparently recognised and endorsed as legitimate by the majority of the population. It is not a recent phenomenon but has characterised English kinship in particular for several centuries. At certain times in the past Governments have sought to define and enforce certain responsibilities, most obviously through the Poor Law. However historical evidence suggests that this was experienced as inconsistent with the way in which family responsibilities were defined in practice and was therefore widely resented, sometimes resisted (Finch, 1989a).

Thus, in the future, family responsibilities cannot be relied upon to deliver a consistent pattern of informal care for elderly people. Although present social and demographic trends will not necessarily undermine this aspect of family life – indeed I have argued that some trends may encourage the growth of committed relationships between parents and children in particular – the basis of responsibilities is likely to remain highly individual in the future, as it is in the present and has been in the past.

Notes

1. The Family Obligations study was funded by the Economic and Social Research Council, 1985–89 (Grant No. G00232197).
2. The Family Obligations Survey was conducted in the Greater Manchester region. A random sample of 978 people were interviewed, covering adults of all ages and drawn from the electoral register.
3. The Family Obligations interview study involved semi-structured interviews with 88 individuals. We drew interviewees initially from the survey population, then where possible we interviewed other members of their own close kin group, thus building up a series of family case studies. Though these families are not a representative sample, they cover a wide range of socio-economic circumstances.
4. The Inheritance study is funded by the Economic and Social Research Council, 1990–93 (Grant No. G00232035). As part of this research a random sample of 800 wills is being analysed, drawn from people who died in the north-west and south-east regions of England in four sample years.

References

Allan, G. (1988) 'Kinship, responsibility and care for elderly people'. *Ageing and Society.* 8.249–68.

Arber, S. and Gilbert, N. (1989) 'Men: the forgotten carers'. *Sociology.* 23.1.111–18.

Brannen, J. and Collard, J. (1982) *Marriages in Trouble: The Process of Seeking Help.* London. Tavistock.

Clark, D. and Haldane, D. (1990) *Wedlocked?* Cambridge. Polity.

Elliott, B. J. (1991) 'Demographic trends in domestic life 1945–87', in Clark, D. (ed.) *Marriage, Domestic Life and Social Change.* London. Routledge.

Ermisch, J. (1989) 'Divorce: economic antecedents and aftermath', in Joshi, H. (ed) *The Changing Population of Britain.* Oxford. Blackwell.

Finch, J. (1989a) *Family Obligations and Social Change.* Cambridge. Polity.

Finch, J. (1989b) 'Kinship and friendship', in Jowell, R., Witherspoon, S. and Brook, L. (eds) *British Social Attitudes: A Special International Report.* Aldershot. Gower.

Finch, J. and Mason, J. (1990a) 'Filial obligations and kin support for elderly people'. *Ageing and Society.* 10.152–75.

Finch, J. and Mason, J. (1990b) 'Divorce, remarriage and family obligations'. *Sociological Review.* 38.2.219–46.

Finch, J. and Mason, J. (1990c) 'Gender, employment and responsibilities to kin'. *Work, Employment and Society.* 4.3.349–67.

Finch, J. and Mason, J. (1991) 'Obligations of kinship in Britain: is there normative agreement?' *British Journal of Sociology.* 42.3.345–67.

Finch, J. and Mason, J. (1992) *Negotiating Family Responsibilities.* London. Routledge.

Firth, R., Hubert, J. and Forge, A. (1970) *Families and Their Relatives.* London. Routledge.

Green, H. (1988) *Informal Careers.* OPCS Series GMS No.15. Supplement A. London, HMSO.

Haskey, J. (1989) 'Current prospects for the proportion of marriages ending in divorce'. *Population Trends* 55, 34–7. London. HMSO.

Lewis, J. and Meredith, B. (1988) *Daughters Who Care.* London. Routledge.

Mansfield, P. and Collard, J. (1988) *The Beginning of the Rest of Your Life?* London. Macmillan.

Mellows, A. R. (1983) *The Law of Succession.* London. Butterworth.

Morgan, D. H. J. (1975) *Social Theory and the Family.* London. Routledge.

Oliver, J. (1983) 'The caring wife', in Finch, J. and Groves, D. (eds) *A Labour of Love: Women, Work and Caring.* London. Routledge.

Parker, G. (1992) *With This Body: Caring and Disability in Marriage.* Milton Keynes. Open University Press.

Population Trends, (1992), No. 69, Autumn. OPCS. London. HMSO.

Qureshi, H. and Walker, A. (1989) *The Caring Relationship*. London. Macmillan.

Rossi, A. and Rossi, P. (1990) *Of Human Bonding*. New York. Aldine de Gruyter.

Social Trends (1993) No. 23. Central Statistical Office. London: HMSO.

Ungerson, C. (1987) *Policy Is Personal*. London. Tavistock.

West, P. (1984) 'The family, the welfare state and community care: political rhetoric and public attitudes'. *Journal of Social Policy*. 13.4.417–46.

Wolfram, S. (1987) *In-Laws and Out-Laws: Kinship and Marriage in England*. London. Croom Helm.

Wright, F. (1983) 'Single carers: employment, housework and caring', in Finch, J. and Groves, D. (eds.) *A Labour of Love*. London. Routledge.

Chapter 4
MIGRATION AND FAMILY CARE

ANTHONY WARNES
AND REUBEN FORD

Introduction

Social reproduction requires migration. When children mature, marry and reproduce, they are expected to leave their parents' (or a parent's) home but not to sever all contact (Finch, 1989). There is, however, no consensus about the degree of concern and care which adult children should provide to elderly parents when sick or frail. Many elderly people say that they wish to preserve their residential independence as long as possible, but not to disrupt their children's lives nor create an obligation to care, yet paradoxically believe that if it became necessary, children could be called upon to provide more than usual support. Among adult children, many are willing to move nearer their elderly parents but not to live with them. Affluent children may willingly provide a flat within their house but resist fully shared living arrangements.

The articulation and resolution of these attitudes into specific forms of instrumental support and care is no doubt specific to each case. The resolution is also moderated by changing social conditions and societal norms and by practicability. For example, high quality residential institutions would be far more attractive to affluent elderly people than depersonalising residential institutions which provide minimal care to the poor. Presumably there would be less resistance to entering them, and less guilt among children about recommending this course to a parent. Expectations, norms and the expressions of family care are also moderated by the history of the relationship between an elderly person and a child; and these in turn are influenced by the residential histories of the participants and their present proximity. In the vocabulary of social psychology, the potential and the practice of family care is related to the participants' personalities and values, and to their calculus of the credits and debits in serial reciprocal relationships.

Migrations are infrequent but commonplace: among elderly people, fewer than 3 per cent move in any year while a majority change address after 60 years of age. Most migrations are short distance and mundane but a few are spectacular – to New Zealand or the move from Bournemouth to Bermondsey. In most parts of the country few make long distance moves around the age of retirement, but at least a fifth and maybe one-quarter leave the metropolitan area of London. And most migrations produce only minor adjustments to the type of residence, daily activities and social networks, while a few radically change people's lives, normally for good but sometimes in very damaging ways. Residential mobility and migration comprise therefore both 'normal' and 'stressful' events, and mainly mundane but occasionally exotic behaviour. This makes it difficult to assess in the round. Impressionistic evidence holds great sway, partly because the data are deficient. This chapter begins with a brief account of our knowledge of migration in later life. It reviews differential migration by age, marital status, household type, housing tenure and recent personal events (notably widowhood), and the relative propensities to make moves of different types and over various distances, e.g. from large cities to remote rural areas or from suburb to suburb. Attention is given to the relationship between the level of residential mobility and the state of the (owner-occupation) housing market, and whether periods of very low activity (as in the early 1990s) increase the prevalence of sub-optimal residential situations among elderly people, including great separation distances from children or other relatives, and therefore the need for help from voluntary and statutory bodies. The chapter then concentrates on the relations between a person's migration history and their current residential situation, including the distributions of family members and social networks and the nature of visiting and interactions.

There is much less evidence about the relationship between visiting, or more generally the integration of an elderly person's and a younger relative's lives and whether or not this promotes instrumental support. There are many degrees of family 'care', from surveillance, such as spotting that an electric socket is dangerous or that a hot tap is causing problems – to nursing care. Co-residence or frequent visits do not guarantee responsible and flexible care, but great separation distances make them nigh impossible.

This account draws from earlier British studies and has theoretical sections informed by American research on social networks among older people. Findings are also discussed from a study investigating the triggers of, and motivations for, moves in the eighth and ninth decades of life, the extent to which moves are desired but frustrated by housing markets, and the extent to which people anticipate changes in their circumstances and overtly negotiate and act upon a residential strategy for their last decades of life. The Study of Mobility in Later Life (MILL) was funded by the ESRC and included an interview and postal survey of 1,912 people.

Understandings from migration and residential theories
Residential stress and changing house

Moving house is one option for an individual who wishes to alter their residential circumstances. Others include property alterations and or a changed social support network (Quercia and Rohe, 1992). Migration is however the most radical change at the community and household level. The study of migration has had a distinguished history since E.G. Ravenstein's formulation of 'laws' in the late nineteenth century, and there have been substantial contributions from demographers, social historians, economists, sociologists and geographers. Contrasting theoretical formulations exist, from 'gravity' models of the spatial allocation of flows to behavioural theories of individual migration decision-making. The behavioural theories are most relevant to family contact and care. They postulate a rational evaluation of comparative 'place utility', viz the advantages and disadvantages of the present residence and location in comparison to those at a different location (Wolpert, 1965). Another concept is that of residential stress, the sum of all 'disutilities', effectively the pressures on the individual to change (or adapt) his or her dwelling (Clark and

Cadwallader, 1973; Reschovsky, 1990). The evaluation of place utility depends upon information about other locations, which explains why most people contemplate moving only to locations they already know.

A perceived net negative utility at the present location establishes a potential to migrate. As Ohm's law explains for an electrical potential, it will be discharged only if the force is greater than the resistance which, in the case of changing house are several *personal and structural constraints*. These include personality, competence, low income, legal impediments as with leases and conveyancing, and the bureaucratic allocation of housing vacancies (Bourne, 1981; Clark and Davies, 1990; Lee, 1966). Allocation procedures in the public sector and housing market fluctuations for owner-occupiers are unusually powerful restraints in Britain. Common personal constraints include physical impairments, such as the inability to climb stairs or hills, the inability to drive, or the need to visit a clinic frequently. Behavioural or personality factors also play a part: some people are timid about moving, or have a deep attachment to the present home; others are exceptionally keen to move, perhaps because of personal insecurity in the present home or of dislike of their neighbours. The interaction of these factors changes through the life course, partly because the expectancy of remaining life falls, and partly in response to life events such as bereavement and illness.

The decision to move

Theories usually ascribe migration decisions to individuals whatever the composition of the household (Castro and Rogers, 1983a, 1983b). In practice, most follow negotiation among those who move, other people who will be affected by the move and professional advisers. Occasionally third parties such as landlords initiate or promote moves. The prevalence and process of negotiation in migration is little understood and, in critical instances will be inextricably bound up with tacit or explicit agreements to mobilise family support and care. Many different outcomes follow. Widowed siblings often agree to form a joint household; a child may move to live very near a parent; or a parent may agree to move in with a younger relative. These decisions deserve study at two levels.

Firstly, the majority of elderly people's long distance moves involve married couples. There is evidence from both Britain and France that men are more enthusiastic than women about moving and are more satisfied with the results. One reason for women's lower satisfaction is the disruption to their social networks. On the other hand, several surveys have found that about one-third of long distance retirement moves brought migrants closer to a child's home. Children are very often consulted and supportive of these moves. In other words, moves may promote family contacts as often as they damage them. Secondly, the decision making process should be studied as a negotiation among many interested individuals. Each participant expands the pooled information, alters the other participants' perceptions, and contributes new insights into the constraints and how to overcome them. A fuller understanding of the decision process may be a foundation for helpful advice for others, particular those with no confidants and few advisers.

Progression through the life course and residential strategies

Residential requirements and preferences differ for each life course stage. Life course analysis originated in demographers' and sociologists' representation of the family's reproductive cycle (Bryman *et al* 1987; Clark and Onaka 1983; Grebenik *et al* 1989). Peter Rossi (1955) applied these ideas in *Why Families Move* to residential selection, emphasising the changed requirements of young families at the childless, child-raising and child-launching stages. The ideas can be extended to old age. Not only is retirement now distinguished as a life course stage, it is increasingly differentiated between early (healthy and active), late (solitary, sick, frail or dependent) and terminal phases (severely ill and requiring constant care), each of which has distinctive residential requirements and different levels of migration (Table 1). The three phases of old age are sequential but not tied to specific chronological ages. They are societally specific and rapidly changing. In the United States each phase is increasingly associated with different commercially provided residential and care services, from the resort communities for the 'young old', through retirement apartments for active but solitary people, to nursing homes for the 'old old'. Such differentiation is not yet common in Britain, still less in other European countries.

The three life course stages of old age imply a sequence of optimal residential requirements. A dwelling that maximises the opportunities to pursue an active, recreationally-orientated life in early retirement *may* remove a retired couple from their family members and be inaccessible except by car to shops or health services. It follows that moves to minimise 'residential stress' in the first old-age life course stage may exacerbate 'stress' at later stages. They may initiate a sequence of migrations, which begin with positive moves, planned in advance and prompted by locational and housing preferences, and followed by responsive moves, necessitated by current or impending 'crises'. *MILL* seeks to establish the prevalence of just such sequences of residential stresses and moves. We are asking whether people conceive old age in these stages and, if so, whether on retirement they evaluate their financial, health and social network resources and in any sense develop a residential strategy for their remaining lives.

Choosing destinations

Behavioural theories have stressed the influence of the amenities and location of a dwelling and neglected housing and social network factors. They also tended to idealise and exaggerate search processes. People rarely engage in elaborate comparisons between many possible destinations and normally search only in districts they already know. Their 'information field' or mental map depends upon previous place experience (Law and Warnes, 1982; Wiseman, 1980). The knowledge of friends, relatives, the media and professional bodies is sometimes drawn upon. Rational decisions are handicapped also by the haphazard availability of housing vacancies at the intended destination. Public sector moves are also faced with institutional rules which suppress moves across housing authority boundaries, whilst in the private sector house-price variations limit options. Different motivations for moves at different life course stages alter the relative importance of housing and environmental influences. The geographical search is likely to be restricted when proximity to potential carers is paramount.

TABLE 1

Life course stages and transitions salient to migration

Life course Stage (S) or _Transition (T)_	Migration rate: Age-relationship during Stage, or peak rate of Transition	Empirical rates: UK 1980–81 NL 1973	Over-represented migration distances and types
S1 Childhood (0–15 years)	Decreasing exponentially with age	0.17–0.06 0.08–0.03	Short distance. Urban to suburban
T1 Passage to Adulthood (16–20 years)	Very high	0.25 0.14	Long distance. Rural and suburban to urban. Inter-urban
S2 Working age (16–60 years)	Decreasing exponentially with age	0.25–0.04 0.14–0.02	Urban to suburban
T2 Retirement (58–65 years)	Low	0.05 0.03	Long distance. Urban to rural and peripheral
S3 Active retirement (55–circa 70s)	Very low rate, decreasing with age	0.05–0.04 0.03–0.02	
T3 Failing capacities or dependency (65 upwards)	Variable age of onset. Rising prevalence with age in population		Short distance. Rural to urban including return migrations
S4 Dependent old age (circa 70s upwards)	Very low rate		Short distance.
T4 Severe or terminal illness (circa 70s upwards)	High rate. Variable age of onset. Rising prevalence with age in population	Not known. 0.04 at 90. 0.25 at 90 in Belgium[1]	Short distance. Moves into institutions.

Notes: The empirical rates are (above) changes of address during 1980–81 from the 1981 UK Census (Stillwell and Boden, 1989, Figure 4.2), and (below) male inter-district migrations during 1973 in The Netherlands (Scholten and Van der Velde, 1989, Figure 4.9).
1. Male inter-communal migration rate, Belgium 1979–82 (Poulain, 1989, Figure 11.2).

Empirical evidence
Migration and residential mobility in later life

Late age migrations have become widespread in affluent nations during the second half of the twentieth century (Meyer and Speare, 1985; Rogers *et al*, 1992). This reflects the extension of retirement, rises in the standard of living, educational receipts, and residential expectations, and constitutes a new form of 'post-industrial' mobility (Zelinsky, 1971). Evidence about them is however partial in all countries and fragmentary in many. Relevant research has had a short history and sundry methodologies and focal interests, including: the consequences for regional population distributions, the evolution of migration motivations, the implications for people's social networks and life satisfaction, and the impact on health or social service demands (Longino, 1990; Rogers *et al*, 1992). There is relatively poor coverage of long-term trends and of migrations very late in life.

Progress has been slowed by methodological difficulties which need brief explanation. One is of inconsistent measurement or *validity*, for the comprehensiveness of empirical migration series varies considerably. Some continuous population registers record all changes of (legal or permanent) address. In most countries, however, the principal data source is a census question, 'What was your address x years ago?' which inevitably under-represents both moves made by elderly people less than x years ago and, more generally, frequent moves and movers. Published tabulations are often richest for moves between a small set of large regions. The difficulty is that age correlates with both the mean distance and the origin-destination patterns of moves. Consequently datasets differentially represent migrations at different ages. Another weakness is that most sources do not give information on both the origin and destination housing type or household, and few cover motivation or co-migrants.

Age and the likelihood of moving house

'The most prominent regularity found in empirical schedules of migration rates is the selectivity of migration with respect to age'. So concluded Rogers and Castro (1981, 1986) from an examination of over 500 age-propensity schedules, now supplemented by European continuous register schedules and census series disaggregated by marital status, household headship status and race. They also developed a model migration schedule which has an age-independent or constant migration rate supplemented by four elements which in ascending age are: (i) an exponentially declining migration rate through childhood, (ii) a left-skewed unimodal curve through the labour force years – the dominant feature, (iii) a low and approximately symmetrical peak around the age of retirement, and (iv) an exponentially rising propensity to move in advanced old age (Rogers, 1988). The two departures through old age from the slowly declining exponential probability of moving are the least prominent and widespread features. Long distance, 'total-displacement' migrations at and around the age of retirement characterise only minorities in societies with long life expectancy, widely distributed affluence, and the legal or corporate backing of age-eligibility to retirement and pensions. They are well identified in Australia, France, Italy, the United Kingdom and the United States, occur without a distinctive pattern of origins and destinations in The Netherlands, and are absent in Japan. Distinctions between moves around the age of retirement and at older ages are recognised in many countries (Litwak and Longino, 1987; Rogers *et al*, 1992; Wiseman, 1980). Later life moves are associated with bereavement, income and health decline, which generate a need for housing readjustment to maintain independence. Last of all, increasing dependence necessitates a third type of move, that into an institution.

The late age slope is least researched and raises interpretational and modelling problems. A rising migration rate after the early seventies is strongly revealed by continuous registration data which records *all* moves by single years of age, rarely specified for advanced old age in census tabulations. In Belgium in 1979–82, inter-commune annual migration rates increased from 12–15 per cent for men and women in their early seventies to 25 per cent for men and 35 per cent for women in their late eighties (Poulain, 1989, Fig. 11.2). The slope is normally interpreted as the transition from healthy, independent early old age to a phase of frailty, sickness, low incomes or widowhood. Many moves follow widowhood or the onset of ill health (Grundy 1987a, 1987b; Harrop and Grundy 1991). They include return moves to areas of previous residence and of family, to conserve income, to bolster emotional or practical support, or to protect an individual's ability to live independently in normal housing. Some moves are into congregate, supported or institutional settings. But the slope also includes moves in the last months of life that are forced upon the seriously ill. If these moves are recorded as migrations, their age-distribution reflects the age distribution of deaths. The late age slope therefore arises from the aggregation of heterogeneous migrations associated with more than one life course stage.

Data from the 1991 GB census show that the percentage who had moved during the previous year fell exponentially from approximately 15 per cent among those aged 1–4 years to 7 per cent at ages 10–14 years. The percentage increased steeply through adolescence to 26 per cent at 20–24 years, and thereafter fell with increasing age, steeply at first but with an exponential moderation, to about 3 per cent at 70–74 years. At older ages, a late age slope was found to 8 per cent among those aged 85+ years. The retirement peak is most evident for long distance (inter-county) moves among married couples and owner occupiers, and the late age slope is strong for short distance (intra-county) moves among widowed females (Warnes, 1983). In Great Britain, for example, 29 per cent of the changes of address by married men aged 65–69 years during 1980–81 crossed county boundaries, compared to 19 per cent of those made by widowed women aged 75+ years. The age-pattern of migration rates among men and women is illustrated with data from the NHS Central Register of patient re-registrations (Table 2).

Geographical patterns of late age moves

Retirement migrations were first evident in Great Britain, France and the United States in the decade following the First World War (Allon-Smith, 1982; Hitt, 1954). They came a generation after the weekly paid holiday, often spent in

TABLE 2

Temporal change in age/sex specific rates of migration within England and Wales, 1975–76 to 1988–89

| | Age group (years) | | | | | | | | | | |
	15–9	20–4	25–9	40–4	45–9	50–4	55–9	60–4	65–9	70–4	75+
Males											
1981/82	3.88	6.22	5.92	2.19	1.72	1.45	1.26	1.52	1.52	1.19	1.24
1987/88	3.73	7.23	7.58	3.26	2.53	2.14	1.88	1.96	2.17	1.49	1.73
Ratio	0.96	1.16	1.28	1.49	1.47	1.48	1.50	1.29	1.43	1.25	1.40
Late 1970s	4.34	7.29	6.70	2.44	1.91	1.60	1.51	1.53	1.76	1.27	1.55
Late 1980s	4.53	6.81	7.08	2.99	2.27	1.90	1.67	1.73	1.94	1.38	1.57
Ratio	1.04	0.93	1.06	1.22	1.19	1.19	1.10	1.13	1.10	1.09	1.09
Females											
1981/82	5.19	9.07	6.42	1.77	1.47	1.30	1.31	1.61	1.34	1.22	1.43
1987/88	4.63	10.6	8.58	2.71	2.24	2.01	1.89	1.98	1.84	1.45	1.92
Ratio	0.89	1.17	1.34	1.53	1.52	1.55	1.44	1.23	1.37	1.19	1.34
Late 1970s	5.99	10.5	7.01	2.07	1.67	1.51	1.60	1.70	1.53	1.28	1.53
Late 1980s	4.72	10.0	8.02	2.46	1.97	1.75	1.66	1.74	1.64	1.33	1.76
Ratio	0.79	0.96	1.15	1.19	1.18	1.16	1.04	1.02	1.07	1.04	1.15

Notes: (i) The rates refer to migrations with identified origins and destinations. Figures for the late 1970s are averages of the annual rates for 1975/76 to 1979/80: for the late 1980s for the five years 1984/85 to 1988/89.

a coastal resort. The development was slowed by the 1930s depression and in Europe by the Second World War (which generated economic recovery and the reverse effect in the USA, notably on Florida). From the mid-1950s, the habit of retirement migration grew strongly. Three stages of development have been proposed (Law and Warnes, 1982). The first was dominated by return moves to dispersed rural areas of nativity, the second by concentrated destinations, mainly selected coastal resorts, and the third by renewed dispersal to newly-serviced rural and non-urban coastal areas. There is a strong relation between city size and population density and the rate of out-migration (Table 3). In Great Britain, the last two decades have seen much diffusion of the most favoured destinations, with North Norfolk, Lincolnshire, North Yorkshire and Powys now attracting high rates of inflows, while the movement into East Sussex has declined (Table 4) (Warnes, 1992; Warnes and Ford, 1993).

Françoise Cribier has detailed the comparable evolution of retirement migration in France, where the substantial exodus from Paris replicates the metropolitan dominance of the British pattern. Cribier's first studies were of a cohort of Parisians born between 1906 and 1912. During the 1970s, half their residential moves were within Greater Paris and half towards the provinces. Relatively high rates of departure were found among those who retire early, particularly from public sector occupations, among more substantial entrepreneurs, those in good health, those with second homes, and those whose children were relatively few and/or resident in the provinces. Several sources established the peak years for departure at around 63–66 years for men and 61–60 for women: these modal ages have been falling. By the late 1970s more than one-half

TABLE 3
Areas of exceptional rates of out-migration of elderly people

Origin FPC Area	Males 65–69 years		Females 60–64 years	
	1975–80	1984–89	1975–80	1984–89
Camden & Islington	4.98(1)	3.67(11)	3.85(4)	3.16(11)
Kensington, C & W	4.76(2)	4.52(2)	4.60(1)	4.14(1)
Lambeth, S & L	4.14(3)	4.51(3)	4.42(2)	3.90(3)
Merton, S & W	3.81(4)	4.18(4)	3.46(6 =)	3.59(5)
Croydon	3.74(5)	4.80(1)	3.33(8)	4.06(2)
City, H, N & TH	3.73(6)	3.91(8 =)	3.93(3)	3.47(8)
Middlesex	3.66(7)	3.84(10)	3.46(6 =)	3.41(9)
Redbridge & WF	3.53(8)	4.13(6)	3.30(9)	3.56(6)
Bromley	3.35(9 =)	4.16(5)	3.63(5)	3.71(4)
Surrey	3.35(9 =)	3.91(8 =)	2.93(12)	3.49(7)

	Males 75+ years		Females 75+ years	
	1975–80	1984–89	1975–80	1984–89
Camden & Islington	2.82(1 =)	2.52(6 =)	2.75(2)	2.76(8 =)
Kensington, C & W	2.82(1 =)	3.37(1)	3.37(1)	3.25(1)
Lambeth, S & L	2.73(3)	3.04(2)	2.61(3)	3.11(2 =)
City, H, N & TH	2.51(4)	2.67(4)	2.35(7)	2.94(4 =)
Bromley	2.46(5)	2.47(9)	2.53(5)	2.74(10)
Surrey	2.43(6)	2.53(5)	2.36(6)	2.70(11)
Richmond & Kingston	2.23(7)	2.49(8)	2.14(10)	2.87(6)
Merton, S & W	2.18(8)	2.52(6 =)	2.05(12)	2.76(8 =)
Isle of Wight	2.10(9)	1.69(26)	1.43(34)	1.75(34 =)
Croydon	2.08(11 =)	2.74(3)	2.25(8 =)	3.11(2 =)
Solihull	2.08(11 =)	2.24(13)	2.57(4)	2.94(4 =)
Middlesex	1.89(17)	2.42(10)	2.25(8 =)	2.60(13)
Manchester	1.83(18)	2.15(15)	1.67(23)	2.77(7)

Notes: (i) Values in parentheses are ranks

TABLE 4
Areas of exceptional rates of in-migration of elderly people: England and
Wales, 1975–80 and 1984–89

| | Males 65–69 years | | Females 60–64 years | |
	1975–80	1984–89	1975–80	1984–89
West Sussex	4.48(1)	4.00(8)	5.10(1)	3.48(9)
Isle of Wight	4.21(2)	5.16(1)	3.75(4)	4.43(1)
Dorset	4.16(3)	4.73(3)	4.09(3)	4.32(3)
East Sussex	4.07(4)	4.09(6)	4.13(2)	3.61(7)
Somerset	3.68(5)	4.05(7)	3.59(5)	3.72(5 =)
Norfolk	3.55(6)	3.59(11)	3.00(10 =)	3.28(10)
Cornwall	3.46(7)	4.23(5)	3.33(6)	3.96(4)
Lincolnshire	3.25(8)	4.89(2)	2.93(12)	4.33(2)
Gwynedd	3.18(9)	3.93(9)	2.86(13)	3.50(8)
Powys	2.28(23)	4.29(4)	3.17(7)	3.72(5 =)
Essex	2.96(14)	2.34(23)	3.14(8)	2.19(22)
Buckinghamshire	3.04(12)	2.65(20)	3.09(9)	2.59(19)
	Males 75+ years		Females 75+ years	
	1975–80	1984–89	1975–80	1984–89
Hertfordshire	2.74(1)	2.16(16 =)	2.94(5)	2.61(13)
West Sussex	2.69(2)	2.58(4 =)	2.67(6)	2.76(11)
Surrey	2.56(3)	2.11(20)	2.60(7)	2.66(12)
Buckinghamshire	2.46(4)	3.03(1)	3.05(3)	3.50(2)
Berkshire	2.44(5)	2.34(10)	3.00(4)	2.88(6)
Dorset	2.29(6)	2.04(24)	2.08(17)	2.21(28)
Solihull	2.17(7)	2.58(4 =)	3.23(1)	3.00(4)
Somerset	2.08(8)	2.46(6)	2.49(8)	2.83(8 =)
Kensington, C & W	2.07(9 =)	1.335(48)	1.14(53 =)	0.96(83 =)
Trafford	2.07(9 =)	1.65(39)	2.07(18)	2.30(22)
Powys	1.62(27)	2.95(2)	2.36(10)	3.53(1)
Sefton	1.96(14)	2.93(3)	1.98(24)	3.42(3)
Hereford & Worcs	1.66(26)	2.42(7)	2.09(16)	2.86(7)
Bromley	2.05(11)	2.40(8 =)	3.07(2)	2.96(5)
Warwickshire	1.78(21)	2.40(8 =)	2.25(12)	2.81(10)
Croydon	2.00(12)	2.07(21)	2.38(9)	2.83(8 =)

of the retired people leaving Paris were doing so before the age of 65 years, anticipating the reduction of the statutory age in France in 1983. A recent paper is an excellent synthesis of the French evidence (Cribier and Kych, 1992). The authors argue that Greater Paris exemplifies the dynamism of retirement migration from a large metropolitan area. A third of the retired population younger than 75 years left the city between 1975 and 1982. Many might suspect that recent improvements in the material and health conditions of elderly people would have raised out-migration to the provinces. The reverse has been the case, while seasonal forms of residential mobility have increased.

Housing tenure in Britain and moving in old age

As with many facets of British life associated with housing, moving in later life shows strong differentials by tenure. The 'parochialism' of local authority housing has never been broken down, despite many attempts to foster national tenancy exchange schemes. This, together with the generally greater enthusiasm of urban councils compared to rural and coastal authorities for developing public housing during the earlier decades of this century, has meant that it is very difficult to arrange transfers between housing authorities, and large flows of tenants away from the main urban areas have never occurred. Long distance retirement migration, as normally understood, is virtually impossible for the urban local authority tenant household unless: (a) they relinquish their tenancy, or (b) purchase their home sufficiently in advance of retirement for it to be saleable at that time. Only a fortunate few, in the best family housing types, could expect to raise sufficient capital with which to finance a move to an owner occupied home on the coast or overseas.

On the other hand, the pressure upon local authority housing departments to make housing available to young couples with very young children leads to active management to match dwelling types and sizes to the tenant household. During the first twenty-five post-war years, the bulk of local authority housing construction was of two- and three-bedroom dwellings suitable for young families. By 1979, the ageing of the council house tenant population resulted in many dwellings being occupied by older working-age and retired tenants, whose children had left home, and including an increasing number of widowed persons living alone. For a decade, central government encouraged local authorities to concentrate their new-build on specially designed small dwellings for elderly one and two-person households. These were skilfully located within existing estates. Various conversions of larger dwellings into structurally separate one-bedroom flats were also tried. Through the 1980s, the role of providing special 'social' housing for small, older households was taken over by the housing associations. During the early 1990s the curtailment of new building and high rates of unemployment sustained the pressure on council house waiting lists people from young, low-income families. To accommodate these demands, local authorities treat favourably (and sometimes encourage) applications from older, small households to transfer to smaller dwellings. Financial incentives at a rate per released bedroom are offered by at least one London Borough.

The overall result is that moving in later life is a common experience among the third of households in the local authority sector. The majority of these moves are short distance. They rarely cross a local authority boundary and only in the largest city authorities and in extensive rural areas are they likely to exceed 5 km. Their impact on the proximity of relatives in different generations is likely to have been less than the 'right-to-buy' policy, for the search for relatively low value housing among older former tenants will have taken many to outer-suburban areas and across local authority boundaries.

Motivations and triggers

It is useful to distinguish between events which trigger a move and the migrants' underlying preferences and motivations. Ceasing work, widowhood and the onset of illness are often triggers, while the underlying motivations are to optimise either amenities or social networks. A few studies have investigated these influences on decisions to move in later life in the United Kingdom (Table 5) (Glyn Jones, 1975; Karn, 1977; Law and Warnes, 1980; Stuart, 1987) and information is also available from unpublished tables of the OPCS *Retirement Survey*.[1] The earlier studies concentrated on movers to regions of high amenity, at or shortly after retirement; the more recent studies consider more general samples. Specialised surveys have normally found environmental preferences (including past associations) and social network factors to be most important in the selection of destinations than housing or health reasons. The *Retirement Survey* provides some information about antecedent events which trigger a move. For one-fifth of respondents, actual or approaching retirement was important, whilst 12 per cent cited their own ill health. At least 40 per cent identified no trigger. In broad terms, respondents report that about one-third of long distance retirement moves take people nearer to children or other close relatives. On the other hand, the *Retirement Survey* finds housing considerations to be the modal reasons for all old-age moves.

Least information is available about the reasons for moves in advanced old age. Recent surveys of sheltered housing residents found unsurprisingly that housing considerations were of primary importance, whilst the *Retirement Survey* found that being near friends was cited by twice the proportion of older post-retirement movers as younger ones (for example, 21 per cent of 65–69 year olds but 10.4 per cent of 55–59 year olds) (Fleiss, 1985; Williams, 1990). The data do not enable disaggregation by either marital status or gender. From the MILL survey, the importance of social and housing factors over environmental and location choice was found to be even greater for older than younger respondents, suggesting that the amenity orientation of retirement moves is less prevalent later in life (Ford and Warnes, 1993).[2] As anticipated, the modal trigger (for one-fifth of respondents) was the choice 'worsening health or increasing age'.

This evidence of the importance of housing and social network factors among older movers implies the wish to maintain independence through later life and in the face of negative life events. *MILL* interviews found many expressions of disinclination to enter an institution and that 70 of 88 respondents expressed the desire to preserve independence. Another dimension of the

76

TABLE 5
Review of reasons for moves and choice of destination in surveys of older migrants

Study	Law and Warnes 1973	Glyn Jones 1975	Karn 1977	Law and Warnes 1977	Stuart 1987	Harris Research 1991	OPCS Ret. Survey 1991	Ford and Warnes 1993
Retirement migrants	Yes	Yes. Who moved since their 'late forties'	Yes	Yes	Households 'thinking of moving'	Sheltered housing residents i) private ii) public	Persons aged 65–69 years, moving in previous 15 years	All who moved since 50th birthday
Location	Llandudno	Exmouth	i) Bexhill ii) Clacton	Dorset and N. Wales	London Borough of Brent	Great Britain	Great Britain	S.E. England
Reason	for moving to Llandudno	for moving to Exmouth	for moving to Bexhill or Clacton	for moving to Dorset or N. Wales	for thinking about i) moving ii) destination	for moving	for moving	i) for moving ii) for choice of destination
Sample size	121	54	i) 503 ii) 487	201	i) 44 ii) 68	i) 942 ii) 330	504	i) 51 ii) 51
% mentioning:					(multiple mention)	(multiple mention)	(multiple mention)	
Environmental preference	31	–	39 24	21	27 35	– –	11	8 18
Health	12	33[1]	11 18	9	– –	11 34	12	22 –
Friends/Relatives	16	24	10 15	21	7 56	19 6	21	18 43
'Want change'[2]	24	–	7 9	6	– –	– –	20	2 –
Push factors[3]	–	–	11 6	11	34[4] 6	16 15	24	8 –
Appropriate dwelling	–	–	4 9	6	18 –	37 27	45	22 –
Financial reasons	–	–	5 9	–	– 10	– –	6	12 6
Past associations	–	43	– –	12[5]	– 18	– –	–	4 10
Events[6]	–	–	5 5	3	– –	3 5	57	4 6
Other/unspecified	16	–	7 6	–	21 8	14 13	3	2 10

Note: columns do not total to 100% due to rounding errors.

[1] Combined health and climate reasons
[2] Includes anticipation of retirement, to change tenure (non-financial reasons).
[3] Includes deterioration of origin environment, security considerations, death and outmigration of friends.
[4] Minimum, those reporting deterioration as reason for considering moves.
[5] Environmental attractions based on established knowledge not distinguished from social attractions.
[6] Includes death of spouse, return to UK, forced moves.
[7] Minimum, reporting death of spouse.

tenacity of independence can be interpreted from attitudes to future co-residence with family or relatives. A widespread wish to promote social and familial networks does not extend to a positive view of co-residence: willingness to contemplate this arrangement was found among only 28 per cent (15 of 53) of those aged 55–74 years, and 29 per cent (10 of 35) of those aged at least 75 years. This limited evidence supports the dichotomy of migration motivations between those at or around the age of retirement, for which environmental attractions hold great sway, and those at older ages, for which coping, preserving independence, and social network considerations including enabling family surveillance or care are more important.

Institutional factors

The influence of triggers and motivations is reduced where institutional factors constrain decision-making. In a minority of cases, moves are impelled by employers, landlords, developers, doctors or social workers against the wishes of the resident. The *Retirement Survey* found that leaving tied accommodation necessitated migration for 7.1 per cent of 60–64 year olds. Around one-in-seven council tenants had been moved in the previous fifteen years by their authority, and expatriates retiring to Britain are another sizable minority. A far from negligible incidence of thwarted moves (20–25 per cent) has been found among non-movers (Law and Warnes, 1980; Ford and Warnes, 1993). For some people, such as those in low grade council housing, institutional or income constraints make unrealistic any aspiration to move voluntarily unrealistic. Some evidence is available on the reasons why people do not move in old age. In a sample of non-movers matched to retirement migrants, more than half (55 of 100) cited proximity to friends and relatives as the reason for not moving, with locational preference and specific ties to local organisations cited by 26 per cent of the sample (Law and Warnes, 1980). Data from MILL on 35 non-movers found one quarter staying for social network reasons, while two-fifths cited locational factors. A low incidence (<5 per cent) of financial or health reasons was found in both studies. Locational convenience and social network considerations appear to be carefully weighed in decisions whether to move or to stay.

Moves to release housing equity have recently received increasing attention and are discussed in detail in Chapter 8 (Mackintosh, Means and Leather, 1990; Mullings and Hamnett, 1992). Rational and behavioural explanations of retirement moves envisage capital release to stimulate moves either to a smaller dwelling or away from high housing-price cities. Respondents to survey questions mention financial motivations remarkably infrequently, but nevertheless census data in many countries show exceptionally high rates of departure from the largest cities. This evidence suggests that house price differentials are important, even when environmental, urban malaise and occupational status effects are recognised (Steinnes and Hogan, 1992). Equity-release schemes for continuing residence have proliferated recently, but today's depressed housing markets do not encourage formal or informal asset conversion and take up has been slow (Mullings and Hamnett, 1992). The risks associated with releasing housing equity to support later life needs (including nursing or health care) and its conflict with traditional wishes to bequest, suppress the enthusiasm for such schemes (Hamnett, Harmer and Williams, 1991). The Retirement Survey found that saving or making of money from moving was important for 11 per cent of all movers aged 55–64 years, but for only 6.3 per cent of 65–69 year olds. More older people (16.3 per cent) reported being able to increase savings as a result of the move, compared with 10.7 per cent and 15.9 per cent respectively of the younger groups.

Negotiation and residential strategies

Law and Warnes (1980) found that among relatively young, retirement migrants, 7.5 per cent of moves were initiated by persons outside the household. For older samples, such as those participating in *MILL* preliminaries, the role of outsiders appears even more important, with over a quarter reporting the principal encouragement to be from outside the household. Among the 201 people who had moved over the five years before the interview, only exactly one-third reported no advice from others and 30 received advice or encouragement from doctors. There have been many studies of the effect of changing social and support networks on older persons, and complex typologies of network type have been constructed (Wenger, 1992). Nevertheless, few have investigated any outcome effect of these diverse sources of encouragement and advice on the propensity to change residence. Housing officers are a prime source of information and advice to public sector sheltered housing tenants, while owners of sheltered dwellings more often rely on family members.

Local authority tenants are particularly exposed to a wide range of formal sources of advice, particularly from housing and health professionals. In the *MILL* postal survey, of the 57 respondents who moved after 1987 into local authority dwellings, 37 (65 per cent) received advice. Ten were advised by council officers, and eleven by doctors. All but one of the 22 people who had moved into a housing or voluntary association flat or house received advice, a majority (12) from doctors.

The frequency and sources of advice to the 79 men and 130 women who had moved (to any tenure) in the last five years were similar, except that doctors were significantly more likely to advise women than men (20.9 per cent to 8.9 per cent). Those living alone were most likely to have received advice (74.4 per cent as opposed to 63.2 per cent for others), particularly from doctors (27.9 per cent as opposed to 8.8 per cent): these exceeded two-thirds of the occurrences of doctors' advice. The lowest income groups (<£80 per week) received advice more frequently (82.1 per cent) than others (64.5 per cent), particularly from doctors (46.2 per cent compared to 9.2 per cent), and from relatives other than a spouse (17.9 per cent compared to 4.6 per cent). Unexpectedly perhaps, the more children an elderly person had, the less likely they were to have received advice (25.0 per cent of the childless reported no advice, but 40.3 per cent of those with three or more children). From the *MILL* interview survey, it was found that when advice came from within the household, it was more likely to be about the type of a dwelling than its location (31 per cent versus 13 per cent), but if it came from outside the converse was found (25 versus 31 per cent). Half of those who did not move had been encouraged to move: such encouragement is not always therefore the trigger for a move.

TABLE 6
Anticipation of negative life events (by age group)

Anticipation of event	Age group (years)			

a) HEALTH CHANGE – such that you are less able to carry out your daily activities

	55–64	65–74	75+	*All*
Won't happen/not thought about it	13	14	21	*48*
Thought about it or have definite plans	9	17	13	*39*
– more likely to move as result	(4)	(11)	(4)	*(19)*

b) LOSS OF SPOUSE/PARTNER

Won't happen/not thought about it	5	8	4	*17*
Thought about it or have definite plans	8	15	14	*37*
– more likely to move as result	(3)	(9)	(2)	*(14)*

Base: MILL, all respondents 'at risk' aged 55 years and over (a: N = 87, b: N = 54).

There is sparse evidence of successful planning or the existence of residential strategies – it does require a careful retrospective or longitudinal study design. Retirement migration studies have asked about the duration of plans to move. For example, Law and Warnes reported that 31 per cent of long-distance retirement movers had planned their move at least five years in advance, while 26 per cent had plans for less than one year. The *MILL* sample, with many older respondents, found a median lead time for all changes of address of 11 months, with only four movers (8 per cent) having planned the move for five years or more. There are many problems with the interpretation of such retrospective estimates as evidence of residential strategies, especially ones incorporating conditional options should certain life events occur. Strategic and responsive elements in achieved motives have not yet been adequately investigated. Expressed predictions of residential change in response to future life events have been collected, and come close to ideas of residential strategies. *MILL* interview respondents were asked about the extent to which they anticipated events associated with their ageing and the plans they had made for those they anticipated. Salient events included health decline and, notably, widowhood (Table 6). A substantial proportion of eligible respondents considered themselves as more likely to move should either of these events occur, although few had definite plans. The older Harris survey respondents were less likely to anticipate moving than the younger, and were more certain that their current home would be the last.

Residential locations and inter-generational relations

A few social investigations have given attention to the role of proximity in structuring social interaction and support (for overviews see Lee *et al.*, 1990; Litwak and Kulis, 1987; Wenger, 1992; Willmott, 1986, 1987). One United States scholar argued that the two fundamental determinants of interaction frequency are 'the degree of kin relationship and the distance of residence', with distance invariably overriding degree of relationship (Adams, 1968). The 'friction of distance' is not however, constant but a function of the prevailing technology and real cost of transport and communications. Distance may predict contact in cross-sectional studies but be of little value in longitudinal or cross-cultural exercises.

The interrelationships between lifetime residential mobility, the net effects on the localization or dispersion of family members, and the association between proximity and patterns of visiting were studied in a survey of 432 elderly married couples and their children in England in 1983 (Warnes, Howes and Took, 1985a, 1985b; Warnes, 1986, 1987). The parents ranged in age from 57 to 89 years (males) and from 46 to 89 years (females). The mean duration at the current address was 24 years. Over one third had not moved since establishing their first home after marriage and another third had moved only once. The moves that had been undertaken had mainly been short distance. Only one fifth of the couples had made a move of more than 30 km but there were very strong social class differentials. These were studied by classifying the social status of both the elderly parents and their children, and by examining social mobility across the generations. The higher status groups moved more and over longer distances and consequently were far more dispersed. 34 per cent of the higher social classes but only 7 per cent of skilled manual workers had made moves of more than 30 km. The adult children had been more migratory than their parents, particularly over long distances. Nearly one half had made a move of more than 30 km, and one quarter had made two such moves. Adult children are likely to be more mobile than their parents as a consequence of their age (whatever the temporal trend in mobility rates).

A large proportion of adult children in 1983 lived close to their parents. Almost 23 per cent lived within 2 km, 38 per cent within 5 km, and half were no more than 10 km away. On the other hand, 19 per cent lived more than 100 km away, but again there were strong status and social mobility differentials. Except among children living very close to their parents, the controlling influence on propinquity and patterns of visiting was the child's achieved social status (Figure 1). Many more children in blue- than white-collar households lived within 3 km of their parents (41 per cent to 16 per cent); and among white-collar children the principal effect of parents' blue-collar occupational status was to raise the proportion living between 3–10 km (31 per cent to 17 per cent). When examined in terms of the distance from the parents of the nearest child, over a third of the retired couples had a child living within 1 km and 58 per cent within 5 km. Only 7 per cent of the elderly couples had both children living more than 100 km away. For the great majority of retired couples in England in 1983, a close relative lived within a short walk or car ride. In London, however, relatively few parents lived either very close to their children or more than

Figure 1

The dispersion of children from retired parents by their respective occupational groups: four districts of England, 1983

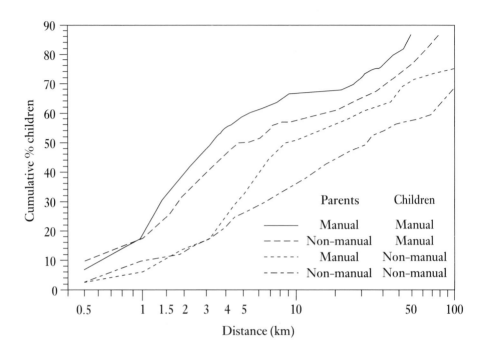

100 km away, and a majority of both sons and daughters lived within 20 km (Table 7).

This survey found a strong relationship between residential proximity and the frequency of visits to and from elderly parents and their children. The relationship is shown by comparing three categories of the children; those living within 2 km, those between 5 and 20 km, and those living more than 100 km away. The percentage of children visiting at least once a week dropped from 81 through 47 to 1.6 per cent, while the percentage visiting less frequently than once a month increased from 5 through 15 to 90 (Table 8). It is not only that very high frequencies of visiting (3+ times per week) are virtually confined to dyads living within 5 km of each other, but also that where the separation is 50+ km, 55 per cent of the children see their parents less than three times per year. Once separation is taken into account, social class has no significant effect upon children's visiting frequency. In other words, the differential visiting frequencies of the different social classes can be almost wholly accounted for by their different levels of residential mobility and consequent propinquity.

Data on the proximity of children has also been collected in the 1993 *MILL* Survey. Among the entire *MILL* sample in South East England, 15.7 per cent of the primary respondents lived with a child (196 of 1,245). Those under 75 years were more likely to be sharing than the older respondents (19.9 per cent

TABLE 7

Proximity of retired married couple's children in the London Borough of Merton and outside London, 1983

Proximity of children (km)	Males		Females	
	Merton %	Index to nation	Merton %	Index to nation
Less than 2.0	7.2	0.25	15.3	0.61
2.1–5.0	15.3	1.07	18.9	1.17
5.1–20.0	28.8	1.82	23.4	1.30
20.1–100.0	36.9	1.87	24.3	1.18
More than 100	11.7	0.54	18.0	0.88
Sample size	*111*	*310*	*111*	*311*

Mean distance between parents and children (km)

| First children | 53.5 | | 32.8 | |
| Second children | 45.0 | | 50.9 | |

Note: The index indicates the ratio of the percentage share in Merton to the percentage share in the survey districts outside

TABLE 8

Frequency of children's visits to retired married couples by the distance of separation in four districts of England and Wales, 1983

| Frequency of visits | Residential separate (km) | | | | | | | | | | | | Total |
| | 0–1.9 | | 2–4.9 | | 5–19.9 | | 20–49.9 | | 50–99.9 | | 100+ | | Sample size |
	No	%	No	%	No	%	No	%	No	%	No	%	
3+ per week	74	39	26	20	7	4	2	2	0	0	0	0	109
1 or 2 week	79	42	58	44	71	43	14	11	4	6	3	2	229
1–3 month	25	13	24	18	65	39	60	48	22	31	16	9	212
4–11 year	5	3	11	8	12	7	34	27	24	34	45	25	131
3 year or less	5	3	13	10	12	7	14	11	20	29	119	65	183
Total	188		132		167		124		70		183		864

Note: columns total to 100% with rounding errors

TABLE 9

Frequency of living with children by two elderly age groups and timing of late age migration:: SE England, 1993

	Aged 60–74 years			Aged 75 years or more		
	Living with child		Sub-group sample	Living with child		Sub-group sample
	Number	%		Number	%	
Non-mover	140	22.5	623	22	8.5	258
Moved at 60–74 years	20	10.9	180	7	6.4	109
Moved at 75+ years	—	—	—	7	9.3	75
Total	160	19.9	803	36	8.1	442

to 8.3 per cent). Migrants were significantly less likely to be sharing than non-migrants (9.3 per cent to 18.4 per cent), particularly those who move in early old age. Among the sub-group aged 75+ years, 8.5 per cent of non-migrants were sharing, 6.4 per cent of early-old age movers, and 9.3 per cent of late old-age movers (Table 9). The location of each respondent and of each child for which an address was given have been located by grid references to the nearest 100 metres, enabling an analysis of the distribution of separation distances by the main tenures and by migration history (Figure 2). Among elderly owner-occupiers (not living in someone else's property), 13 per cent lived within 100 metres of a child. Over one-quarter lived within one kilometre and just under one-half within 5 km of a child. Seven in ten of the elderly owner-occupiers had a child no further than 11 km away. The cumulative distribution of the separation distances of 'early movers', those who moved at ages 60–74 years, is consistently to the right of the general curve. Less than 13 per cent lived within one kilometre, just over one-third no more than 5 km, and only 42 per cent within 10 km from a child. After this distance, however, the cumulative percentages of 'early movers' progressively approaches the general curve. Overall, early retirement movers to their own owned homes live further away than others from their nearest child but the greatest differentials are in shared house and, as shown by the 1983 survey, to around 10 km.

Moves after 75 years of age to self-owned housing are associated with a different and intriguing pattern of separation distances. As with the 'early movers' only 4 per cent live with or next to a child, but no less than 14 per cent are found between 100–325 metres, more than three times the fraction of the general sample. Beyond this distance, the cumulative distribution of 'late movers' rises step-by-step with the total sample, to one-half living within 5 km of a child. Between 5 and 11 km, a widening gap between the 'late movers' and the general sample occurs, and only 18 per cent are beyond 11 km compared to approximately one-third of all. The overall effect is that while owner-occupiers' moves made at 75 years and more (with any concurrent children's moves) 'pull' the parent-child separation distances to within 16.5 km or 11 miles, they do not substantially increase the prevalence of co-residence at these advanced ages.

Figure 2
The residential dispersion of the nearest child from (a) owner-occupiers, and (b) social housing tenants, aged 60 years or more: SE England, 1993

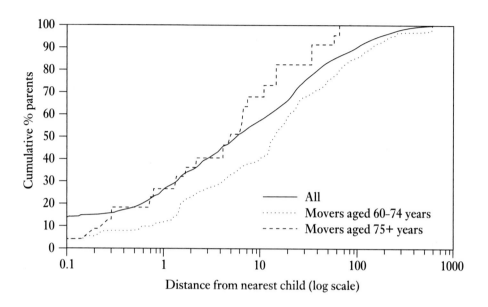

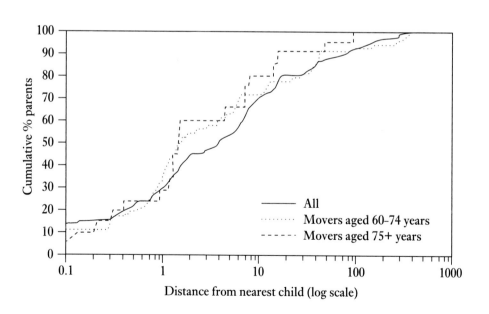

A similar analysis of propinquity by migration history among social housing tenants (local authority and housing association) reveals that social renters are generally living slightly closer to their children (the two cumulative dispersion curves are very similar but the social renters' is to the left) and one clear contrast. 'Early movers' to social tenancies live closer to their children than non-movers and particularly increase the share living with 0.8–1.3 km from a child. This is little different to the effect of 'late-moves' among social housing tenants, but the latter also 'pull' the dispersion tighter in the range 7–12 km. It is, however, in clear contrast to the dispersing effect of early moves among owner-occupiers. Overall it is found that movers in early old age are significantly more independent residentially of their children than those who do not move. In terms of propinquity, however, there is a clear tenure difference. Early-movers to owner-occupation tend to disperse from their children, while among social renters they tend to come closer. Those who move in late old age have an insignificantly different likelihood of living with a child than those who never move but the clear effect in both tenures is to reduce progressively the shares separated by distances in excess of 10 km (Table 9).

Discussion and prospects
Migration and family care

The implications of migration and residential proximity for family care are not straightforward. Social network studies suggest that if there are relatives in the same household, interaction beyond is comparatively weak. Beyond the household, when there are children, one or more are normally prominent in social interaction. But the covariant variables, distance of separation and socio-economic group (or income), do strongly structure the frequency and nature of contacts. Long distances make feasible only limited instrumental care and emotional support by telephone, and among higher socio-economic groups, opportunity costs and status considerations decrease the preference for providing domiciliary instrumental help but raise the opportunities for changing house and for joint or contiguous living arrangements. High quality or frequent care is near contingent upon proximity (Litwak and Kulis, 1987). While those in need of family care may wish to move near to those willing to provide it, institutional constraints, difficult housing market conditions and the unavailability of suitable dwellings in desired locations often intervene. These and personal impediments to moving may prevent incremental adjustments and continued independence. As a result, both thwarted moves and migrations may raise or decrease the feasibility of family care.

To the extent that an individual's morale (at any age) is dependent upon interaction with others and their esteem and regard for the subject, then adverse impacts, perhaps with implications for formal services, may result from the trend towards solitary households. This trend is itself partly a consequence of decreased family size and the greater geographical dispersion of children. But high morale is not dependent upon living with others and can be associated with independent living with a rich and rewarding social network. It may be that the progressive raising of the population's occupational and educational status or, following Wirth and Tönnies, that economic and attitudinal changes result in the declining importance of sibling and extended family relationships, an increasing emotional focus on vertical consanguineous relationships, and a differentiation of the emotional and psychic content of family relationships from the sources of instrumental and nursing support. Residential independence can be preserved alongside progressively closer proximity and interaction with children or carers, and this has been the effect on propinquity of the residential moves made after the age of 60 years in South East England in the current elderly population.

Cohort succession will alter the characteristics of future retired people and their inter-generational relations and residential behaviour. The principal changes that we can anticipate are: continued rises in the rate of household headship among the retired population; that succeeding cohorts will have had more education and higher status occupational histories, higher rates of owner occupation, greater assets, and a greater disposition to consider retirement residence overseas; that successive cohorts will have had lower completed family sizes and younger ages of birth of the last child, more erratic marital histories, and that, among long term couples, there will be greater variation in the ages of men and women. How these socio–demographic and personal resource changes interact with changing patterns in the supply of and charges for care and supported residences can only be anticipated in general terms.

If, however, we are to reach a penetrating understanding of how people's lives in old age are changing and of future aspirations and needs among old people, some attempt must be made to understand these complex interacting forces. Without such understanding, social policies will be guided unrelievedly by short-term expediency, pragmatism and ideological simplicities. Peter Laslett's (1989) vision of a distinctive 'third age' may be indirectly prescient. The proposition that the healthy retirement years will convert to a self-actualising 'third age' implies a complement, that there is a fourth stage of life associated with illness and frailty. These decrements are normally seen as synonymous with dependency. This complement has invoked heated criticism of Laslett's view, for it carries the danger of a stereotypical misrepresentation, that all those who attain some advanced age will be impaired, or that all positive, developmental or rewarding attitudes and exertions will cease. But even if the fourth stage is marked by frailty, restriction and social decrements, the level of consequent dependency may not be high and may be changing. Impairments are consistent with a preference to remain residentially independent. Living arrangements and activity patterns can be sustained that support rather than undermine people's morale, self-worth, autonomy and contributions to others (as through 'grand-parenting roles'). The successful accommodation of frailty and declining abilities is largely a matter of financial and psychological resources and of people's ability to express their preferences.

A free interpretation of the survey evidence does suggest that among the present cohort in advanced old age, the ability to move nearer a child but to retain residential independence has been successfully exerted. This result is entirely consistent with the proposition that inter-generational and other family relationships for social interaction, mutual affirmation and psychological support have been strengthening, even while the prevalence of shared living arrangements declines. Whether the increased ability to make residential changes which achieve these conjoint aspirations extends to a more general rise in people's competencies in their own affairs or even to a rising preference for non-familial instrumental support is not known. It is clear, however, that the elderly population's preferences are sophisticated and complex, moulded by attitudes and experience, constrained by economic resources, limited by housing and environmental opportunities, and most of all constantly in flux.

Endnotes

1.   The OPCS Retirement Survey was carried out on behalf of the DSS, primarily to aid planning and policy on pensions and provisions. The target population comprised people aged 55 to 69 years at the time the study was carried out (December, 1988). Interviews were conducted with 3,543 persons in the target age range and 609 outside the target age range who qualified as partners of initial contacts. Various weighting factors were applied to allow for regional disparities in response rates. As the sample characteristics of principal interest to the survey were economic and employment related, the available data presented here is the weighted responses of the 3,543 eligible respondents (since the sampling of persons outside the 55–69 year age group was unrepresentative).

2.   11 of the 22 respondents who moved when 64 years or younger gave environmental preferences as the most important reason for their choice of district, compared to the 9 of the 29 who moved when older.

References

Adams, B. N. (1968) *Kinship in an Urban Setting*, Markham: Chicago.

Allon-Smith, R. (1982) 'The evolving geography of the elderly in England and Wales', in Warnes, A. M. (ed.) *Geographical Perspectives on the Elderly*, Wiley: Chichester, Sussex, 35–52.

Bourne, L. S. (1981) *The Geography of Housing*, Edward Arnold: London

Bryman, A., Bytheway, W. B., Allett, P. and Keil, T. (eds.) (1988) *Rethinking the Life Cycle*, Macmillan: London.

Castro, L. J. and Rogers, A. (1983a) 'Patterns of family migration: two methodological approaches'. *Environment and Planning A*, 15, 237–54.

Castro, L. J. and Rogers, A. (1983b) 'What the age composition of migrants can tell us'. *Population Bulletin of the United Nations*, 15, 63–79.

Clark, W. A. V. and Cadwallader, M. (1973) 'Locational stress and residential mobility'. *Environment and Behavior*, 5, 29–41.

Clark, W. A. V. and Davies, S. (1990) 'Elderly mobility and mobility outcomes: households in the later stages of the life course'. *Research on Aging*, 12, 430–462.

Clark, W. A. V. and Onaka, J. L. (1983) 'Life cycle and housing adjustment as explanations of residential mobility'. *Urban Studies*, 20, 47–57.

Cribier, F. and Kych, A. (1992) 'La migration de retraite des parisiens: une analyse de la propension au départ'. *Population*, 3, 677–718.

Finch, J. (1989) *Family Obligations and Social Change*, Polity, London.

Fleiss, A. (1985) *Home Ownership Alternatives for the Elderly*, Her Majesty's Stationery Office, London.

Ford, R. and Warnes, A. M. (1992) *Residential mobility in later life: the revised research design*. MILL Working Paper 1, Occasional Paper 32, Department of Geography, King's College London.

Ford, R. and Warnes, A. M. (1993) *Residential Strategies in Later Life: Focus Group and Interview Study Results*, MILL Working Paper 3, Occasional Paper 38, Department of Geography, King's College London.

Glyn-Jones, A. (1975) *Growing Older in a South Devon Town*, University of Exeter: Exeter.

Grebenik, E., Hohn, C. and Mackensen, R. (eds.) (1989) *Later Phases of the Life Cycle: Demographic Aspects*, Clarendon: Oxford.

Grundy, E. (1987a) 'Retirement migration and its consequences in England and Wales'. *Ageing and Society*, 7, 57–82.

Grundy, E. (1987b) 'Household change and migration among the elderly in England and Wales'. *Espaces, Populations, Sociétés*, 1987/1, 109–123.

Hamnett, C., Harmer, M. and Williams, P. (1991). *Safe as Houses: Housing Inheritance in Britain*, Paul Chapman: London.

Harrop, A. and Grundy, E. (1991) 'Geographic variations in moves into institutions among the elderly in England and Wales'. *Urban Studies*, 28, 65–86.

Hitt, H.L. (1954). 'The role of migration in population change among the aged'. *American Sociological Review*, 19, 194–200.

Karn, V. (1977). *Retiring to the Seaside*, Routledge: London.

Laslett, P. (1989) *A Fresh Map of Life: The Emergence of the Third Age*, Weidenfeld & Nicolson: London.

Law, C. M. and Warnes, A. M. (1980) 'The characteristics of retired migrants', in Herbert, D. T. and Johnston, R. J. (eds.) *Geography and the Urban Environment, Volume III*, Wiley: Chichester, 175–222.

Law, C. M. and Warnes, A. M. (1982) 'The destination decision in retirement migration', in Warnes, A.M. (ed.) *Geographical Perspectives on the Elderly*, Wiley: Chichester, Sussex, 3–81.

Lee, E. (1966) 'A theory of migration'. *Demography*, 3, 47–57.

Lee, G. R., Dwyer, J. W. and Coward R. T. (1990) 'Residential location and proximity to children among impaired elderly parents'. *Rural Sociology*, 55, 579–589.

Litwak, E. and Kulis, S. (1987) 'Technology, proximity and measures of kin support'. *Journal of Marriage and the Family*, 42, 923–34.

Litwak, E. and Longino, C. F. (1987) 'Migration patterns among the elderly: a developmental perspective'. *The Gerontologist*, 27, 266–72.

Longino, C.F. (1990) 'Retirement migration streams: trends and implications for North Carolina communities'. *Journal of Applied Gerontology*, 9, 393–404.

Mackintosh, S., Means, R. and Leather, P. (1990). *Housing in Later Life: The Housing Finance Implications of an Ageing Society*, School for Advanced Urban Studies: Bristol.

Maddox, G. L., 'Long-term care policies in comparative perspective'. *Ageing & Society*, 12(3), 1992, 355–68.

Meyer, J. W. and Speare, A. (1985) 'Distinctive elderly mobility: types and determinants'. *Economic Geography*, 61, 79–88.

Mullings, B. and Hamnett, C. (1992) 'Equity release schemes and equity extraction by elderly households in Britain'. *Ageing & Society*, 12, 413–42.

Poulain, M. (1989) 'Changes in the life space during the final stages' in Grebenik *et al* (eds.), *op. cit.* 208–21.

Quercia, R. G. and Rohe, W. M. (1992) 'Housing adjustments among older home owners'. *Urban Affairs Quarterly*, 28, 104–125.

Reschovsky, J. D. (1990) 'Residential immobility of the elderly: an empirical investigation'. *AREURA Journal*, 18, 160–183.

Rogers, A. (1988) 'Age patterns of elderly migration: an international comparison'. *Demography*, 25(3), 355–70.

Rogers, A. and Castro, L. J. (1981) 'Age patterns of migration: cause-specific profiles', in Rogers, A. (ed.) *Advances in Multiregional Demography*, Research Report RR-81-6, International Institute for Applied Systems Analysis: Laxenburg, Austria, 125–159.

Rogers, A. and Castro, L. J. (1986) 'Migration', in Rogers, A. and Willekens, F. (eds.) *Migration and Settlement*, Reidel: Dordrecht, Netherlands, 157–209.

Rogers, A., Frey, W. H., Rees, P. H., Speare. A. and Warnes, A. M. (eds.) (1992) *Elderly Migration and Population Redistribution: A Comparative Study*, Belhaven: London.

Rogers, A. and Woodward, J. (1988) 'The sources of regional elderly population growth: migration and aging in place'. *Professional Geographer*, 40, 450–459.

Rossi, P. (1955) *Why Families Move: A Study in the Social Psychology of Urban Residential Mobility*, Free Press: Glencoe, Illinois.

Steinnes, D. N. and Hogan, T. D. (1992) 'Take the money and sun: elderly migration as a consequence of gains in unaffordable housing markets'. *Journal of Gerontology: Social Sciences*, 47, S197-S203.

Stuart, A. (1987) 'Migration and population turnover in a London Borough: the incidence and implications of retirement out-migration'. *Espaces Populations Societes* 1987/1, 137–151.

Warnes, A. M. (1983) 'Migration in late working age and early retirement'. *Socio-Economic Planning Sciences*, 17, 291–302.

Warnes, A. M. (1986) 'The residential histories of parents and children, and relationships to present proximity and social integration'. *Environment and Planning A*, 16, 1581–1594.

Warnes, A. M. (1987) 'Microlocational issues in housing for the elderly', in Maddox, G.L. and Busse E.W. (eds.) *Aging: The Universal Phenomenon*, Springer Publishing Co.: New York 534–554.

Warnes, A. M. (1992) 'Temporal and spatial patterns of elderly migration', in Stillwell, J., Rees, P. and Boden, P. (eds.) *Migration Processes and Patterns: Volume II, Population Redistribution in the 1980s*, Belhaven: London, 248–70.

Warnes, A. M. and Ford, R. (1993) *Migration and the Distribution of Elderly People in Great Britain*, MILL Working Paper 2, Occasional Paper 37, Department of Geography, King's College London.

Warnes, A. M., Howes, D. R. and Took, L. (1985a) 'Intimacy at a distance under the microscope', in Butler, A. (ed.) *Ageing: Recent Advances and Creative Responses*, Croom Helm: Beckenham, Kent. 96–112.

Warnes, A. M., Howes, D. R. and Took, L. (1985b) 'Residential locations and inter-generational visiting in retirement'. *Quarterly Journal of Social Affairs*, 1, 231–247.

Wenger, G. C. (1992) *Help in Old Age – Facing Up to the Challenge: A Longitudinal Network Study*, University of Liverpool Press: Liverpool.

Williams, G. (1990). *The Experience of Housing in Retirement*, Avebury, Aldershot, Hampshire.

Willmott, P. (1986) *Social Networks, Informal Care and Public Policy*, Policy Studies Institute, London.

Willmott, P. (1987) *Friendship Networks and Social Support*, Policy Studies Institute, London.

Wiseman, R. F. (1980) 'Why older people move'. *Research on Aging*, 2, 141–154.

Wolpert, J. (1965) 'Behavioural aspects of the decision to migrate'. *Papers and Proceedings of the Regional Science Association*, 15, 159–69.

Chapter 5
THE LABOUR MARKET AND UNPAID CARING: CONFLICT AND COMPROMISE

HEATHER JOSHI

The labour market context

Paid work is an input into the economy and, for the individual, the major source of livelihood. Besides income, it is often a source of social identity, self esteem, contact with others and of autonomy. Most people, women as well as men, can expect to spend most of their lives between education and retirement in the labour force. Even for most of those not currently in it, opportunities for employment are a relevant alternative. Carers are drawn from the general population. Informal caring may indeed be an important job in itself, as recognised by the House of Commons Social Services Committee (1990), but it is by definition different from the formal economy of paid work. Consideration of the structure and trends in the labour market as a whole is necessary background to the specific questions of whether caring and paid work conflict or combine. This opening section of this chapter takes a brief overview of trends in the labour market and its structure in contemporary Britain.

Over the post-war period, trends in male labour force participation have moved in the opposite direction to that of females, although by the beginning of the 1990s male participation rates are still above females, who in 1991 formed nearly 48 per cent of the labour force. More than nine out of ten males at 'prime' ages (20–54) were still in the labour force in 1990, but the age span would have extended to age 59 in the early 1970s (Smyth and Browne, 1992, Table 9.3). Employment rates of men aged 55–64 have fallen even more dramatically than their economic activity rates. An upward trend in the unemployment of older men was briefly halted in the booming labour markets of the late 1980s. These developments partly reflect voluntary earlier retirement, facilitated by improved pensions, but they also reveal massive age discrimination in employment practices (Trinder *et al.*, 1992).

Women's employment is not only, still, a little less universal than that of men's, it is very much more likely to be part-time. 22 per cent of women under 60 worked part-time in 1991 (Great Britain) compared to under 1 per cent of men under 65. Full-time employment accounted for 37 per cent of all women under pension age and 86 per cent of men (Employment Department, 1992). Women's participation in the labour force falls below men's largely because of their domestic roles. The gap is at its greatest around age 30 where the presence of young children is concentrated. The raised participation rates of women in mid-life are accounted for by part-time employment, often taken on by 'women returners' to paid work after or during child rearing. A break in employment around childbearing has been characteristic of the post-war period in Britain, but the average length of this interruption has diminished for successive generations. As the minority who never resumed paid work disappeared, another minority emerged, in the 1980s, of mothers who never interrupted their employment except for maternity leave. This applies particularly to highly qualified women who have been numerically unimportant until recently. A longitudinal perspective of trends up to 1980 is given by Martin & Roberts, (1984) and plotted graphically in Joshi (1990).

Until the late 1980s, virtually all the increase in the female participation rate was accounted for by the emergence of the part-time sector for those aged 30–59. As discussed elsewhere (Joshi, 1990; Joshi and Hinde, forthcoming), part-time employment represents the compromise which enabled British women to combine motherhood and paid work. The same argument would also apply to the roles of wife or carer. The compromise was achieved at a price, for part-time employment on the whole offers poor terms such as rates of pay, job security, promotion prospects and pension coverage. Women, older men and ethnic minorities are also over-represented in some other forms of 'non-standard' employment outside the privileges of the internal labour markets said to operate in about half of UK firms (Trinder et al., 1992). 7 per cent of female employees and 4 per cent of male employees had temporary or casual contracts in 1991 (Employment Department, 1992). Self employment is more common among men than women, but has been increasing for both. The same is true of unemployment, not only of the male-biased official count of claimants but also of unemployment as revealed in surveys, increasing over the long view as well as in the years since 1990.

A notable feature of paid work is the high and apparently unchanging degree of occupational segregation. Women concentrate in service and 'caring' occupations, men more in occupations connected with manufacturing. Part-time female employment is particularly concentrated in a few categories, mostly particularly poorly paid, such as cleaners, shop assistants and waitresses.

The increase in female participation has meant that two-earner couples have become more frequent than the traditional partnership of the breadwinner and his housewife. This does not mean that the patriarchal tradition has disappeared. Divisions of labour between the sexes persist not only in paid work but in the unpaid work of the home, where it is still unusual for husbands to take or share responsibility for all but a few domestic tasks even where the wife is employed full-time outside the home (British Social Attitudes Survey, 1988, cited by Kiernan and Wicks, 1990). Caring for an infirm elderly person would generally be considered more appropriate for a woman than a man (Dalley, 1993); indeed the notion of caring is very much bound up with women's gender identity.

'The experience of caring is the medium through which women are accepted into and feel they belong in the social world...It is through caring in an informal capacity – as mothers, wives, daughter, neighbours, friends – and through formal caring – as nurses, secretaries, cleaners, teachers, social workers – that women enter and occupy their place in society...' Graham (1983 p30).

Another corollary of the female duty to keep the home fires burning is a corresponding obligation on men to keep the family finances going. Despite the increase in two-earner couples this dependence of women on men's earnings is not obsolete. There is asymmetry in the bringing in of cash just as there is in unpaid work, even in two-earner couples. Because so much of women's employment is part-time, and because even more of it is poorly paid, husbands tend to earn much more than their wives – roughly twice as much on average. In many couples the second earner is a secondary earner. If she is not totally dependent, she is partially dependent on her husband's employment (Joshi, 1989). Wives are even more likely to be fully or partially dependent on their husband's pensions in old age – and may be particularly hard hit if they divorce (Joshi and Davies, 1991). As divorce is increasingly likely, the importance of married women maintaining contact with the labour market is also increasing.

Prospects for employment over the rest of the 1990s have been assessed by the Institute for Employment Research. As an underlying trend, setting aside the immediate recession, they expect between 1990 and 2000 a more or less static male labour force, with a growing part-time component. The female labour force is expected to continue to rise, although with a slowing of the growth in participation rates particularly among older age groups. Part-time employment, as with men, is the growth area (see Trinder et al., 1992; and Dex, 1992). The occupational mix projected is for further growth towards service industries and occupations likely to favour females and, perhaps, older men. The Institute points out that outcomes will be affected by whether policies are pursued to maintain and improve the quality of the labour force. In their absence, a 'cost-cutting', or cheap labour, scenario would result in less rewarding jobs for both workers and the economy.

In the next section of this chapter we examine details of carers' access to the labour market. The final part outlines measures which might improve the terms on which it is possible, for those who so choose, to combine caring and paid work.

The employment of carers

Table 1 shows estimates of the participation in employment of carers and non-carers under state pension age from the 1985 and 1990 General Household Surveys. Carers were less likely than their non caring counterparts to have paid work, but the margin is not great. Men carers have employment rates much closer to men without caring responsibilities (around 80 per cent), than to women's (around 60 per cent). The net effect of trends between the two GHS enquiries on carers was to raise employment rates generally for carers and others alike.[1] One may surmise that the downturn in employment since 1990 has also reduced employment rates of both carers and non-carers alike. We turn shortly to see how these and other data can address the question of how the labour market experience of carers and non-carers differ.

Carers of the elderly compared to all carers

First, since most of this kind of evidence concerns care recipients of all ages, not just the elderly, consider Table 2, which compares employment rates for carers of all ages with carers of persons over pension age. It is not surprising that the

TABLE 1

Employment Rate of Non Elderly Respondents to two General Household
Surveys by whether or not caring

Men under 65 Women under 60 in 1985, under 64 in 1990 Recipients of care all ages	Percentage Employed	
	1985	1990
Men	%	%
Non-carers	79	81
Carers	73	77
Married Women		
Non-carers	59	66
Carers	57	62
Non-married Women		
Non-carers	64	61
Carers	61	53
	Sample numbers	
Men		
Non-carers	6260	5722
Carers	805	874
Married Women		
Non-carers	4036	3969
Carers	831	999
Non-married Women		
Non-carers	1938	2000
Carers	262	339
Care recipients all ages		

Source: 1985, Evandrou and Winter (1992 Table 2)
    1990, OPCS Unpublished table of General Household Survey

two sets of rates are close, as the majority of care recipients are elderly. The slight
employment lead of those caring for elderly people indicates that employment is
less common among those caring for younger people (see also Baldwin and
Parker, 1991 Table 8.4). For the most part it can be assumed that the labour
market implications of caring for the elderly are fairly well represented in
accounts covering care for all ages of recipient.

Ages of carers

The tabulation by SPRU (Table 2) showed that almost exactly half the under 65
year old men caring for elderly people were also under 45. Among female carers
of the elderly, those under 45 slightly outnumbered those aged 45–59. Parker
(1992) shows that carers under 45 were somewhat more likely to be in separate
households. Among in-household carers of parents or parents-in-law, 37 per
cent were under 45. Although women aged 45–59 are most likely to be most
heavily committed to caring (Dalley, 1993), it would be a mistake to think of
carers of the elderly solely in terms of women over 45.

TABLE 2

Carers of the elderly compared to all carers: Employment participation profiles 1985 General Household Survey

	Men under 65		Women under 60	
of those who were: Caring for an elderly person percentages employed		All caring	Caring for an elderly person	All caring
	%	%	%	%
Full-time	71	69	25	25
Part-time	4	3	35	32
All Employed	75	73	61	58
Sample Numbers	766	805	1057	1093

Source: Special analysis of the 1985 GHS of caring relationships involving elderly recipients, Gillian Parker, SPRU University of York, and recalculation of analyses reported by Evandrou and Winter (1992, Table 2).

TABLE 3

Percentages of Women Providing care, 1965 to 1990, by employment status

	1965 %	1980 %	1985 %	1990 %
Not employed	13	15	18	20
In employment	10	13	15	18
Full-time	7	11	12	15
Part-time	15	16	19	21

Notes: 1965 and 1980 data apply to non-students under 60.
1985 and 1990 figures apply to all women 16–64.
Care recipients all ages
Sources: 1965 Hunt (1968) as cited by Martin and Roberts (1984, Table 8.34) also the source for 1980. 1985: General Household Survey, Green (1988 Table 2.9), 1990: General Household Survey, OPCS Monitor SS92/2 Table 6.

Trends in women's caring and employment

Before the General Household Survey (GHS) brought male participation in caring to light, some nationally representative evidence was collected in two major surveys on women's employment. This evidence is combined with that of the GHS in Table 3, showing participation rates in caring by employment status, rather than participation rates in employment by carer status. In 1965, the proportions of women under 60 caring for an elderly or infirm person were low: 13 per cent of those not in employment and 10 per cent of those with a job. Although caring still only affects a minority, the proportion involved has gone up to nearly one in five. The upward trend has involved women both with and without paid work. The margin between their caring rates has not opened up. Part-timers remain somewhat more likely than those without paid work to report caring responsibilities. This development is contrary to fears that increased labour force participation would draw women away from caring (see Parker 1985, 1982).

There are also parallels with the increased employment of women with dependent children (though the proportion of women with this type of responsibility has fallen). In 1973, 17 per cent of mothers of dependent children had full-time paid jobs and 30 per cent had part-time paid jobs. By 1990 these had risen to 21 per cent and 39 per cent respectively, together a rise of 14 points. The economic activity rate of these mothers went from under a half to approaching two thirds (Smythe & Browne, 1992 Table 9.5). The growing issue of how families cope with combining employment of mothers with bringing up children is also relevant to the issue of carers of the elderly and the labour market. The analogy of caring for the older and the younger generation has its limits. The type of care required is by no means identical. Schools and child day care are not identical to day centres and residential facilities for the old. The uncertainties involved are different, probably greater in the case of elderly people, in contrast to the normally diminishing demands of growing children. Those of elderly people are likely to increase, until the unpredictable point where the older person dies, or goes into residential care. Note that in the latter case, demands on the carer's time and energy have not finished.

Given these features of caring for elderly people, the question arises as to what extent carers' responsibilities are an impediment to employment in practice.

Effects of caring on labour force participation

Caring, as broadly defined in nationally representative sample surveys, is so heterogeneous, and involves such a range of time commitment, that its effects on labour force participation are also likely to be very varied. The effects appear to depend upon which carers are considered, whether they are compared with otherwise comparable non-carers (and by what method this is done) or with what the carers themselves would otherwise have been doing.

Crude differences in employment rates between carers and others may just reflect differences in the group's composition in terms of factors predisposing employment. Only when these are controlled can one start to think of the comparison as revealing the **effect** of caring. Even then one has to be careful about interpretation. The acquisition of caring responsibilities may not be random but tends to be bestowed upon those with lower labour force attachment. Little is known (from quantitative evidence) about the selection of individuals into caring, apart from the obvious gender bias in social expectations (possibly weakening in practice). Following Evandrou and Winter (1992) we proceed here without tackling this problem of who becomes a carer. It is assumed, with this caution, that differences between carers and others can be interpreted as the outcome of caring rather than its cause.

Linear comparisons

First consider evidence that compares people with caring responsibilities with that of comparable people in nationally representative samples. Parker and

Lawton (1990) compared the employment rates of all carers (broadly defined, recipients of all ages) with matched samples of non-carers. They found differences in the employment rate of 3 percentage points for females and 7 points for males. In each case the 'impact' on full-time work was greater, offset by more part-time employment of carers. These estimates were felt to be reasonably similar to the 'all else being equal' effect reported by Joshi in a linear probability regression on the 1980 Women and Employment Survey – of 9 percentage points reduction on employment, 6 points full-time, for women under 60 (Baldwin and Parker 1991, Joshi 1987). The uncontrolled difference in the employment rate of carers and non-carers in the Women and Employment Survey was less than 2 percentage points (derived from Martin & Roberts, 1984, Table 8.35)

Non-linear methods

When the same data were subject to a more rigorous estimation method (multi-nominal logit) by Davies and Joshi (1992), the estimated impact of caring on employment came out at a reduction of 12 percentage points at the mean, 10 on full-time, 2 part-time. These reductions would vary in magnitude across women, greater for those most likely to participate on other grounds, less for those anyway less likely to participate. They should be comparable with the General Household Survey in that the Women and Employment Survey (WES) asked a similarly broadly defined question about caring. Non-linear methods have also been applied to the 1985 GHS by Evandrou and Winter (1992). On their analysis, the impact of caring on employment comes out, at their sample mean, as a reduction of 3 percentage points for women and 5 for men.

Cross tabulation

Table 4 gives details, from the 1990 General Household Survey, of the pattern of participation, by age, sex, and for women, marital status, according to whether people had any caring responsibilities and, if so, whether they were co-resident carers. The small group caring for someone in the same home are discussed after a consideration of the more broadly defined group of carers from which they are drawn. The distribution of non-carers in each group over full-time and part-time employment, unemployment and economic inactivity mirrors the rates in the population at large. Almost everyone over 65 is 'inactive', most men are otherwise in full-time employment, and the employment of women, particularly if married, is more evenly spread between full- and part-time jobs. The pattern among carers broadly defined is also similar.

Table 5 shows the differences between non-carers and carers in the rates shown on Table 4, although they control only for age, sex and female marital status. Tables 4 and 5 also suggest that the overall impact of caring responsibility

TABLE 4

Participation in Paid Work by Caring and Age Group GHS 1990

TABLE 4 part (a)

	Men		
	No caring	Any caring	Co-resident Care
16–29			
Fulltime	70%	64%	48%
Part-time*	7%	6%	6%
Unemployed*	13%	18%	18%
Inactive	10%	12%	27%
Sample numbers	1864	140	33
30–44			
Fulltime	86%	85%	78%
Part-time*	3%	3%	4%
Unemployed*	7%	7%	12%
Inactive	4%	5%	6%
Sample numbers	1953	255	50
45–64			
Fulltime	73%	70%	56%
Part-time*	3%	4%	3%
Unemployed*	5%	4%	7%
Inactive	19%	22%	34%
Sample numbers	1905	479	123
Over 65			
Fulltime	3%	2%	2%
Part-time*	6%	6%	3%
Unemployed*	0	0	0
Inactive	90%	92%	95%
Sample numbers	1289	218	98

Part-time* includes a few workers with unknown hours
Unemployed* includes those on Government Schemes
Care-recipients all ages

Source: OPCS Unpublished tabulations.

TABLE 4 part (b)

	Non married women		
	No caring	Any caring	Co-resident Care
16–29			
Fulltime	46%	39%	43%
Part-time*	17%	20%	13%
Unemployed*	11%	13%	17%
Inactive	26%	28%	26%
Sample numbers	1138	103	23
30–44			
Fulltime	50%	34%	35%
Part-time*	19%	20%	15%
Unemployed*	7%	7%	0
Inactive	24%	40%	50%
Sample numbers	391	92	20
45–64			
Fulltime	30%	22%	34%
Part-time*	19%	26%	12%
Unemployed*	4%	4%	0
Inactive	46%	48%	54%
Sample numbers	471	144	41
Over 65			
Fulltime	0	0	0
Part-time*	1%	5%	13%
Unemployed*	0	0	0
Inactive	98%	95%	87%
Sample numbers	1151	114	15

Part-time* includes a few workers with unknown hours
Unemployed* includes those on Government Schemes
Care-recipients all ages

Source: OPCS Unpublished tabulations.

TABLE 4 part (c)

	Married & cohabiting women		
	No caring	Any caring	Co-resident Care
16–29			
Fulltime	49%	29%	10%
Part-time*	18%	23%	30%
Unemployed*	4%	4%	0%
Inactive	29%	43%	60%
Sample numbers	907	95	10
30–44			
Fulltime	32%	29%	18%
Part-time*	40%	42%	31%
Unemployed*	3%	3%	4%
Inactive	25%	26%	47%
Sample numbers	1631	365	55
45–64			
Fulltime	24%	23%	14%
Part-time*	33%	35%	22%
Unemployed*	1%	1%	1%
Inactive	41%	41%	64%
Sample numbers	1419	556	111
Over 65			
Fulltime	1%	0	0
Part-time*	3%	3%	3%
Unemployed*	0	0	0
Inactive	96%	97%	97%
Sample numbers	701	154	89

Part-time *includes a few workers with unknown hours
Unemployed *includes those on Government Schemes
Care-recipients all ages

Source: OPCS Unpublished tabulations.

TABLE 5
Differences of carers' rates from non-carers

	Men		Women Non married		Married & cohabiting	
	Any caring	Co-resident	Any caring	Co-resident	Any caring	Co-resident
16–29						
Fulltime	6	22	7	3	19	39
Part-time*	0	1	−4	3	−5	−12
Unemployed*	−5	−5	−2	−6	−1	4
Inactive	−2	−17	−2	0	−14	−31
Sample numbers	140	33	103	23	95	10
30–44						
Fulltime	2	8	17	15	3	14
Part-time*	0	−1	−1	4	−3	9
Unemployed*	0	−5	0	7	0	−1
Inactive	−1	−2	−16	−26	0	−22
Sample numbers	255	50	92	20	365	55
45–64						
Fulltime	2	16	8	−4	1	11
Part-time*	−1	0	−6	7	1	12
Unemployed*	1	−2	0	4	0	0
Inactive	−3	−15	−2	−7	0	−23
Sample numbers	479	123	144	41	656	111
Over 65						
Fulltime	2	1	0	0	1	1
Part-time*	0	3	−4	−12	0	0
Unemployed*	0	0	0	0	0	0
Inactive	−2	−5	3	11	−1	−1
Sample numbers	218	98	114	15	154	89

Care-recipients all ages
See Table 4 for definitions and sample size of comparison group
Source: OPCS Unpublished table of the 1990 General Household Survey

is modest. The gaps in employment rates vary from 1 to 16 percentage points. This mostly involves full-time employment, especially for men. Part-time differentials are sometimes offsetting. There is no consistent pattern to suggest that either men's or women's employment participation is more affected.[2]

Whatever the precise number, and whether or not it has been changing over time, adjusted or not, the difference between the employment rates is not spectacular. This means two things. First, carers tend to be drawn from groups who would otherwise be participating normally in paid work. Secondly, the majority of carers combine paid work with their caring responsibilities. Just as the responsibility for children can be combined with paid work, so can (some) responsibilities for extra care. Figure 1 shows how the participation profile of caring for elderly people resembles that of women with dependent children in data for 1985. This is particularly so for those in the 45–64 age group, where employment of other women is also similar. For women over 45, neither carers of the elderly nor carers of children have employment rates as big as the group with no dependent children (some carers are included among the latter). Carers under 45 had higher employment rates than mothers, due to full-time employment. Despite the difficulties outlined above, there is not here any sign that care of elderly people is a greater deterrent to labour force participation than motherhood. In the WES analysis (Joshi, 1987) the 'impact' on employment participation of caring came out about the same as that of the average dependent child.

Effect on what?

As with dependent children, the effect of caring on labour force membership has further dimensions. We need to ask what kind of employment and what kind of caring. We see from Tables 4 and 5 that full-time employment is less compatible with caring than part-time employment. The larger care-related gap in employment rates of men compared with women in 1985 is thought to reflect the greater difficulties of men in finding part-time employment. Evandrou and Winter (1992, Table 11) estimate that employed carers, at the mean of their 1985 sample, would work about one hour more per week if they had no caring responsibilities.[3]

The unemployment experience of the carers might be thought to be less affected than that of non-carers because they are more likely to be out of the labour force altogether. On the other hand, those who are in the labour force may find more difficulty than non-carers in finding, or retaining, a job to suit their circumstances. Table 4 suggests that the result in 1990 was that carers under 30 had even higher chances of unemployment than non-carers, whereas those aged 30–64, male and female, had about the same chances of unemployment as non-carers in their own group.

Intensity of caring

On the question of what kind of caring responsibility affects employment there are a number of dimensions that might be considered – the type of attention

Figure 1
Employment by Care of Old and Young

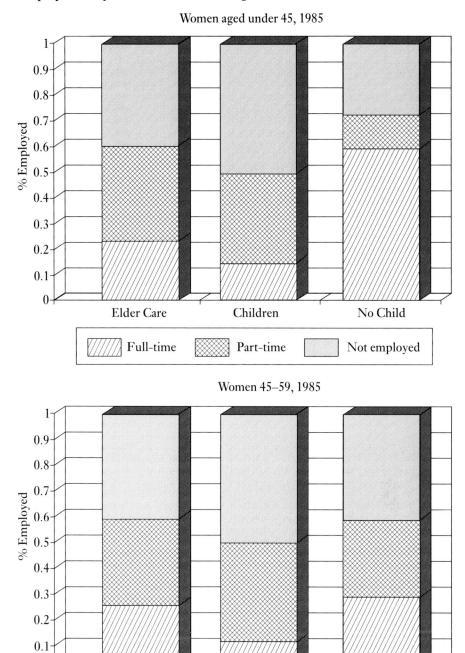

Women aged under 45, 1985

Women 45–59, 1985

Source:
General Household Survey 1985 Report for women with and without dependent children. Those involved in eldercare also, in a few cases, have dependent children. Likewise, a few of the women with no children are caring for the elderly. Data on elder care supplied by Gillian Parker, from her analysis at the University of York of the 1985 Household Survey.

needed (from errands to heavy personal care), the hours devoted to care, how many other people share the care, whether the caring is within or outside the carer's household, the age of the recipient and their relationship to the carer. For most of the analyses under review here, data on age or relationship of recipient is not linked to employment data. Suffice it to say that the majority of the care recipients in the GHS were elderly. Hours of care is not taken as an independent variable here, on the grounds that how much paid work and how much caring is done may be jointly determined. On the whole, those spending over 20 hours per week caring are not in much paid work, though some carers combine full-time employment with as many or more hours of caring. Half the male and just over one third of the female carers doing over 50 hours of caring also had paid work in 1985 (Evandrou and Winter, 1992). Leisure is the forgone opportunity.

The multivariate analysis by Evandrou and Winter put the effects, at the mean, on participation of caring for more than 50 hours per week at 16 and 14 percentage points for men and women respectively. The estimate for in-household care is 5 points for men and 4 for women. Being the sole carer of a co-resident reduces women's employment by 7 points and men's by 29 points (Evandrou and Winter, 1992 Tables 7 and 9).

Co-resident care

The subset of carers who give care to someone else in their household is distinguished in Tables 4 and 5. On the whole this captures the people with the greater caring demands. It includes those situations where the carer moved in with a parent (or vice versa) because of the need for close and constant attendance (see Arber and Ginn, 1991). It also includes cases where the carer looks after a spouse or a child, and hence includes a higher proportion of non-elderly care recipients (46 per cent in 1990) than carers taken as a whole (21 per cent).

It is immediately obvious from Tables 4 and 5 that co-resident care is less compatible with paid work than the broad definition of care. In virtually all the cells for carers under 65, co-resident carers are more than 10 percentage points less likely than non-carers to be in full-time employment. This could also be true of the cases where it does not appear to hold, given the margin of sampling error around the relatively small cells concerned. The association of co-resident caring with part-time employment is weaker and in varying directions. The raised unemployment of younger carers noted above also applies to young co-resident carers, and to some extent to men over 30. It is for this, as yet small, 'hard core' of carers of elderly people that loss of earnings and pension rights is likely to be severe, particularly if the situation is prolonged and residential care is not an alternative. Such 'hard core' situations of conflict with employment could well grow in number, as more of the elderly are to be cared for, for longer, in the community.

What carers say about the effect on employment

Another approach to estimating the impact of caring on employment is to ask those who are involved whether they think their employment is or was affected by caring. This can be made most explicit if they are asked whether they left employment as a result of caring responsibilities.

National surveys

Nationally representative evidence on this question is available from the 1980 Women and Employment Survey and the 1988 OPCS Retirement Survey (Martin & Roberts, 1984; Bone et al., 1992). In the former survey, of those caring for a sick or elderly dependant, 12 per cent with paid work and 29 per cent of those not employed said caring affected their work. In the latter case most of the effects reported were in having to give up work; for the employed carers, restricted hours of work and having to take time off were most frequently mentioned. Martin and Roberts (1984) expressed surprise that the numbers reporting an effect were so low, but they are in line with other surveys and, even more surprisingly, the multi-nominal logit analysis. Had the 29 per cent of non-employed carers, who said they had been affected, switched back into employment, the employment rate of carers would have been raised by 12 per cent, exactly the estimate offered by Davies and Joshi (1992).

In the 1988 Retirement Survey, respondents aged 55 to 69 looked back over their lifetimes. Women were more likely to have left a job to look after a 'sick or disabled or elderly relative' than men, co-resident and ex-carers more likely to have done so than other current carers. The highest proportions reporting an effect were 18 per cent and 10 per cent among women and men co-resident carers, with 17 per cent of the numerous women ex-carers also affected. 14 to 15 per cent of co-resident carers (men and women) and of female ex-carers reported having become unemployed as a result of caring. In relation to other effects on employment (taking a lower paid job, having difficulty getting a job, or losing pay through taking time off), the small group of male co-resident carers reported the highest, though perhaps modest, rates of disruption (6 per cent, 8 per cent and 18 per cent) (Tinker et al., 1992, Tables 3.9 3.10). Those retired informants who had been pre-retirement carers were asked whether caring had affected the timing of their retirement. The vast majority (84 per cent of women and 89 per cent of men) said it had not, reinforcing the impression of the cross-sections that caring and employment are not all that incompatible (Bone et al., 1992, Table 8.45). Further analysis reported by Tinker et al (1992) shows that co-resident carers were, as we might expect, more likely to have been affected. 29 per cent of women among them had brought forward their retirement, as had 26 per cent of the men, but these were a small group.

Small-scale surveys

Smaller scale studies add depth, if not necessarily representativeness, to the picture. In the 22 married couples studied by Nissel and Bonnerjea (1982) and the 58 single carers studied by Wright (1983), the impression of the disruption of female employment is dominant. Nissel and Bonnerjea (1982) report a small but intensive study of married women caring for severely handicapped elderly people. The majority (15) of this sample were out of paid work, and most of those would have been employed had it not been for their caring role. The seven women with paid jobs (2 full-time, 5 part-time) in this sample reported a variety of difficulties and stresses in combining their roles.

Carer surveys

In a 1990 survey, focused on 'full-time' carers not in paid work, more than half reported earlier employment disruption (60 per cent said they had given up paid work because of caring or had taken early retirement; 57 per cent said they would be employed were it not for caring). This is more than would have been expected from the Retirement Survey evidence. In a survey of employed carers, 47 per cent of women and 35 per cent of men felt that caring had a detrimental effect on their working lives (Opportunities for Women, 1991, quoted by Brotchie and Hills, 1991). The Eldercare Survey (Whatmore and Mira–Smith, 1991) sent out a questionnaire to a quota sample of carers identified by a number of organisations, receiving 1,946 replies. Again a similar rate of giving up work because of caring emerged – 40 per cent of the total, of whom 28 per cent were in employment, ie 56 per cent of the non-employed. Effects on employment other than giving up were mentioned almost as frequently. These included having to take time off, arriving late and leaving early, loss of promotion chances and so on. When asked to identify statements which best summed up their attitude to caring, conflicts with work were not, however, the most salient notions. Both women and men carers were more likely to mention worry about not having time for oneself (around a half), and women to mention strains on relationships. About one third mentioned difficulties of combining work and care, and about the same proportion mentioned financial difficulties. Future carers, particularly women, were more worried about the prospects of difficulty about employment.

In another recent survey of the members of the Carers National Association (1992), a self-selected and largely female sample of 2,916 carers, the rate of employment was also as low as 28 per cent, like the Eldercare Survey, but unlike the General Household Survey. Employment did not emerge as a salient issue, perhaps because of the focus of the questionnaire. Employment opportunities were not mentioned among things that would improve the quality of life. Most respondents were receiving Invalid Care Allowance or Income Support and may have thought of themselves as out of the labour market. The CNA also contacted 834 ex-carers who described their problems after giving up the role of main carer. Only 9 per cent of these mentioned difficulties finding paid work.

Effects on employment reviewed

Two out of three of these carer surveys suggest a more severe impact of caring on employment than the national surveys. The contemporary evidence on the impact of caring on employment is a bit confusing, as so many factors vary. It will obviously depend upon the degree of infirmity of the elderly person, and on the availability of other sources of help, formal and informal. On the potential carer's part it will also depend on a number of factors – whether she or he was expecting to be in employment in any case, how much they might earn, how easy it is to combine employment and caring, at what cost in terms of hours and rates of pay, as well as how they perceive their alternatives. In some situations the severe loss of employment described in earlier surveys still affects some caring situations, and these will appear in small-scale studies specifically designed to look for them. When a nationally representative net is thrown out, evidence emerges of what is probably a growing phenomenon of the combination of employment and caring. Policies need to address the problems of each situation: on the one hand the total loss of earnings where this occurs, and on the other, the terms upon which it is possible to combine paid work with caring.

Effect on earnings

The consequence for earnings of carers' lower participation and lower hours are compounded if the rate of pay per hour is also affected. This might come about because of poor time-keeping and absenteeism, loss of seniority because of past breaks in employment, loss of promotion opportunities, the limited opportunities for earning high pay while working part-time *inter alia*. Whatever the reason, Evandrou and Winter (1992) found evidence of depressed wage rates, especially for some types of commitment. The average hourly wage rates of in-house carers were 12 per cent below those of non-carers for males and 17 per cent for females (unadjusted for differences in sample composition). Analysis of WES (Wright and Ermisch, 1991, in Davies and Joshi, 1992) suggests that both men and women gain in pay as their employment record builds up. Therefore an interruption in earning could have a long-term effect on pay (and on final salary for pension purposes), particularly if taken before age 45. Beyond that age such effects appear to be negligible. There is also an effect on hourly wage of working part-time rather than full time. The penalty for part-time work for a woman with an otherwise uninterrupted full-time employment record is estimated as 21 per cent at age 30, 28 per cent at age 40 and 29 per cent at 50. For a woman with the employment record characteristic of a married mother of two, these factors are 11 per cent, 15 per cent and 19 per cent at these ages. The impact of these effects is often experienced on re-entry to employment after a break when job downgrading into part-time work is common.

Opportunity costs

If caring has an effect of reducing someone's paid work, then the resulting loss of earnings can be seen as the opportunity cost of the caring activity. The total opportunity cost for any given carer depends on the combination of (i) effects on employment, hours and rates of pay during, and perhaps, beyond the period of caring, (ii) whether the carer has difficulty returning to paid work, and (iii) if she does return, whether she suffers adverse consequences from the loss of employment experience. Adverse effects on the rate of pay are more likely if the break in employment comes in the carer's twenties or thirties. The effect on earnings will also affect pension entitlement.

A case study

Nissel and Bonnerjea (1982) estimate replacement costs and opportunity costs of their sample's caring activities for the current period, not allowing for any long-term effects. Replacement costs were conservatively estimated on the basis of buying-in help for the hours actually devoted to caring activities in their time budget data (3.5 to 4 hours per day) at an hourly rate a little above home helps and nursing auxiliaries, but below that of registered and enrolled nurses. As they point out, this is optimistic because of the disjointed and unpredictable nature of the care needed. Replacement costs came out at £2,500 per annum at 1980 wage rates. The opportunity cost for the (10 out of 15) non-employed carers who would wish to be employed again, measured as average full-time earnings in their former occupations, was nearly twice this – £4,500. Had those employed part-time been able to work full-time, their forgone earning opportunities amounted to rather less than replacement – £1,900. Given the particular composition of this sample, and allowing no earnings opportunity cost to the non-employed who were not interested in employment or the two employed full-time, the average opportunity cost for the sample as a whole is about the same in cash terms as the replacement cost. But, as should be clear, the relative size of the replacement cost and the opportunity cost varies with circumstances.

Pay and pension forgone: a few examples

It is possible to calculate the long-term effects on earning and pensions for the relatively simple case of carers in their 50s, where induced effects on subsequent pay can reasonably be ruled out (to be more precise, we know workers in this age group do not gain much from accumulating further experience, and there is little evidence about the effect on pay of late re-entry). Consider a woman in her fifties who would otherwise work full-time and earn £15,000 per annum, who does give up employment entirely for a 5 year stint of caring (the median reported in the Retirement Survey). She forgoes £15,000 for each of those five years (assuming no inflation), a total of £75,000. If she had been an otherwise fully paid-up member of an occupational pension scheme, expecting two thirds of her final salary at age 60 (£10,000), this will be reduced by her lost years of contribution to £8,750 if she draws it at that age, a forgone pension stream of £1,250 per annum. The cut in the value of the pension could be more than doubled if it was drawn early, according to the practice of the individual scheme. Entitlement to State Basic pension would not be affected if she qualified and claimed Home Responsibility Protection or was credited with contributions because claiming ICA. If she was not contracted out into the scheme outlined above, any Home Responsibility Protection would in due course also cover her SERPS entitlement, although the forgone years of earning might have raised her lifetime average, and hence her SERPS pension slightly. If the woman were expecting to work full-time until 60, but had earlier interrupted her pension contributions the proportional loss of pension results would be greater. If the carer in this example were a man, his annual salary would be somewhat higher, say £17,000, so that the total of the hypothetically forgone earnings over 5 years mounts to £85,000, and the forgone pension drawn at 65 to £1,420. If the carer were a woman who would otherwise be employed part-time, the earnings costs would be lower, say around £8,000 per annum, £40,000 in total. Effects on occupational pension can be ignored until enrolment of part-timers becomes more common. At least within a few years, these estimates can all be varied in proportion to the number of years assumed. If the carers had been younger, say in their 30s, it would be more complicated to calculate forgone earnings. Direct earnings loss would be less as salaries would not have reached their peak, but there would also be losses from the effect of lost work experience on pay. Younger women are also likely to be responsible for children, and this would anyway reduce the commitment of many of them to the labour force.

Costs and rewards

Those who maintain their employment alongside their caring commitments may be juggling their lives to avoid just these sorts of financial consequences, along of course with the hope of preferring the other benefits from being in paid work noted at the outset. Those who do give up, or stay away from, paid work to care are actually incurring these opportunity costs. Cash benefit for carers can start to redress the opportunity costs, but at present only do so very partially and conditional upon very limited employment participation. Better long-term protection of employment and pension rights, as well as cash supplementation of incomes that are reduced rather than eliminated by caring, could help to protect the incomes of carers, and make the caring role a little more rewarding for those who have yet to take it on.

Other effects

Caring may have a number of other effects on the carer, for example on their health, social life, leisure and family relations (see Nissel and Bonnerjea, 1982). Those who combine paid work with caring have additional sources of stress, maintaining the appearance of reliability at work for example, and pressure on time. Dalley (1993) quotes a case study of a woman who kept her job and her marriage going through six years of caring for her mother after a stroke, but who took no care of herself and lost confidence and, she felt, her youth. Though not inevitable, such reactions are commonly reported.

The health consequences of combining paid work with caring are not necessarily adverse. Caring can take a toll of physical and mental health even if the carer is not in paid work, perhaps particularly so. Bartley et al. (1992) estimate that domestic workload, including care of the elderly among other tasks, had an adverse effect on both physical symptoms reported to the Health and Lifestyle Survey and, more strongly, the psychological malaise score, independent of employment status in a multivariate analysis. In a review of

British and American research of the health consequences of women's paid employment, Macran (1993) found that the evidence, largely for mothers with young children, for a positive effect of role enhancement on the whole outweighed evidence of role strain. This does not mean that strains of combining employment and domestic responsibility never occur. It indicates either that the disadvantages are outweighed by the advantages (pecuniary and other) of working for pay, or that they can precipitate a withdrawal from paid work, as reported by a number of carers, for example in the Eldercare Survey.

The problems of caring and of combining it with employment are worse for those with low economic resources (Arber & Ginn, 1991). They are compounded when the carer faces gender, age or race discrimination in the labour market. The problems of ignorance and poor communication that feed racism also apply in making access to support services particularly difficult for some ethnic minorities (Brotchie & Hills, 1991). Quantitative evidence on this is still scarce because of the relatively small numbers, as yet, of black elders. As their numbers grow the multiple problems facing their carers are likely to become a large issue.

As many carers of old people as mothers at home with children?

It has been conjectured that the numbers of people caring for elderly people has come to outnumber the number of people caring for children. What light does the latest nationally representative survey, the GHS of 1990, throw on this proposition? There were roughly equal numbers of people involved in some way in informal care as mothers of dependent children (equivalent to approximately 7 m). This superficial correspondence compares carers of both sexes with parents of one, giving no credit to fathers for parental responsibilities, and it also involves a broad definition of care, and recipients of all ages. There is some overlap. Mothers of dependent children may also count as carers of disabled children (just over 1 per cent did so in 1990).

It is also possible to make a comparison of the numbers more heavily involved in the two types of care. One step is to exclude people who also have paid work. Mothers who were at home with dependent children and without paid work (around 3 million) also numbered roughly the same as carers broadly defined who were not employed (2 million women, 1 million men, very approximately). This mirrors the statement that participation in paid work by carers is not very different from that of mothers. Turning to more demanding situations, there were about twice as many mothers with at least one child under 5 as there were carers (both sexes) living in the same household as at least one dependant. Nearly 2 million of the mothers of children under 5 are 'at home', not doing paid work, compared to 1 million carers of co-residents with no paid job (0.6 million women, 0.4 million men), not all of whom care for the elderly. Co-resident carers would begin to outnumber mothers as the age band of children considered is narrowed. There are more of them than there are women who have had a baby in the past year, for example. They will also tend to grow, relative to the number of mothers of young children, unless growth in the annual numbers of births keeps pace with growth in the number of very elderly people receiving care from a co-resident.

112

TABLE 6
Percentage of the workforce who were carers

	Men	Non-married women	Married women	All women	Persons
Employed					
Full-time					
1985	11	10	13	12	11
1990	13	11	17	15	13
Part-time					
1985	12	17	20	19	18
1990	12	18	22	21	20
All workforce					
1985	11	12	17	15	13
1990	13	13	20	18	15
Sample numbers					
Full-time					
1985	5315	1021	1334	2355	7670
1990	5017	967	1571	2538	7555
Part-time					
1985	223	382	1629	2011	2234
1990	259	427	1647	2074	2333
All employed					
1985	5538	1403	2963	4366	9904
1990	5276	1394	3218	4612	9888

Source: 1985 GHS, Green (1988) Table 2.9
1990 GHS OPCS Monitor SS92/2 (OPCS 1990) Table 6.
Care recipients all ages.

Concluding remarks: compensation and compatibility

The evidence surveyed suggests that caring activity for women has grown alongside the growth in their labour force participation. For men, caring has probably increased, while employment trends decline. In both cases, employment and informal care, or at least some types of it, are not incompatible. Another perspective is to review the extent to which the workforce is already involved in care. Table 6 shows that in 1990, around one in seven in the workforce – men as well as women – had some involvement in caring. Over a longer time span more people, and more workers, are likely to face the challenge of giving care. Demographic and institutional changes mean that more than a small minority will be involved. This final section discusses policies that might be adopted, by government, firms and families, to cope with caring alongside individual need to retain a foothold in the labour force.

Over the next 40 years demographic trends alone suggest increasing demand for 'elder care' while the numbers of young children are not expected to rise much, (if at all). Whether this actually means that housebound care of the elderly will overtake housebound care of the new generation depends on a number of other factors besides the demographics – on the health of older people, and on how the family, the state, and the market evolve to provide a range of alternative ways of providing help to those who need it, at both ends of the lifespan. The model of childbearing as being the sole responsibility of an unpaid female is gradually changing. Fathers are more involved in child-rearing than they used to be. Mothers have long since shared responsibility for their children with schools, and increasingly, during the 1980s, other non-parental facilities for childcare – paid and informal – are being taken up by a growing minority.

The model of a network of care also seems more promising for elderly people than that of a sole carer, for whom Invalid Care Allowance (ICA) seems to have been designed. Such a person gives up paid work to provide near-constant attendance (over 35 hours), usually on a one-to-one basis, of a heavily disabled person. Some carers may gladly take on the often thankless task, being committed round the clock to social isolation and excluded from the financial and other rewards of the labour market, but others might like some alternatives. The recent (1992) increase in earnings permitted to ICA recipients from £30 to £40 per week, was intended to make it more suitable for people who combine caring with paid work, as so many do. This may or may not have overcome the other reasons why so few carers actually received Invalid Care Allowance (134,000 in 1990 compared to about a million non-employed co-resident carers). The earnings limit was raised again in 1993, to £50 per week net of work expenses and costs of paying someone to care for a child or other cohabiting person while at work. By 1994 the numbers claiming ICA had risen to over 200,000.

Income replacement, of which ICA is a rather limited form, is not the only type of help that carers need. The evidence assembled here suggests that the problems facing the employed carer need also to be addressed. Such people would not qualify for income replacement, but they could often do with some supplementation to their earnings. A version of Family Credit for carers might be considered. It is also important to give attention to protecting their pension rights somewhat better than do Home Responsibility Credits in their present form. Years of part-time earnings may, in some circumstances under these rules, reduce entitlement to SERPS. It is fairly difficult for carers to qualify and claim Home Responsibility Protection at the moment. It has to be claimed (it is not awarded automatically as to those drawing Child Benefit) and the person cared for has to be sufficiently disabled to qualify for Attendance Allowance. There is virtually no home responsibility protection for occupational and personal pensions (Joshi and Davies, 1991 and 1992).

Policies extending cash to carers need to be complemented by policies affecting employment itself. These should improve the terms on which carers can earn for themselves and enable them to benefit from the other advantages of paid activity out of the home. Longer-term employment policies by firms seeking to avoid the labour shortages expected in the 1980s involved, among other forms of human resource development, the notion of 'family friendly' employment practice. Such policies have been primarily framed with the mothers of young children in mind, but they can in principle be applied to all parents as well as to those caring for the older generation.

A few employers already operate such policies. Employed carers in the Opportunities for Women survey in 1990 quoted arrangements to work part-time in 22 per cent of cases, flexi-time in 20 per cent, 5 per cent were able to take unpaid leave, and 8 per cent had carer leave schemes. Even where there were arrangements, there were restrictions, such as the need to plan in advance. Carer leave schemes were valued, but were highly discretionary, with a lack of clear terms and conditions. In many cases they were not extended to men (Brotchie and Hills, 1991). Most of the measures mentioned are policies which would also benefit those responsible for children. Job sharing and career break schemes may also be adaptable to the circumstances of carers of the elderly, despite the differences between rearing healthy children and caring for someone near the end of life.

Among the types of support needed, survey respondents mentioned career guidance, flexi-hours credit, workplace counselling, specific training, emergency care procedures, domestic help and respite care arrangements. The latter forms of support would come from the local community, private, voluntary or state sector, rather than employers, but they would be at least as relevant to carers with jobs as those at home. A few carers purchase paid labour of various sorts from home help and sitters to agency nurses. Thought needs to be given to how such help can be made more affordable, and also how conditions of employment in this sector might be monitored.

It is important that policies to support carers by statutory and voluntary services are not designed only for those who would otherwise be at home all the time. There is more of a challenge to fit the schedules of formal services around the formal work of carers. Flexibility is required on all sides. Training should be designed to recognise the constraints (for example time) on those with family responsibilities, and also to develop the skills that are acquired at home.

With the prospect of greater demands on informal carers likely to follow the implementation of the NHS and Community Care Act, the question of an impact on carers' earnings, income and contribution to the formal economy through the labour force will remain. While it is undoubtedly an advance for the elderly people to remain at home as long as possible, it would also be an advance to organise services and working life so that their carers could remain in the labour force should they so choose. Not to think along these lines would, as a consultant to the Carnegie Enquiry on the Third Age points out, be short-sighted and wasteful.

'Middle aged people these days not only have kids, they also have parents alive and they are going to have those sorts of responsibilities whether employers like it or not. Now if employers restrict themselves to people who are going to give their total commitment to their work, they are going to lose out on quite a lot of talented people. That will be their loss and the nation's...' (Charles Handy quoted in Brotchie and Hills, 1991).

So far informal care and the labour market have co-existed in compromise rather than conflict. They will doubtless continue to do so, but on what terms, and at what quality of the two sorts of work, will depend on deliberate effort.

ACKNOWLEDGEMENTS

I am grateful to the OPCS for supplying unpublished tabulations of the 1990/1 General Household Survey, and to Gillian Parker and Dot Lawson, Social Policy Research Unit, University of York, for providing a special analysis of the 1985 General Household Survey.

Endnotes

1   The exception to this is a fall among non-married women, particularly those with caring responsibilities which may not be significant. It does not appear in the tabulations of the slightly different samples in Table 9.4 of the 1990 GHS Report (Smythe and Brown, 1992). The discrepancy arises partly because this analysis did not count being on a Government scheme as employment. There may also be an effect of different samples.

2   The tabulation does not permit us to test the finding by Evandrou and Winter for 1985 that employment differences between carers and non-carers were least for the never-married, nor are other variables controlled.

3   ie average paid hours worked by women carers would go up from 25.4 to 27.0, those by men from 37.6 to 38.2 per week.

References

Arber, S. and Ginn, J. (1991) *Gender and Later Life*. London: Sage.

Askham, J., Grundy, E. and Tinker, A. (1992) *Caring: the Importance of Third Age Carers*, Research Paper no 6 Carnegie Enquiry into the Third Age. Dunfermline: The Carnegie Trust.

Baldwin, S. and Parker, G. (1991) 'Support for Informal Carers – the Role of Social Security', in Dalley, Gillian (ed) *Disability and Social Policy*, London: Policy Studies Institute, pp 163–198.

Bartley, M., Popay, J. and Plewis, I. (1992) 'Domestic conditions, paid employment and women's experience of ill-health'. *Sociology of Health and Illness*, Vol 14, 3, 313–343.

Bone, M., Gregory, J., Gill, B. and Lader, D. (1992) *Retirement and Retirement Plans*, London:HMSO.

Brotchie, J. and Hills, D. (1991) *Equal Shares in Caring*. London: Socialist Health Association.

Carer's National Association (1992) *Speak Up, Speak Out*. London: Issue Communications Ltd.

Dalley, G. (1993) 'Caring, a legitimate interest of older women' in Bernard, Miriam and Meade, Kathy (eds), *Women come of age: Perspectives on the Lives of Older Women*, London: Edward Arnold pp 106–125.

Davies, H. and Joshi, H. (1992) 'Constructing Pensions for Model Couples', in Hancock, R. and Sutherland, H. (eds) *Microsimulation Models for Public Policy Analysis: New Frontiers* 67–96. STICERD Occasional Paper 17. London: LSE, 1992.

Dex, S. (1992) 'Labour Force Participation during the 1990s: Occupational Mobility and Part-time Employment', in Lindley, Robert (ed) *Women's Employment: Britain in the Single European Market*, Equal Opportunities Commission, London: HMSO pp 56–70.

Employment Department (1992) 'Women and the Labour Market: results from the 1991 Labour Force Survey'. *Employment Gazette*, September, pp 433–459.

Ermisch, J. and Wright, R. (1991) 'Welfare Benefits and Lone Parents in Great Britain'. *Journal of Human Resources*, 26, pp 424–56.

Evandrou, M. and Winter, D. (1992) *Informal Carers and the Labour Market in Britain*. Paper presented to the International Conference, Social Security 50 Years after Beveridge. STICERD LSE.

Graham, H. (1983) 'Caring – a Labour of Love' in Finch, J. and Groves, D. (eds) *A Labour of Love: Women, Work and Caring*, London: Routledge, pp 13–30.

House of Commons Social Services Committee (1990) Fifth report *Community Care: Carers*, 9 May, London: HMSO.

Hunt, A. (1968) *A Survey of Women's Employment*, London: HMSO.

Joshi, H. (1987) 'The cost of caring', in Glendinning, Caroline and Millar, Jane (eds) *Women and Poverty in Britain*. Brighton: Wheatsheaf Books (pp 112–133). Revised edition 1992.

Joshi, H. (1989) 'The Changing Form of Women's Economic Dependency', in Joshi, H. (ed) *The Changing Population of Britain*, Oxford: Basil Blackwell, pp 157–176).

Joshi, H. (1990) 'Changing Roles of Women in the British Labour Market and the Family', in Deane, P. (ed) *Frontiers of Economic Science*, Macmillan (pp 101–128) (Birkbeck Discussion Paper in Economics, 88/13).

Joshi, H. and Davies, H. (1991) *The Pension Consequences of Divorce*. CEPR Discussion Paper 550.

Joshi, H. and Davies, H. (1992) 'The Paid and Unpaid Roles of Women: How should Social Security adapt?', in Baldwin, S. and Falkingham, J. (eds) *Social Security: New Challenges to the Beveridge Model*, Hemel Hempstead: Harvester Wheatsheaf (in press).

Joshi, H. and Hinde, A. (forthcoming) *Employment after Childbearing: Cohort Study Evidence*. European Sociological Review . NCDS Discussion Paper 35, Social Statistics Research Unit, City University.

Kiernan, K. and Wicks, M. (1990) *Family Change and Future Policy*. York and London: Joseph Rowntree Foundation and Family Policy Studies Centre.

Mcran, S. (1993) *Role Enhancement or Role Overload? A Review of Research on the Health Consequences of Women's Domestic and Paid Work*. CPS Research Paper 93–1, London School of Hygiene and Tropical Medicine.

Martin, J. and Roberts, C. (1984) *Women and Employment: a Lifetime Perspective*, London:HMSO.

Nissel, M. and Bonnerjea, L. (1982) *Family care of the Handicapped Elderly: Who pays?* London: Policy Studies Institute.

Opportunities for Women (1991) *Care to Work 1990 Survey Report*, Vol 1 for a National Carers Survey.

Parker, G. (1992) *Informal Care of the older People in Great Britain: evidence from the 1985 General Household Survey*. Typescript, University of York SPRU CP 851 9/91 GP.

Parker, G. (1985) *With Due Care and Attention: a Review of Research on Informal Care*, London: Family Policy Studies Centre.

Parker, G. and Lawton, D. (1990) *Further Analysis of the 1985 General Household Survey Data on Informal Care: the Consequences of Caring*. University of York, SPRU Working Paper DHSS 716.

Smyth, M. and Browne, F. (1992) *General Household Survey* 1990 Series GHS no 21 OPCS London:HMSO.

Tinker, A. McCreadie, C. and Hancock, R. (1992) 'The Financial Costs of Caring' in Askham, J. *et al.* pp 33–74.

Trinder, C. Hulme, G. and McCarthy, U. (1992) *Employment: The Role of Work in the Third Age*, Research Paper No 1, The Carnegie Enquiry into the Third Age. Dunfermline: the Carnegie UK Trust.

Whatmore, K. and Mira-Smith, C. (1991) *Eldercare in the 1990s*, National Carers Survey Research Team

Wright, F. (1983) 'Single Carers: employment, housework and caring', in Finch, J. and Groves, D. (eds) *A Labour of Love: Women, work and caring*, London: Routledge and Kegan Paul pp 89–105.

Wright, R. and Ermisch, J. 'Gender discrimination in the British Labour market'. *The Economic Journal*, 101 pp 508–522.

Chapter 6

LOVE AND MONEY: THE FINANCIAL CONSEQUENCES OF CARING FOR AN OLDER RELATIVE

SALLY BALDWIN

Introduction

The last twenty years have seen an enormous change in public awareness of family caregiving as an activity which saves the state large amounts of money but can involve heavy costs and sacrifices for the carers (Parker, 1990). The credit for this must go to feminist scholars who, since the early 1970s, have identified the labour involved in caring as well as the love (Graham, 1983), and have amassed a wealth of detailed information on the financial and other costs of caring for frail or disabled kin.

The background to this chapter is set by two related concerns: whether the supply of family care for older people will fail to match the need for it over the next twenty years; and whether the financial penalties of caring will act as a disincentive to begin, or continue, caring for an older relative. The chapter's point of departure was a set of questions about the role of material factors in influencing decisions about caregiving. Do people base their decisions on whether they can *afford* to care for a parent – on the amount of earnings they stand to lose, the replacement value of social security benefits, or hopes that current losses will be balanced by future inheritances? What might the answers to these questions suggest public policy should do to sustain the supply of family caregivers? Is this, in any case, a legitimate or sensible policy goal? Might it not be more just to reflect on what is owed to people who invest time and effort in supporting older relatives; or on how public policy can best protect the dignity and quality of life of both parties in the relationship and the relationship itself?

These would be difficult questions, even if the empirical data to address them were available. A search of the research literature indicates that they are not. We are only beginning to understand the complex rules which govern family obligations in relation to caregiving and the equally complex norms which relate to financial transfers (Finch, 1989; Finch and Mason, 1993). This chapter therefore reports what is currently known about the financial consequences of providing care for an older relative – which is considerable. It also gleans information on the extent to which finance is an issue in beginning or continuing to provide substantial amounts of care. These serve as the basis for discussion of future trends and how policy might anticipate them.

Two kinds of research material are drawn on. First, there is a body of qualitative research focusing in some detail on particular issues or types of carer – financial consequences (Nissel and Bonnerjea, 1982; Glendinning, 1992); daughters caring for mothers (Lewis and Meredith, 1988); sole carers (Wright, 1986) and so on. Secondly, there are larger scale, population based, survey data, notably the 1985 and 1990 General Household Surveys (GHS) and the 1985 OPCS surveys of disability. Both are useful and provide complementary evidence. However, it is particularly important to test claims that are made about the financial consequences of caregiving using data from the general population. This chapter therefore relies extensively on the important data collected in the 1985 and 1990 GHS. As a basis for that discussion, it is useful briefly to assess the proportions of care provided to older people by the statutory and informal sectors; and to distinguish the different activities that 'caring' can consist of, the different characteristics of 'carers' and the different contexts in which caregiving is done.

What counts as caring and who does it, where, for whom?

It has been amply demonstrated from a large body of research that older people who are highly dependent only receive significant amounts of statutory support when they live alone. Arber and Ginn's re-analysis of the 1985 GHS, for example (1991, p. 150), finds only six to seven per cent of the personal care provided to severely disabled elderly people living with spouses or children coming from the formal sector – as against one third to similar elderly people living alone. The same is true of social services such as home help. The OPCS Disability Survey data show that services such as home help and meals on wheels are much less likely to be received by older people living with others, even when they are extremely disabled. A re-analysis of those data for this chapter, for example, found that 61 per cent of people over 75, who were severely disabled and living alone, had a local authority home help, as against 13 per cent of equally disabled older people living with other people. Hence Arber and Ginn's observation that 'where elderly disabled people share their households with others, household members perform virtually all of the necessary personal and domestic care tasks for them, and state services are provided at a very low level' (*op. cit.*,p. 151).

As the first reliable source of population data on family caregiving, the 1985 and 1990 GHS create unprecedented scope for mapping in great detail the prevalence and intensity of family care for older people and its consequences. 12 per cent of respondents to the 1990 GHS identified themselves as providing care for an older person – the vast majority (78 per cent) for a relative. The care they provided ranged from small amounts of practical help – with shopping, for example – to very intensive involvement in personal care and practical help. Such intensive levels of care were provided by a much smaller proportion of respondents to the 1990 GHS – only two per cent of respondents were providing more than 20 hours a week to an older relative. (This was 14 per cent of all who identified themselves as caring in any way for an older relative.)

Analyses of the GHS carers data (Parker and Lawton, 1990; Evandrou, 1990; Arber and Ginn, 1991) identify important distinctions within the carers of older people, which are associated both with differences in the kind and level of care given and with its impact on carers' financial circumstances. A major distinction is whether care is provided to someone living in the same or a different household. That provided to people in the same household is more intensive and more likely to include personal care. Co-resident carers of older people in the 1985 GHS spent an average of 53 hours a week on caregiving activities, as against the average of nine hours spent by people looking after an older relative in another household. (While this distinction between co-resident and separate household carers is important, it should not be allowed to hide the fact that an important minority of 'out of household' carers do provide significant amounts of care to older relatives. 43 per cent of the people in the 1990 GHS who gave more than 20 hours of care a week to an older person lived in a separate household. This, mainly younger, group were not all caring for relatives and did not give such high levels of care, on average, as co-resident carers.)

Co-resident care is done on the basis of very different relationships. People who look after an elderly person in the same house are predominantly spouses (40 per cent in the 1985 GHS) and adult children or children-in-law (47 per cent). 'Other household' carers are predominantly adult children and their partners (54 per cent), but over a quarter are caring for a friend or neighbour, not a relative. Co-resident spouse carers provide almost half (48 per cent) of the total hours of care provided to older people. They are the group who spend most time of all – an average of 65 hours a week (distributed equally between husbands and wives); as against the 55 and 50 hours spent by co-resident daughters and daughters-in-law, and the 40 and 30 hours by sons and sons-in-law. Retired people are also significantly involved in providing care to older people in other households – though on a less intensive basis (Arber and Ginn, *op. cit.*, pp. 132–134).

It is important to signal the extent to which 'family care' for older people is provided by people themselves over retirement age, particularly in relation to the large amounts of care provided by spouses. There has been little acknowledgement of their contribution in policy and academic debate so far. The feminist debate has tended to focus on younger women caring for parents. This focus has contributed to the lack of prominence given, until recently, to co-residence and marriage as important predictors of intensive caregiving. We do not yet have a thorough analysis of available survey data on the consequences of caring for an older spouse nor, indeed, has there been detailed qualitative work on this topic. Indeed, caregiving within marriage has only recently (Parker, 1993) been identified as an important subject for research. The lack of available data will inevitably mean that this chapter has more to say about the consequences of caregiving for younger carers. This should not be taken as lack of awareness of their situation, or of concern.

One further, important, distinction to emerge from recent research concerns the size of the household within which caregiving occurs, and in particular differences between households composed only of two persons (the older person and the carer) and those containing three or more adults (often a married couple looking after a parent or parent-in-law, plus adult children). Almost two thirds of the co-resident carers in the 1990 GHS giving more than 20 hours care a week (63 per cent) lived alone with the person they looked after. These 'sole' carers were both spouses and adult children, but predominantly spouses (73 as against 27 per cent). Younger sole carers differ in important respects from spouse carers. As Wenger (1987, 1990), Lewis and Meredith (1988), Glendinning (1992) and Ginn and Arber (1991) have all argued, younger 'sole' carers experience caregiving, and the constraints it imposes on their lives, in quite different ways from spouse carers. For the latter, caring is more likely to be accepted as the central focus of their lives – implicit in the marriage contract. In the case of younger carers, caregiving may displace or distort the previous balance of relationships (Wenger, 1990, p. 199). It will disrupt employment and affect income in different ways. It may also provoke a different response from statutory service providers because they recognise employment as a legitimate aspiration for younger people and therefore provide support to make at least part-time work a possibility.

The population data provided by the GHS has thus allowed us to move away from notions of carers as a homogeneous group, or of gender as the only significant variable discriminating between carers. We have identified three key distinctions in addition to gender which are associated with different kinds and levels of caregiving and seem likely to create different effects on work and income. These are the carer's age, the size of the household, and whether the older person is part of it or lives separately.

The next section summarises the existing state of knowledge on the extent to which caregiving affects carers' personal incomes, via effects on employment and earnings. We focus mainly on co-resident carers under retirement age, giving more than 20 hours care a week. These are the carers likely to experience the greatest effects.

Effects on carers' personal incomes
Employment

A large number of studies (reviewed by Parker, 1990) have reported that caregiving adversely affects carers' opportunities for paid employment, and thus their incomes. In general, these studies have not allowed comparisons with the general population and have been based on small, and often special, groups. The GHS data for 1985 and 1990 do allow such comparisons – though considerable care is needed to make sure that it is the effect of caring that is being identified (Parker and Lawton, 1990). And, importantly, data of this sort can not tell us whether people may become carers because they already have low earnings, or are not employed. The GHS data do, even so, tell us much more than was previously known about the impact of caring on carers' personal and household incomes and about the living standards of the households in which they live.

As Joshi notes (Chapter 5), most available evidence on employment concerns care recipients of all ages, not just the elderly. In her view it can, for the most part, 'be assumed that the labour market implications of caring for the elderly are fairly well represented in accounts covering care for all ages of recipient'. This remains to be tested. However, in the absence of alternative data, much of the data in this section also cover care recipients of all ages, though a small number of analyses of the 1990 GHS, done for this chapter, refer specifically to elderly care recipients.

As Joshi's and Parker and Lawton's analyses demonstrate, carers of working age do, in general, have depressed levels of labour force activity – though the difference between them and 'non-carers' is less spectacular than might be expected from the findings of earlier research. Both male and female carers are less likely than their age peers to be in full time paid work. However, the effect is greater among men. This is partly because women's participation is *generally* lower and partly because men are less likely to find part-time work and more likely to give up paid work altogether.

This general picture conceals the greater effects experienced by people more intensively involved in caregiving. 31 per cent of the most heavily burdened carers in Parker and Lawton's analysis, as against 47 per cent of matched non-carers, were in full-time work. Co-residence and household size also play a part. Carers who live alone with the person they support, and who spend more than 20 hours per week caring are unlikely to do significant amounts of paid work unless, as smaller scale studies indicate (Wright, 1986; Glendinning, 1992), they are in work which is highly paid and thus can afford to pay for substitute care. A number of studies of different sorts, quantitative and qualitative (Glendinning, 1992; Matthews and Truscott, 1990; Martin and White, 1988; Baldwin and Parker, 1991), indicate that carers in larger households (married couples caring for parents or parents-in-law, for example) have a greater chance of sustaining paid employment, even when moderately high levels of care are needed. The 'growing' phenomenon noted by Joshi – the combination of caregiving with paid work – is more common among co-resident carers in large households, sole carers with well paid jobs and carers who live separately and give fewer hours of care. Carers living alone with an older relative needing a lot of care and who have low earnings potential will find it much more difficult.

Earnings

Joshi's chapter identifies the different ways in which carers' restricted employment opportunities can affect their incomes: earnings loss due to non- or part-time employment; and opportunity costs, encompassing shorter term losses; effects on career prospects; and loss of pension rights. It also models the effects for carers in different circumstances. Joshi's figures are necessarily speculative but give a compelling idea of the magnitude of the overall effect for different types of carer – greater, for example, for a professional man who leaves full-time employment entirely in his fifties than for a woman who does so at the same time –and her 'cost' greater in turn than that of a woman who gives up part-time employment.

At a more immediate level, data from the GHS provide convincing cross-sectional evidence of the result of carers' less secure attachment to the labour force. The picture that emerges is that while carers' earnings are, in general, consistently depressed, the magnitude of the effect is strongly influenced by whether they live with the person they care for, the size of household in which they live, and their sex.

Parker and Lawton's analysis of the 1985 GHS, for example (1990), identifies two main effects on carers' personal earnings – an overall depressive effect because they are less likely to be in paid work, and lower earnings among those who *are* in work, because of their shorter hours. (Joshi adds to this the effect of lower hourly rates of pay.) Thus, carers in general earned an average of £8 a week less than non-carers. The size of the effect was greater for men (£16 a week on average) than for women (£4 a week). Since women *in general* experience the cost of child-rearing, the effect of additional caring responsibilities is smaller. The effect is also greater among co-resident carers. In-household carers in the 1985 GHS earned an average of £15 a week less than non-carers; for out-of-household carers the difference was £6 a week. This analysis did not identify the earnings of sole carers. Preliminary analysis of the 1990 GHS carers data indicates that for men these are substantially less than those of similar men in non-carer households. For women, however, the differences are negligible.

Personal incomes

Other forms of income such as social security benefits and investment income can, of course, supplement or substitute for earnings. The 1985 GHS carers data indicate that other income played virtually no role in boosting income among women carers, and only a slightly bigger role for men. Female carers' average personal incomes were very low, but on average only £3 a week less than those of counterparts without special caring responsibilities. For male carers, on the other hand, other sources of income modified an original earnings gap of £16 a week on average to a personal *income* gap of £12 (Parker and Lawton, *op. cit.*, p. 19).

As with earnings the picture is different among different carer sub-groups. Evandrou's analysis of the 1985 GHS data, for example (1990), indicates the much larger income effects experienced by co-residents, and particularly sole co-resident carers. This analysis finds 25 per cent of carers with dependants in the same household in the bottom quintile of incomes, as against 16 per cent of those caring for someone in another household. Sole carers are much more likely to be in the bottom quintile – 22 per cent, as against 11 per cent of joint carers. Sole and co-resident carers were also more likely than other carers and non-carers to be living in, or on the margins of, poverty; 35 per cent of co-resident carers and 30 per cent of sole carers, as against 17 per cent of joint carers and 25 per cent of non-carers had incomes at or below 140 per cent of supplementary benefit.

The 1985 GHS data predate social security changes which might be expected to improve these income figures – notably the extension of Invalid Care Allowance (ICA) to married women in 1986, increases in the ICA earnings limits and the introduction of a carers' premium in Income Support. Preliminary analysis of the 1990 GHS carers data broadly confirms the patterns found in the 1985 GHS – but also shows intriguing differences. Again, the incomes of male carers are more affected than those of female carers in a similar situation – the personal incomes of male co-resident carers are an average of £115 lower than those of male non-carers. Women carers in a similar situation have incomes virtually identical to those of female non-carers. The intriguing finding is that these female sole carers have incomes significantly higher than men living alone with the parent they are looking after – an average of £29 a week higher. This could be the result of greater possibilities of combining part-time earnings with ICA. However, the data suggest that the difference is largely due to much higher earnings by these women. This suggests that the earnings potential of women and men who become 'sole' carers may be different (Parker, 1993). This needs closer scrutiny – the numbers involved are small and the differences observed could be caused by sampling error.

Older carers' personal incomes

As noted earlier, many of the GHS analyses reported here do not distinguish older and younger carers. (For this analysis, 'older' carers were defined as over retirement age i.e. over 60 for women and over 65 for men, and 'younger' carers were defined as under retirement age.) Preliminary analysis of the 1990 GHS, looking at the incomes of older carers in two person households, finds a picture very similar to that among younger carers. Both older male and female carers had incomes considerably lower than similar non-carers, but the gap was greater for men (an average of £32 a week) than women (£9 a week). Again, this mirrors the lower earnings of women in general. Older male carers' personal incomes were on average £44 a week higher than those of similar female carers; for male and female non-carers the gap was £67.

These findings on the much lower personal incomes of older carers are troubling – particularly in the context of older people's generally low incomes. It is worth noting that 38 per cent of elderly carers in the 1985 GHS were in, or on the margins of, poverty; and that this rose to 53 per cent of those aged 75 or over (Evandrou, 1990).

Savings

Savings are an important resource. Parker and Lawton's analysis of the 1985 GHS revealed that carers providing the most intensive levels of care were substantially less likely than their non-carer equivalents to have any income from savings. They conclude that this is a real, and important, effect of caregiving. Glendinning's study of the costs experienced by carers under pension age (1992) provides detailed supportive evidence of how lower income both makes it difficult to save and creates pressure to spend down existing savings. As Parker and Lawton note, 'this has clear and serious implications for carers' standard of living in their own old age' (*op. cit.*, p. 23).

Household incomes

We have seen that carers' personal incomes are lower than those of non carers, and in some instances very low in absolute terms. Is this moderated by access to household incomes that are moderately prosperous?

The concept of family incomes is widely recognised as problematic (Pahl, 1989). The more complex structure and history of carer households, where not only spouses, but siblings and adult children may be involved, means that these households constitute difficult and unmapped territory in terms of understanding the allocation of resources. It is useful, however, to begin by assessing whether the financial resources of other members bring the household's income to the point where it *could* balance a carer's lower income if all members had access to that income on an equal basis.

The general picture to emerge from analyses of GHS and OPCS Disability Survey data (Baldwin and Parker, 1991; Martin and White, 1988; Matthews and Truscott, 1990) is in fact that, with the exception of 'pensioner' households,

households containing both disabled people and carers have substantially lower incomes than similar households in the general population. The magnitude of the difference is strongly influenced by household size – essentially via the number of earners in the household (Matthews and Truscott, 1990, p. 13). Thus, Parker and Lawton's analysis of the 1985 GHS, using the Luxembourg Income Scale to control for differences in household composition, finds carer-household incomes to be £4 a week lower on average than those of non-carer households. Much greater differences are found in two, overlapping, sub-groups – those where the most intensive forms of care are required (an average of £15 a week) and those containing co-resident carers (£14).

The household incomes of people who live alone with the person they look after are particularly low. Preliminary analysis of the 1990 GHS finds the household incomes of younger carers providing more than 20 hours a week to be an average of £155 a week lower than those of non-carer households when the carer is male, and £106 when she is female. Previous research (Martin and White, 1988) finds older households with a disabled member to have slightly higher incomes than similar households in the general population – the result of generally lower incomes in old age and the availability of disability benefits. The 1990 GHS contradicts this – at least for older people needing significant amounts of care and living only with another person over retirement age. Two-person households where both were over retirement age and more than 20 hours of care supplied, had substantially lower incomes than similar households in the general population – by an average of £31 a week where the carer was male and £49 where she was female.

By and large, then, carers do not live in prosperous households – though as we will see, they are sometimes subsidised by other household members, including the older person they look after.

Assets

Pleasant surroundings and the availability of assets such as cars and washing machines can make caring easier and improve the quality of life of both care giver and recipient. Twigg and Atkin's research (1993) draws attention to the importance of the material conditions of caring and particularly the role of appropriate housing – in terms both of space and the fitness of dwellings for the management of incontinence and restricted mobility, for example.

The 1985 GHS provides useful information on housing as a resource – in terms both of tenure and of space. Parker and Lawton's analysis of these data indicate that, while carers in general were no less likely than similar people in the general population to be in owner-occupied accommodation, co-resident carers were significantly less likely to be (63 per cent and 55 per cent respectively). Moreover, particular carer sub-groups were significantly more likely to be living in overcrowded housing. These included women and co-resident carers and carers providing personal care. 7 per cent of female carers lived in houses below the bedroom space standard, compared with 3 per cent of their peers; 13 per cent of in-household carers as against 3 per cent of their non-carer equivalents similarly lived in homes below the bedroom space standard. Glendinning's (1992) study also identifies both space and suitability as difficult and sometimes costly issues for, particularly, households that are extended by the arrival of an older parent or, conversely, a carer's decision to move into a parent's house. Her study also indicates that the resolution of these problems can be difficult, depending either on the availability of personal finance or on generous assistance from local authorities – not often given to adapt a carer's home.

In relation to consumer durables, Parker and Lawton's analysis finds that, while carers in general have equal or higher access to a range of consumer durables, the most heavily burdened carers, and particularly those who live with the older person, are less likely than non-carer households to own assets such as washing machines and cars. This is disturbing, given the role these particular commodities can play in making carers' lives easier.

Real resources
Financial management systems, subsidies and transfers

The real amount of money carers actually have at their disposal depends not only on their personal incomes but on income flows and transfers between them and the person they care for, and between them and other relatives – particularly when they live in the same household.

Little is known on a systematic basis about financial transfers within extended families and households. Existing research on family finances and allocation patterns (Pahl, 1989; Brannen and Wilson, 1987) deals almost exclusively with the nuclear family. Glendinning's qualitative study of the costs experienced by younger, co-resident, carers (1992) is an exception. It provides important insights both into the ways caregiving affects carers' employment and incomes and the financial arrangements that determine their real access to financial resources.

This study echoes and amplifies the GHS findings discussed earlier. Combining caregiving with paid work was important for psychological as well as financial reasons and for longer term, not just immediate, considerations. However, caregiving almost invariably restricted carers' employment possibilities. Some carers had given up paid work altogether. Around half of those who were managing to continue in their previous jobs now had lower earnings or incomes greatly reduced by paying for substitute care. Having previously reduced their hours and earnings they could no longer combine work and caregiving. Carers in larger households had more chance of keeping in touch with the labour market, but they were likely to find part-time work more suitable. Male carers were more likely to give up altogether when caregiving became more demanding. Factors, other than household size, which made it possible to combine employment and caregiving, included earnings high enough to make the purchase of substitute care possible, work reasonably near to home, and employers who offered a degree of flexibility about hours.

Glendinning's study breaks new ground in exploring the factors that shape financial management systems in different kinds of 'caregiving' households and the extent and direction of any subsidy between care givers and recipients. She identifies different types of household formed in different circumstances: adult children who have never left home and are now caring for a parent; others who have left but returned after divorce; married couples caring for a parent who has come to live with them when his or her care needs became too heavy to manage at a distance; others who have moved in with a parent whose house is more suitable. Glendinning thus identifies the key variables in predicting the overall 'cost' of caring and who will bear the brunt of any costs or subsidise the other: the circumstances in which people have come together; the history of the relationship; the status and authority of different relationships; and the resources commanded by each unit. It is clear from this study that the rules governing the allocation of financial resources between care giving and receiving 'units' are highly complex, as Finch's (1989) work confirms.

Glendinning is principally concerned with three issues: the costs of caregiving for carers in different situations; the relationship between care giver and recipient, in terms of managing and controlling the household's money; and the overall financial balance between them. Her original contribution is to explore in detail how 'caring' households' financial arrangements work. Like Pahl (1989) she finds that allocation systems vary with the level of income – the poorest households are more likely to pool their resources and delegate management to one person. In most cases the carer will manage households' budgets on a day to day basis – and in that sense they have access to a high proportion of household monies. However, **control** of the household's finance is not invariably delegated to carers – particularly where they have not previously been housekeeper or householder. Glendinning finds three variants: complete control by the carer; joint control, with the older person significantly involved in decision-making; and separate areas of control. In the last, the older person retains considerable control over his or her own money and assumes responsibility for particular areas of household expenditure – often certain bills.

Which of these patterns emerges is partly a function of the household's total income and of caregiver and recipient's relative income levels. In practice, however, the key issue is how much control the older person exercises. That, in turn, hinges on two factors: who, historically, has been responsible for budgeting in the dwelling and the elderly person's mental capacity. In households where sons or daughters had never left home, or had returned, and a mother was still mentally alert, she was likely to be at the very least an equal partner in managing the household's finances – with all that implied for the carer's freedom of manoeuvre. That was much less likely if she had gone to live with a son or daughter; and not possible if she was mentally very confused.

Glendinning's second novel contribution is to go behind 'official' figures on the personal incomes of care giver and care recipient to explore the real level of resources each has access to, and the size and direction of any subsidy between them. She teases out the circumstances in which a caregiver subsidises a higher standard of living than an older person could sustain, and those in which it is the carer who is subsidised. At one extreme, an older person with no savings joins the household of a daughter working part time whose husband is in full-time employment. At the other extreme is a son who has never left his parents' house and has given up his job to look after his mother. She, in addition to her retirement pension, has higher rate Attendance Allowance, a small occupational pension from her deceased husband's firm and some income from savings. The former is heavily subsidised by her daughter's income; the latter by his mother's. Both situations occur in Glendinning's study but she also finds variations: a few elderly people have capital from the sale of former homes; a few co-resident children maintain well-paid jobs. Sole carers who have had to give up paid work to care for an older relative they live with, lose out substantially in terms of earnings but may be subsidised from a parent's resources – even if only by living rent-free. Like Wright (1986), Glendinning is particularly conscious of the dependency of this group of carers. However, she also signals the vulnerability of all carers whose responsibilities lead to financial dependence on other family members. Her study group contains both a young unmarried carer whose low income from part-time work leaves her financially dependent on a brother's earnings; and several women whose inability to resume paid work leaves them financially dependent on their husbands. Though Glendinning's work does not explicitly address the issue of the older person's feelings about financial and physical dependency on children, these also deserve recognition. In both situations there must be possibilities for the abuse of power.

Extra costs

Carers' financial resources may also be reduced by special demands on the household's budget. There is by now a substantial body of research evidence that disability creates extra costs. The evidence that caregiving causes extra expenditure is less clear, though a number of qualitative studies report that it does. The distinction between costs arising from disability and from caregiving is not always easy to make. Is an extension to accommodate an older relative, for example, a cost of caring or of disability? What are we to make of the fact that the carer may have to meet the costs created by a parent's disability or, in some circumstances, the older person the costs of caregiving? Perhaps the important task is not to attempt this distinction but to identify both kinds of costs, their level, and who pays for them. (See McLaughlin, 1991, p. 29 for a more detailed discussion of the conceptual and measurement problems involved.)

McLaughlin's evaluation of ICA (*op.cit.*, 1991) indicates that such extra expenses are common. The great majority of her sample (87 per cent of current recipients of ICA, 71 per cent of past recipients and 91 per cent of unsuccessful applicants) said they incurred extra expense in looking after their dependant. This included costs associated both with disability and caregiving. Extra expense was more common among the households providing the highest hours of care.

In the majority of cases the care giver and recipient shared the extra costs; over 80 per cent of the carers living with the adults they were looking after received a financial contribution from them. Most, however, (between two thirds and three quarters) 'thought the contribution did not cover all the extra expenses involved' (McLaughlin, *op.cit.*, p. 31). Both this study and Glendinning's (1992) provide detailed, qualitative, information on extra costs incurred and who met them. Glendinning's study identifies a number which arise directly from the disabled person's needs: 'specialised housing adaptations, extra heating, additional laundry, clothing, bedding and toiletries' (p. 82). Nevertheless some, and in some cases all, these costs were met by *carers* – usually because the older person's resources were inadequate but sometimes because resources were pooled. In some cases – paying for adaptations to housing and for extra heating, for example, the costs could be substantial.

She also identifies costs incurred as a direct result of caregiving. These were not offset by contributions from the older person. Some of the heaviest related to substitute care – particularly where sole carers were striving to maintain their employment. One self-employed (male) carer, for example, spent £180 a week on an agency nurse to look after his mother. Carers whose relatives moved in with them frequently spent money on their homes – quite apart from extensions and adaptations – to accommodate the person without inconveniencing other household members. This was for furniture, beds, decoration and so on. Two other clusters of care-related costs are identified. One reflects the pressures on carers' time caused by the demands of caregiving. To accommodate this they 'bought' time using convenience foods, their cars or taxis instead of public transport, employing decorators and cleaners and so on. Finally, there is a miscellaneous group of care-related items 'such as cleaning and replacing carers' own clothes which were soiled or disproportionately worn, telephone charges to keep in touch with other relatives about the health of the disabled person and fares and other expenses when visiting the disabled person in hospital' (p. 83).

Glendinning does not attempt to quantify these 'care-related' costs. They were highly variable and clearly reflect carers' ability to spend on them. She reports that for some carers they were considerable – though the extra costs created by disability, many of which also fell to carers, were more common and carers were more conscious of them.

A balance sheet?

Available survey data do not allow us to model the overall impact of earnings loss and extra costs on carers in different situations. Glendinning's study goes some way towards that by constructing an individual 'balance sheet' for each household – though the qualitative nature of the study means that it should be regarded as exploratory. It was clear from this exercise that, for virtually all this group of carers, the financial balance was negative. Caregiving adversely affected financial resources – via effects on employment, extra costs or both. The nature and intensity of the effects varied substantially between different types of household. The differences Glendinning finds echo the findings reported above from the GHS data. They relate to differences between carers in two–adult and larger households, and arise both from these households' overall income levels and from differences in the *relative* income levels of care-givers and recipients.

The larger households in Glendinning's study were in a better position to maintain their incomes from employment. In most cases their incomes and savings were substantially higher than the older person's. Almost invariably, caregivers subsidised their older relative's living standards – by providing a higher living standard than he or she could have afforded, including rent-free accommodation, and helping with costs arising from disability.

'Sole carer' households were less well placed. Only carers with high earnings could afford to stay in full-time work, because only they could afford the costs of substitute care. The final balance sheet in two-person households thus varied according to the carer's earnings potential and the older person's resources and needs. Glendinning identifies three different patterns among these 'sole-carer' households. In the first, the carer has a higher disposable income from employment, heavily subsidises the older person's living costs and incurs substantial caregiving costs – particularly for substitute care. In the second, the incomes of both parties come only from basic maintenance benefits. These households are poor but both parties contribute on roughly equal terms. In the third, the older person has income from retirement pension, and perhaps disability benefits, occupational pension and savings; the carer receives only a basic maintenance benefit. The living costs of carers in this situation are subsidised by the older person, though usually at a low level, because her own income is not high.

In both the first and the third situations a high degree of financial dependence occurs. It is arguable that this is more worrying in respect of younger, sole, carers. This is partly because they are younger, very disadvantaged in relation to people of their own age, and isolated. It is also because their longer term situation is so precarious. The carers in Glendinning's study who were in this situation were extremely aware of, and troubled by, their dependency on a parent. What would happen when caregiving came to an end and they had to earn a living after years out of work?

At 47 years of age I can't see why I should have to live off my mother, because if I have to live off my mother to that extent, what happens when she dies? Who do I live off then? (Glendinning, *op.cit.*, p. 99)

As Glendinning notes, the cost of caring for this group 'was impoverishment and a return to a degree of financial dependency on a parent which had been characteristic of their younger, pre-adult, status... For these carers current poverty was compounded by considerable longer-term financial insecurity'. McLaughlin's findings (*op.cit.*, 1991) on the patchy employment patterns and low incomes of ex-carers suggests that their anxieties were well-founded. Finally, it should be noted that no research, to date, has focused on the impact of extra costs on older carers and their households – whose incomes are extremely low in general.

It is not surprising, then, given the very low incomes of many carer households that the carers in both McLaughlin's and Glendinning's studies reported both using up their own and the older person's savings and a range of other strategies for making ends meet and providing for the disabled person's special needs. These included cashing-in insurance policies, borrowing, and cutting back on 'normal' expenditure such as food and clothes. In both studies, the strategies adopted varied with the household's income: households in McLaughlin's study who had higher incomes were more likely to report using up savings, while poorer households borrowed. Glendinning relates the differences she finds to differences in household composition. The more impoverished sole carer households were likely to report signs of financial distress – where they drew on savings this was to pay for ordinary living costs. Larger, and better-off households were less likely to draw on savings; where they did, it was to pay for improvements to housing or major consumer durables, not for everyday living costs. By and large, while these households were not immune to the effects of caring on their financial resources and living standards, the effect was less severe than on 'sole-carer' households.

Financial support from other relatives

Do other relatives who are not bearing the costs of caregiving make good part of a carer's losses or contribute to a parent's costs? Evidence on such financial transfers is sparse but suggests that this does not happen to any extent. Financial costs, like caring itself, are not shared to any extent. A study currently underway in PSI, for example, finds only a small number of regular financial transfers from adult children to parents – mainly to pay for bills or large items of household equipment. These are balanced by a similarly small number of transfers from parents to adult children or grandchildren (Perkins, E., personal communication). Regular transfers between siblings were even less common. None of the carers in Glendinning's or McLaughlin's studies received financial help from brothers or sisters outside the household.

Finch and Mason's work (1993), which has begun to unravel the complex rules governing such transactions, identifies reasons why regular financial commitments of this sort are not likely to be common. Obligations to one's own children are accepted as 'legitimate excuses' (Finch and Mason, pp 97–128) for not offering help to a brother or sister caring for a parent. Giving regular financial help might be regarded as problematic in threatening the important balance between dependence and independence, and thus the carer's standing in the family. Pride on the carer's part may hide the need for help. Such issues warrant further investigation. The crude reality, however, is that carers' financial resources seem not to be boosted by regular financial support from relatives outside the household. Indeed there is evidence that in some cases they pay relatives to provide occasional substitute care.

The role of social security

It is clear, from the research evidence cited above, that social security does not to any extent mitigate the financial losses carers experience or compensate them for the work they do. This may be because policy in relation to carers has developed in an *ad hoc* way, in response to lobbying. The goals of policy for carers have not been explicitly addressed in any of the social security reviews that have taken place since 1940, including the recent review of disability benefits.

The British social security system does not identify the need to receive care in later life, or to give it, as risks to be covered by social insurance. Carers qualify for three forms of support at present: ICA; a carers' 'premium' on Income Support; and home responsibilities protection of basic retirement pension rights. They are also exempt from having to register as available for employment when on IS.

Invalid Care Allowance

The main carers' benefit, ICA, as been the subject of intense criticism since its introduction in 1975. This was initially because of the exclusion of married women. However, ICA is also seen as an ambiguous and inadequate response to the financial sacrifices carers experience and the savings they create for society at large (House of Commons, 1990, a and b). Among the criticisms mad four stand out as particularly important.

Purpose and scope

ICA benefits only a small minority of carers providing a lot of care. It is targeted at people giving more than 35 hours care a week. However, since its purpose is not to compensate for caregiving as such, but for earnings lost as a result of caregiving, carers over retirement age are ineligible. Other, complex, criteria further reduce the number eligible: an earnings cut-off at £50 a week; 'overlapping benefits' regulations which mean that it cannot be paid to someone already receiving a maintenance benefit or dependant's addition; and the necessity for the care-recipient to be in receipt of attendance allowance. Thus, in 1989 only 109,000 people received ICA while upwards of 1 million were estimated to be providing more than 35 hours of care each week. In 1994, over 260,000 people claimed ICA.

Adequacy and effectiveness

At its current level ICA is insufficient to live on. Most people giving more than 35 hours of care a week have to supplement it by claiming IS or by relying on relatives or the person they care for (McLaughlin, 1991). That eligibility for ICA depends on the care-recipient's receipt of Attendance Allowance and is compromised by a spouse's receipt of maintenance benefits, further limits its role as an independent income.

ICA, caregiving and paid work

Carers who can maintain their relationship with the labour market are at least risk financially and psychologically. Currently £50 a week can be earned net of work expenses and the costs of paying someone to care for a child or cohabiting person while at work before the benefit is lost (see Joshi, Chapter 5, this volume). This is still not enough to allow a useful mix of employment and caregiving. The use of an income cut-off does not reflect the gradual shift of many carers from full- to part-time work before giving up completely, or earnings lost in the move to part-time work, from lost time, promotion or inability to accept promotions or career moves.

ICA and the particular situation of carers

The argument here is that ICA fits very poorly with the real consequences of caregiving. As a benefit paid at one, low, level, it does not reflect the work involved or the extra costs. Nor does it reflect long-term earnings losses and their impact on pensions. Thirdly, it stops abruptly when the person cared for dies or enters residential care. At that point, carers are required to register for employment, which they are usually ill-equipped to find, and do not even qualify for unemployment benefit.

McLaughlin's evaluation of ICA (1991) provides supporting evidence of these criticisms and suggests a number of ways in which social security protection for carers could be improved and better targeted. The House of Commons Social Services Committee's report on policy in relation to informal carers and community care (1990a) goes further, arguing for a fundamental rethinking of both social security and social services support to carers. There is wide agreement, then, that social security provision for carers is in serious need of review. Twigg and Atkin's research (1993), like that of McLaughlin (1991), indicates that, quite apart from the coverage and level of ICA, carers have serious problems in understanding what ICA is for and in claiming it. This is partly because of the need for the person they support to receive Attendance Allowance, but it is also difficult for carers to grasp the fact that ICA is not a benefit for caregiving as such but partial compensation for earnings loss. This creates difficulties in understanding, and accepting, the logic of overlapping benefits regulations.

Do financial considerations influence carers' decisions?

The question, here, is whether the financial drawbacks involved in caring prompt relatives to refuse to become involved, or force them at some point to give up. The answer depends on who is asked. The literature quoted refers almost exclusively to people currently looking after an older relative or who have recently stopped – not those who have refused. It indicates that for many, the process of becoming significantly involved in caregiving is gradual. The financial consequences unfold gradually over time and are, by and large, accepted – though with a degree of dissatisfaction that, in addition to the often difficult and unsupported work of caring, financial penalties are also incurred. Both Glendinning's and McLaughlin's studies indicate that financial implications are usually not worked out in advance, while knowledge of social security benefits is hazy and often inaccurate. The picture is slightly different when major decisions have to be taken – for example about whether a parent should move in with a daughter and her family; or whether a sole carer should give up paid employment altogether. At these points, financial implications loom larger and are more often worked through. Evidence from those who have decided to go on caring suggest that, even here, detailed and accurate calculations are not the norm except in relation to giving up employment; the expenses side of the equation is hazy and usually underestimated.

The question of whether current income sacrifices are balanced by anticipation of future capital windfalls from inheritance has not been tackled directly in most of the studies quoted here. It seems unlikely that it will not be a factor in some cases, but relatively few carers seem likely to gain sufficient to balance their losses. First, few of the current generation of older people will have significant resources to dispose of when they die (see Groves' and Hamnett's chapters in this volume). Some will simply not have accumulated much – even in the form of housing equity. Others will have spent down resources: in joining a son or daughter's household; supplementing a carer's living standards; or contributing to the costs of residential or nursing home care before they die. When significant financial resources do remain these are likely, where a will has been made, to be divided between children and grandchildren, not left solely to a carer – although she may receive a larger share. The one situation where a clear 'gain' is likely is where a carer living in a parent's house inherits the house, or security of tenure for as long as they want it. The value of such inheritances to carers is not known at present, although current work by Finch and Mason will provide important insights. Existing research does not suggest that this is a major factor influencing decisions to begin or continue caring.

However, two factors are important in balancing the picture that emerges from talking to carers which seem to indicate that financial considerations are *not* a factor in beginning, or continuing, to care for an older relative. First, we have no evidence from people who have decided not to assume responsibility. Secondly, there is evidence that family negotiations, and decisions about who does assume responsibility, are strongly influenced by ideas about who can be expected to carry the costs of doing so. Having children to bring up, or what is seen as too good a job to give up, are accepted as 'legitimate excuses' for not bringing a parent into one's home, or moving back to one's home town and parental home. Clearly, then, there is a level at which financial considerations do strongly colour decisions about becoming a carer.

The future supply of family care

The history of demography shows that attempting to anticipate human behaviour is both seductive and rash. In this case it is particularly difficult. Against the push of demographic factors we have to balance, not only the pull of economic factors, but also the influence of powerful motivations arising from love, reciprocity, and family obligation, rooted in societal norms and expectations. We are, fortunately, better placed to speculate than policy analysts in many other countries because of the wealth of data now available.

We have moved from simplistic assumptions that the care of older people is predominantly provided by daughters. Analyses of the GHS carers' data identify three groups of people heavily involved in their care: married women under retirement age; single, adult children; and spouse carers. In relation to future trends and policy developments the last group is very different from the other two. It is hard to see why spouses should become less willing to care for each other. On the other hand, the numbers of older people living alone is set to increase, implying a greater demand on younger kin.

Among younger carers it is important to distinguish those giving intensive amounts of care from those helping out in various ways. If we focus on those who are providing a lot of care, we find that among those who provide more than 20 hours a week married women currently supply the greatest volume. However, the most intensive *levels* of care, in terms of hours, are supplied by a smaller group of single, co-resident, daughters and sons.

The future of caregiving by younger kin thus depends to a very great extent on the behaviour of women – and particularly married women. Four factors seem likely to reduce their ability, and willingness, to go on providing substantial levels of care:

- the numbers who will be available close at hand;
- changes in employment patterns;
- shifts in the perceived costs of intensive caregiving;
- changes in the financing of community care.

It has been argued (see Parker, 1992) that the extent of reductions in the availability of female kin because of greater geographical mobility has been overstated. Nevertheless, the combination of smaller family size and greater geographical mobility will reduce the number of daughters and sons living close to their parents. More important will be changes in women's employment patterns. Long-run restructuring of the labour market, with associated reductions in 'male' and increases in 'female' jobs will mean that more married women become, and are increasingly recognised as, joint breadwinners. Women's lower wage rates will mean that many have to work longer hours to complement lower earnings by partners to achieve desired living standards. They will thus find it more difficult to combine paid work with significant levels of caregiving – and obligations to their own families will more generally be accepted as constituting 'legitimate excuses'. Alongside these developments, continuing increases in the numbers of women entering higher education and improving their employment and earnings prospects will, for some women, sharpen the trade-off between employment and caregiving. The choice between maintaining secure and well paid employment with good prospects and giving it up to become an unpaid carer will become more stark, and more of a deterrent – not least because awareness of the possibility of divorce has grown, and with it awareness of the need to secure an income and pension independently. In essence, there will be stronger incentives to behave like those who opt out of caring at the moment, and whose reasons for doing so are regarded as legitimate. Current moves to charge for domiciliary services received by older people under the new community care arrangements will also increase pressure on carers' finances. And prospects of inheritance may also be reduced by local authorities' powers to impose a charge on an old person's estate to pay for any residential and nursing home care received before dying.

One group that seems less likely to change its behaviour is those whose lower skills and earnings potential make the trade-off between paid work and caregiving less clear. This will include some married women who have not yet re-entered the labour market, but also a significant proportion of male carers who have never left their parents' home, and possibly of those who **have** done so, but have returned. (The GHS carers data suggest that co-resident male carers are a group with lower earnings potential than women in the same position (Parker, 1993)). This group, however, forms a very small proportion of carers under retirement age.

By and large, then, the number of younger women supplying substantial amounts of care to an older relative seems bound to fall if current trends continue – unless there is a significant redistribution of caregiving responsibilities between husbands and wives or significant change in the policy environment.

A policy for family care?

Can anything be done to maintain – or increase – the supply of family care for older people? It is not difficult to outline the elements of a policy that would ease the strain, and reduce the financial penalties, of caregiving. Any such policy has, first, to recognise the different kinds and levels of care that relatives give. The majority provide practical help to those who are relatively fit; a significant minority provide more intensive levels of support. It also has to recognise the different relationships and contexts within which, particularly, more intensive levels of support are given. The needs of older spouse carers living in the same house will be different in important respects from those of married daughters with teenage children to whose home a parent has moved. Their needs will differ from those of an unmarried son who has never left home. To be successful, policy has to recognise and respond to the heterogeneity of carers.

For carers under retirement age, the key elements of a successful policy straddle employment, financial security and services in kind. The central element needs to be the creation of opportunities for maintaining contact with employment and minimising earnings loss. This means developing employment protection – in the form of entitlements to negotiated flexi-time, part-time work, job sharing and career breaks. As Glendinning (p. 105) points out, such provisions need to be flexible enough to accommodate the degree of employment that an individual carer can actually manage.

Social security could also play a major role. At present, its objectives in relation to carers are ambiguous and the level of support inadequate. As McLaughlin notes, ICA can only be regarded 'as a kind of honorarium' – not as a thoroughgoing response to the financial penalties carers incur or the work they do. In no sense could it be seen as an incentive to take on caregiving responsibilities. Even as an earnings replacement benefit, it is worth less than short-term benefits such as unemployment and sickness benefit and much less than longer term benefits such as invalidity benefit. This is difficult to understand or defend.

The inadequacies of current social security provision for informal carers have been rehearsed in detail elsewhere, together with suggestions for change (House of Commons, 1990 a and b; Baldwin and Parker, 1991; Glendinning, 1992). The need for review is long overdue. Attention most urgently needs to focus on:

- the creation of a truly independent income for carers, at a reasonable level and covering longer term as well as shorter periods of caregiving;
- ways of making it easier to combine significant levels of paid work and benefit receipt;
- ways of easing the transition from caring back into paid work;
- protection of pension entitlements, particularly in relation to the higher levels provided by occupational and earnings-related schemes.

At a very basic level, the objectives of social security policy for carers need clarification. Is it sensible to focus on earnings loss, or should caregiving itself be the focus of a benefit? If the former, what can be done about the fact that overlapping benefits regulations negates the value of ICA for many carers? Is there a case for a carers' costs benefit? Should the caregiving done by older carers be recognised in social security?

For both younger and older carers the 'costs' of caring could clearly be reduced by the delivery of more and better support in the form of services provided, or financed, by the statutory sector. This is particularly true of carers who live in the same household as the person they support. At present they stand very little chance of receiving domestic help, help with housing adaptations, laundry services, day and respite care. These are 'targeted' on older people living alone.

A better focus for policy?

In theory, then, a set of policies could be constructed which would maintain – or possibly increase – the supply of family care. There are strong reasons, however, to question whether this is a sensible, productive or just focus for policy. As Arber and Ginn (1991) argue, the prior need is for policies which recognise older people's individual rights as citizens and the contributions they have made and continue to make to society. Focusing on family carers and their needs is understandable, and welcome – but no substitute for the development of sound policies for later life.

Sinclair *et al*'s important review of research on welfare provision (1990) concludes that, while better support of family carers is one, necessary, element for the success of community care policies, it is far from sufficient. Community care needs to be identified not simply with keeping elderly people out of expensive residential forms of care, but with policies to improve their general well-being. This necessarily involves discussion of pensions, tax, and housing policy – not just services. The feasibility of effectively targeting statutory 'care' services on the elderly people who really need these – the very frailest – depends on developing a wider set of policies for older people in general. This means:

- improving older people's capacity to function independently and support themselves for as long as possible: via better incomes in retirement; access to better housing; effective health promotion and better health care;
- developing the capacity of the voluntary sector;
- identifying older people with greater need for support, identifying their and their carers' capacities and preferences and delivering the levels of publicly funded care needed;
- better coordination of the 'kaleidoscope' of statutory, voluntary, private sector and family care – including social security.

Others have expressed similar views (for example, Arber and Ginn, 1991; Baldwin and Twigg, 1991; Baldwin, 1993). At their heart lies the conviction that, while family care is an important resource that should be nurtured, the primary goal of policy must be to secure the dignity and quality of life of older citizens, and to ensure that they receive the support they need in the place, and manner, they prefer. The evidence from research (Arber and Ginn, 1991, p. 143) is that in most cases this would mean reducing dependence on the next generation – not increasing it – in order to preserve the essential qualities of these relationships.

References

Arber, S. and Ginn, J. (1991) *Gender and Later Life: A Sociological Analysis of Resources and Constraints*, London: Sage Publications.

Baldwin, S. M. (1993) 'The need for care in later life: social protection for older people and family caregivers', in Baldwin, S. M. and Falkingham, J. (eds) *Social Security: New Challenges to the Beveridge Model*, Hemel Hempstead: Harvester Wheatsheaf.

Baldwin, S. M. and Parker, G. (1991) 'Support for informal carers – the role of social security', pp 163–198 in Dalley, G. (ed) *Disability and Social Policy*, London: Policy Studies Institute.

Baldwin, S. M. and Twigg, J. (1991) 'Women and community care – reflections on a debate', pp 117–135 in Maclean, M. and Groves, D. (eds) *Women's Issues in Social Policy*, London: Routledge.

Brannen, J. and Wilson, G. (eds) (1987) *Give and Take in Families: Studies in Resource Distribution*, London: Allen and Unwin.

Evandrou, M. (1990) *Challenging the Invisibility of Carers: Mapping Informal Care Nationally*, Discussion Paper WSP/49, London: STICERD.

Finch, J. (1989) *Family Obligations and Social Change*, London: Polity.

Finch, J. and Mason, J. (1993) *Negotiating Family Responsibilities*, London: Routledge.

Glendinning, C. (1992) *The Costs of Informal Care: Looking Inside the Household*, London: HMSO.

Graham, H. (1983) 'Caring – a labour of love', pp 13–30 in Finch, J. and Groves, D. (eds) *A Labour of Love: Women, Work and Caring*, London: Routledge and Kegan Paul.

House of Commons (1990a) *Community Care: Carers*, Social Services Committee Fifth Report 1989–90, London: HMSO.

House of Commons (1990b) *Community Care: Social Security for Disabled People*, Social Services Committee Ninth Report, HC646, London: HMSO.

Lewis, J. and Meredith, B. (1988) *Daughters Who Care: Daughters Caring for Mothers at Home*, London: Routledge.

Martin, J. and White, A. (1988) *The Financial Circumstances of Disabled Adults Living in Private Households*, London: HMSO.

Matthews, A. and Truscott, P., (1990) *Disability, Household Income and Expenditure: A Follow-up Survey of Disabled Adults in the Family Expenditure Survey*, DSS Research Report No. 2, London: HMSO.

McLaughlin, E. (1991) *Social Security and Community Care: The Case of the Invalid Care Allowance*, London: HMSO.

Nissel, M. and Bonnerjea, L. (1982) *Family Care of the Handicapped Elderly: Who Pays?*, London: Policy Studies Institute.

Pahl, J. (1989) *Money and Marriage*, Basingstoke: Macmillan.

Parker, G. (1990) *With Due Care and Attention: A Review of Research on Informal Care* (2nd Edition), London: Family Policy Studies Centre.

Parker, G. and Lawton, D. (1990) *Further Analysis of the 1985 General Household Survey Data on Informal Care. Report 2: The Consequences of Caring*, unpublished paper, Social Policy Research Unit, University of York.

Parker, G. (1993) *With This Body: Caring and Disability in Marriage*, Buckingham: Open University Press.

Sinclair, I., Parker, R., Leat, D. and Williams, J. (1990) *The Kaleidoscope of Care: A Review of Research on Welfare Provision for Elderly People*, London: HMSO.

Twigg, J. and Atkin, K. (1994) *Carers Perceived: Policy and Practice in Informal Care*, Buckingham: Open University Press.

Wenger, G. C. (1987) 'Dependence, interdependency and reciprocity after eighty'. *Journal of Ageing Studies*, 1, 4: 355–77.

Wenger, G. C. (1990) 'Elderly carers: the need for appropriate intervention'. *Ageing and Society*, 10, 2: 197–219.

Wright, F. (1986) *Left to Care Alone*, Aldershot: Gower.

Chapter 7
COSTING A FORTUNE? PENSIONERS' FINANCIAL RESOURCES IN THE CONTEXT OF COMMUNITY CARE

DULCIE GROVES

'despite these friendships and despite her stoicism, Mary Sheepshanks found old age very hard to bear. She who had once travelled across whole continents, making speeches on the great twentieth century issues of feminism and internationalism, was now confined to one room and even to one (wheel) chair. In 1958 Mary Sheepshanks' daily help had a quarrel with the people above her and told Mary, then aged eighty-six, that she wanted to leave her. Mary could see nothing but compulsory institutionalization ahead. Very nearly blind and paralysed, but still competent to the last, Mary Sheepshanks wrote a loving note to her nephew John, and then killed herself.'
Sybil Oldfield, *Spinsters of this Parish: the Life and Times of F.M. Mayor and Mary Sheepshanks*, (1984)

Introduction

This commentary on the incomes and assets of elderly people is written in the context of newly enacted community care legislation. The White Paper *Caring for People* (1989) made it clear that while ability to pay should not influence decisions on assessment of need, local authorities would be expected to develop 'effective costing and charging procedures' as a means of 'achieving the best use of resources across the range of personal social services' (Department of Health, 1989, p. 28). Once accepted for service, a client's capacity to pay for or contribute towards charges has the potential to become a critical issue in determining the ingredients of the 'community care package', especially where, despite all best intentions to keep a frail, elderly person 'within' the community, it is residential (or even more expensive) nursing home care which is agreed upon as the most appropriate form of care.

As will be seen, most pensioners are far from affluent, though a substantial and increasing number do own their own homes (see Hamnett, Chapter 8, Tinker, Chapter 9, this volume). Many pensioners are income poor. Among the poorest are 'very elderly' non-married women, who form a large majority among that 75+ age group most at risk to the type of physical and/or mental infirmities which can trigger the need for substantial amounts of 'front-line' caring beyond routine family support and neighbourly help (Groves, 1992; Walker, 1992). It is for this age group that issues around 'paying for care' are most pertinent. There are few 'woopies' (Well Off Older People) in the very oldest age cohorts (Falkingham and Victor, 1991). And even the greatest mega-woopie (or his accountant) might well blanch when faced with the realities of funding an indeterminate amount of care in a private nursing home. Paying for care can, quite literally, cost a fortune.

Paying for care

One aim of the new regime is to prevent public money being spent on expensive residential care for people who can be cared for more cheaply 'in' the community. Hence the decision to make local authorities, rather than the Department of Social Security, responsible for funding and means-testing those elderly applicants accepted for service, though a small amount of income support will still be paid to eligible pensioners admitted to residential care (Department of Health, 1993, p. 7). Community care policies are in fact predicated on the availability of much unpaid care, especially from close relatives, 'in' the community. However, not all very elderly people have close relatives, nor are all relatives (who may themselves be elderly) able to provide substantial amounts of daily 'front-line' care. Where local authorities organise service, they are expected to use voluntary and private social care agencies to a considerable extent (Walker, 1993). It is to such agencies that elderly people, assessed by local authorities as not being in 'need' and hence as able to organise and fund their own care, may well turn, or to which others may turn on their behalf.

Oldman (1991) has addressed the issues surrounding personal funding for social care, that is, long-term or chronic care. In 1989, weekly fees for private nursing home care were estimated at £258 (single) or £229 (shared room), while private residential charges were £183 or £169. Facilities provided by voluntary agencies were slightly cheaper (Oldman, 1991, Table 2, p. 8). Oldman comments that it was 'not difficult to find nursing homes with fees in excess of £400 a week'. As Corden (1992) has explained, charges in individual facilities vary considerably. More recent unit cost estimates for 1993/4 suggest £345 for a private nursing home and £250 for residential care (Netten, 1994). A local authority residential home (a dwindling commodity and an unlikely destination for clients with 'means') costs £327. Thus, without making any allowance for personal needs, here is a basis for annual charges of £17,940 for a nursing home place and £13,000 for a residential home. Fees vary regionally and appear to bear a close relationship to local house prices (Oldman, 1991, p. 9). (See Hamnett, Ch. 8, this volume).

The Independent Living Fund (now closed) had experience of routing fee-paying clients through to independent and voluntary domiciliary service agencies. A 1992 study identified 32 agencies in the East Midlands supplying such care, of which 8 had started up within the previous 12 months: most were small, with a high turnover and a disconcerting tendency to go bust (Kestenbaum, 1993, p. 17). Typical agency rates were £4.50 hourly for an unqualified care assistant and £6 for a (daytime) nurse, with slightly higher charges for nights and weekends. A qualified registered or enrolled nurse to 'sleep in' on a week-night would cost anything from £19–£42 and more at weekends. Unqualified care assistants were only marginally cheaper (Kestenbaum, 1993, Appendix II, p. 34). Netten (1994) estimates £8 (per hour of client-related activity) as the unit cost of a local authority home care assistant, £3 outside London for a meal-on-wheels or £23 for a visit from a physiotherapist.

The main purpose of this chapter is to comment on the financial circumstances of the current generation of retirement pensioners and examine the various components which typically make up their total income and assets. To what extent might people now of working age expect to be better off than the current pensioners when they themselves retire? Some sample estimates of the costs of residential and domiciliary care have been given. The concluding section attempts to tease out issues relevant to the incorporation of 'paying for care' into the new regime. It needs to be borne in mind that the rules commonly require that the financial resources of married and cohabiting couples be aggregated when tests of means are applied. And it is elderly people's potential capacity to pay towards the costs of care themselves which is the pivotal question, not their willingness to do so or the availability (or otherwise) of services in the real world, nor any potential financial or other support available from relatives, charitable agencies or other sources.

Elderly people's incomes and assets

Elderly people typically derive their incomes from state pensions, income support, occupational pensions from previous employment, earnings, savings, investments and other capital assets. The current generation of female pensioners, most of whom have been married, have had far less access than men to pension provision in their own right. Husbands were expected to 'provide' for their wives in old age. For those pensioners with capital assets, the main component is likely to be a mortgage-free owner-occupied house or flat.

a) State pensions
The National Insurance basic state retirement pension, conceptualised as 'the foundation from which those retiring in the future can build their own additional pension' is provided on the principle that current employees pay NI contributions towards state pensions for the already retired (DHSS, 1985, II, S1.41, p. 5). This pension, worth £56.10 (1993–4) for an individual and £33.70 for a 'dependent' wife is universally claimed with no sense of stigma. People feel that they have 'paid in' for it, though, strictly speaking, they 'paid in' for their parents' generation. Just over ten million people were claiming the pension in 1991 (DSS, 1992, Table B1.01, p. 102). A full pension is based on contributions for 90 per cent of a notional 'working life' of 49 years (men) or 44 years (women) (Matthewman, 1992, S18.10, pp. 457–459). In 1991, 91 per cent of male pensioners were receiving a full basic retirement pension (DSS, 1992b, Table B1.08, p. 111), but only 15 per cent of women were getting a full 'single' pension from their own contributions (EOC, 1992, p. 28). Only 60 per cent of the very youngest female pensioners (60–64) had any entitlement in their own right (DSS, 1992b, Table B1.01, p. 103).

Women become eligible for any self-funded state pension entitlement at 60. It will be some years before an equal pensionable age (65) is implemented, in stages, between 2010 and 2020 (DSS, 1993a). There is a long history of differential treatment of men and women within the state pension scheme (Groves, 1983: 1993a) which, along with women's typically lower lifetime levels of economic activity (see Joshi, Chapter 5, this volume) has meant that, to date, far fewer women than men have qualified for an individual state pension. Many women have been penalised in particular by the 'half-test' applied for nearly three decades to wives who, once married, had to pay full employee contributions for at least half their married lives to qualify for a self-funded pension. Otherwise all contributions, including those made before marriage, were void (Groves, 1993b, pp. 43–47). Not surprisingly most newly married women, anticipating motherhood and uncertain as to the duration of future employment, took their option to cease making full contributions. A 'dependent wife's' retirement pension at 60 per cent of the single rate has always been guaranteed on a husband's full record, once he reaches 65. The 'half-test' was abolished in 1979 (Drabble, 1977, p. 18) and wives were later allowed to count all self-funded contributions into their record.

Where married couples are both over pensionable age, a wife may add a small individual retirement pension to a small dependent wife's pension to make the whole amount up to a full dependent wife's pension (Matthewman, 1992, S18.14, p. 460). A woman widowed when over pensionable age becomes permanently entitled to a 'single' retirement pension in her own right based on her husband's record, not subject to forfeit on cohabitation or marriage (Poynter and Martin, 1993, pp. 96–97). Women widowed before 60 are subject to rules which can result in partial or total loss of widows' pension before reaching pensionable age or ineligibility for such a pension, with eventual impact on their derived rights to a retirement pension on their late husband's record (Matthewman, 1992, S9–7-9.46, pp. 230–247). At pensionable age, however, a widowed/divorced woman can add her late/ex husband's contribution (to the point where the marriage ended) to her own record, if this is an advantage (Matthewman, S18.12, p. 459). Also, since 1978, 'home responsibilities' credits have been allowed to prescribed categories of carers looking after dependent children or severely incapacitated adults. There are long-standing provisions for crediting Class I contributions to registered unemployed people and others incapable of paid work. Class III (voluntary) contributions can also be made, but there is a six year time limit (Poynter and Martin, 1993, pp. 180–4).

The Social Security Pension Act 1975 introduced a second-tier state pensions scheme. All employees liable to pay NI contributions and not 'contracted-out' into an approved occupational (or, since 1988, an approved personal) pension scheme will eventually become entitled to an additional State Earnings Related Pension (SERPS) based on their record since 1978. This pension was originally based on an individual's 'best twenty years' of earnings, revalued in line with increases in national average earnings (Matthewman, 1992, S18.35, p. 467). It was geared to favour low earners, along with others at risk of major interruption of their 'working life' or whose earnings peaked well before pensionable age. Such an arrangement is potentially favourable to women, immigrants or people with disabilities or who suffer substantial unemployment (Groves, 1991, pp. 43–4). However, the Social Security Act 1986 severely downgraded the value of SERPS benefits from the end of this century and the 'best twenty years' rule will never operate as intended. Whereas at present a widow may inherit the whole of her husband's additional pension and combine it with her own to the theoretical maximum for a single person, in future, only half the pension may be inherited. Widowers' additional pensions are also paid where both spouses were over pensionable age when the wife died (Matthew-man, 1992, S18.30–18.42, pp. 466–70).

SERPS pensions in payment for 1991 ranged from modest to minuscule and were drawn by a total of 3,389,000 'younger' pensioners. The theoretical maximum pension which could be paid to someone with a 'full' record who retired in 1992 was £67.97 weekly, based on the NI upper earnings limit (Matthewman, 1992, S18.38, p. 469). Among all pensioners 65–69 in 1991, 90 per cent of men were getting some additional pension (average £19.07) as were 31 per cent of women (average £7.72) (DSS, 1992, Table B1.12, p. 116). Of the men, 39 per cent were getting under £10 and a further 11 per cent less than £1: the equivalents for women were 51 per cent and 16 per cent. Only 3 per cent of male pensioners were getting more than £40 weekly and 6 per cent between £30–£40. These were the 'winners', whose female equivalents scored at 1 per cent and 3 per cent. Of the remaining men, 14 per cent got between £20–£30 and 27 per cent between £10–£20. Only 7 per cent of women got £20–£30 and 21 per cent got £10–£20 (DSS, 1992, Table B1.13, p. 117).

The other 'second-tier' pension for which some current pensioners are eligible is the 'graduated retirement benefit' which existed between 1961 and 1975 and was targeted at 'middling' earners not in approved occupational pension schemes. The maximum male pension in payment is £6.10 weekly, while for women the amount is actuarially reduced to £5.10 (Matthewman, 1992, S52–56, pp. 476–8).

Thus retired people's state pensions come in various combinations. Some pensioners also qualify for additions for dependent children, disability or other non-means tested benefits which are not retirement benefits as such, though payment of 'over-lapping' benefits is not normally permitted. Yet when all these pensions are added together (excluding dependants' allowances) as of 30/9/91, only 10 per cent of recipients ended up with an income of more than £75 weekly, of whom 67 per cent were men. Only 7 per cent of self-funded married women and 8 per cent of widows ended up with at least that amount. Some of these 'high income' pensioners would have had their income 'inflated' by entitlement to an attendance allowance (DSS 1992, Table B1.07, p. 110). The average male wage for all occupations in 1991 was £313 (Employment Gazette, 1993, 101:1, Table 5.6, p. 525) so even the best off 10 per cent of pensioners were getting a total state pension income which was only equal to at least 24 per cent of the average male wage. The median widow's or self-insured woman's income was £50–£54 and for dependent wives was under £40. Men did better than women, but few people of either sex were drawing other than very modest amounts of state pension (DSS, 1992, Table B1.07, p. 110).

b) Income support

Not surprisingly, given the low value of some state pensions in payment, 1,675,000 pensioners were claiming means-tested income support in 1991, of whom 84 per cent were female. No fewer than 546,000 claimants were women over 80, of whom around 80 per cent were non-married (DSS, 1992, Tables A2.10, 2.12–3, pp. 24–25). Around 18 per cent of British pensioners were successfully claiming benefit, which under-represents those technically eligible to apply. Johnson and Falkingham (1992, p. 79) state that Johnson and Webb (1990, p. 11) estimate that 900,000 pensioners failed to claim in 1987.

The 1992–3 basic income support allowance is £44 for a single claimant and £69 for a married/cohabiting couple. Premiums are payable to pensioners at age-related rates, giving 'single' pensioners total incomes of £60.70 (under 75), £62.65 (75–79) and £66.75 (over 80). Couples get £94.35 (under 75), £97 (75–79) and £101.55 (over 80). The capital disregard is £8000 for individuals or couples: notional interest at a very high rate around 20 per cent, unchanged since 1987, is imputed to capital between £3000–£8000 (Matthewman, 1992, S4.27, p. 57: S4.51, p. 67–8). Where a claimant is over 80, a severe disability premium (£32.55 single: £65.10 couple) may be payable in addition, if attendance or high disability allowance is being claimed and there is neither a 'carer' drawing ICA nor any non-dependent adult actually living in the same household (Matthewman, 1992, S4.50–3, pp. 66–8).

Most elderly claimants are not relying wholly on income support but 'topping up' their available income, from whatever source, to the permitted level. Apart from any housing benefit, council tax benefit, and the occasional severe weather (heating) allowance, no other cash benefits are available to claimants, though pensioners can apply to the Social Fund for community care grants or repayable loans to meet major cash outlays. There are over a million local authority/private tenant retirement pensioner units not drawing income support, but sufficiently poor to qualify for means-tested housing benefit (DSS, 1992, Table A3.20, p. 75).

c) Occupational pension from previous employers
It is access to lengthy membership of good 'final salary' (defined benefit) occupational pension schemes and good pay at around the point of retirement which is the key to an adequate income in old age. Most schemes approved under the Social Security Pensions Act 1975 were 'final salary' but employees are contracted in to such schemes by occupational group, not as individuals, which arrangement has disadvantaged women in particular, given widespread occupational segregation by sex. Access to occupational pension provision mirrors the inequalities of the labour market (Groves, 1992: Walker, 1988).

Analysis of pensioners' 1982 incomes showed that married couples over 75 were less likely (59 per cent) than younger couples (70 per cent) to have employers' pension income. Lone women over 75 were less likely (28 per cent) to have such income than younger (60–64) women (40 per cent), in the group that are now on the threshold of 'old' old age (DHSS, 1984, Table 7, p. 19). Now, as then, it is 'younger' pensioners who tend to be better off than the 'very old'. Recent analysis of pensioners' 1989 incomes estimates that 75 per cent of couples (65–69) have occupational pension income as compared with 55 per cent of non-married men (65–69) and women (60–64) (DSS, 1993b). Younger pensioners, and men especially, have had better access than older people to occupational pension schemes, provided that their employment career was full time and uninterrupted. In addition, they experienced considerable growth in the real value of the earnings on which their pension entitlements are calculated (Walker, 1988).

'Very old' pensioners have inevitably experienced an erosion in the value of their occupational pensions, with the best being linked only to the RPI (Walker, 1988). In addition, some former private sector employees were in 'money purchase' (defined contribution) schemes whereby employer/employee contributed to an individualised fund invested on the employee's behalf. In the 1970s, such schemes went out of favour as high inflation eroded the value of both long-term investments and of the annuities purchased to produce pension income (Hannah, 1986, pp. 107–8). It was poverty among widows which persuaded more occupational pension schemes to offer widows' benefits in the 1960s, to the point where all schemes 'approved' from 1975 had to offer survivors' benefits to all widows who meet the criteria for eligibility for a state pension (Groves, 1991). Widows' benefits can be particularly generous (incorporating large lump sums) when death has occurred in service, thus potentially enhancing the income and assets of a woman widowed below pensionable age, well into old age. The risk of early widowhood is, however, decreasing (CSO, 1993, Table 1.12, p. 18).

Although access to an occupational pension is widely acknowledged as a passport to income adequate for day-to-day living in old age, a 1988 study of net payments actually in receipt by 'younger' pensioners shows how modest the typical payment is. The **median** amount being drawn by retired men (65–69) was £16.42 and by women (60–64) nil. Due to the presence of a small minority of extremely well pensioned men and never-married women with lifelong, full-time earnings, the **average** for men was £33.06 and for women £7.78 (Bone *et al.*, 1992, Table 7.18 a and b, p. 129). It is unfortunate that statistics on pensioners' incomes are so often presented to the public as averages undifferentiated by gender. A recently retired Grade I civil servant could well have a half pay occupational pension of around £40,000 a year (Whitaker's Almanac, 1993, p. 284). He and his like comprise a tiny minority of truly affluent pensioners who are apt to 'skew' pensioner incomes statistics based on averages.

The OPCS retirement study showed 70 per cent of men (65–69) and 27 per cent of women (61–63) with occupational pensions in their own right (Bone *et al.*, 1992, Table 7.4, p. 115). Among graduates, 91 per cent of men and 71 per cent of women (55–69) had retained rights in an employer's scheme, as had a further 86 per cent of men and 61 per cent of women with qualifications above A-level (Table 6.6, p. 81). It is among this group that the 'highly pensioned' are to be found, especially where good pay has been combined with lengthy service. On average men already retired (55–69) had 23 pensionable years and women 17 (Table 6.25, p. 90). Prior to the 1975 legislation it was permitted (and common) to 'cash in' employee pension contributions on leaving a job. Around half of all the retired people had done this at least 16 years earlier: of all the people over 55 still at work, 32 per cent of men and 48 per cent of women had 'cashed in' at least 25 years earlier (Table 6.17, p. 87).

In 1988 the gross basic state retirement pension was £41.15 (single) and £24.75 (dependent wife). The OPCS retirement study showed that among all retired respondents (55–69) only 6 per cent of men and 1 per cent of women were drawing a net occupational pension in excess of £150 weekly, with a further 10 per cent of men and 2 per cent of women drawing between £100–£149 (Table 6.54, p. 102). The median net pension being drawn by a man of 65 in 1988 was £20.81 (average £32.29) and by a woman (60) was £14.28 (£22.26). Early retired men (55–59) acknowledged (30 per cent) financial inducements to retire (Table 5.10, p. 64). It was noticeable that early retired pensioners of both sexes had bigger pensions than the age group just past pensionable age. Median net pensions in payment to 55 year olds were £80.54 men (average £73.29) and £33.46 women (£34.79) (Table 6.58, p. 103).

Estimates for 1989 based on data from the Government Actuary's Department and the Family Expenditure Survey show that the percentage of pensioner couples with occupational pension income had risen by 8 per cent since 1979 to 73 per cent with an average gross pension of £62.70. There had been a 15 per cent increase in single pensioners to 47 per cent, with an average pension of £41.60. Younger couples (65–69) were very marginally better off at £65.60, whereas single pensioners at £41.40 were not. These were men (65–69) and women (60–64) (DSS, 1993b, Table 7). This evidence does not in fact suggest that younger pensioners are in general markedly better off than older pensioners in terms of the occupational pension component of their incomes, though it does suggest that there has been an appreciable increase in the number of 'single' people with an occupational pension. It is likely that they are women with small individual or survivor's pensions.

d) Earnings
There has been a steady decline in the economic activity rates of people over pensionable age, to around 12 per cent (men) and 19 per cent (women) by 1988. It is estimated that economic recovery, allied to the recent abolition of the 'earnings rule' which previously placed a ceiling on the amount of money which could be earned by people wishing to retain their pension, may result in a slight upturn in pensioner employment (Trinder *et al.*, 1992, Figs. 2.1 and 2.2, p. 5: p. 6). People over pensionable age tend to do casual, part-time, self-employed work, with women in particular in low-skilled manual work (see Trinder *et al.*, 1992, pp. 2–19). The 1988 OPCS retirement survey found that retired pensioners 55–69 had nil median earnings, though men 65–69 earned an average £3.91 and women (60–64) £2.02 (Bone *et al.*, 1992, Tables 7.18a and b, p. 129). It is exceptional for 'very old' pensioners to earn and they are least likely to do so if frail enough to need care.

e) Capital assets and investment income
Hamnett (1995) and Tinker (1995) (this volume) have analysed the growing importance of housing as a component of capital assets and have discussed some implications of the increased level of home ownership among the pensioner population. But as Gibbs (1992, pp. 36–37) illustrates, there are considerable regional variations in the extent of home ownership and in property values. The OPCS 1988 retirement survey found that among home owners (55–69) roughly a third of those men and women who were home owners had property worth under £50,000, slightly over a third had a house or flat worth £50,000 to £100,000 and 17 per cent had property worth £101,000 to £150,000. Property worth over £150,000 was owned by 14 per cent (Bone *et al.*, 1992, Table 7.77, p. 169). The value of this property has not necessarily held up, given the recent recession. The house/flat was the main capital asset for most of those younger pensioners.

In the same survey, retired men and women 67–69 reported, in general, a low level of savings and investments. 17 per cent of men and 23 per cent of women had none, while a further 48 per cent of men and 58 per cent of women had assets up to £8,000, the current 'ceiling' for capital which can be retained under the income support rules. Only 35 per cent of men and 19 per cent of women had assets over £8,000 and of these, only 15 per cent of men and 7 per cent of women had assets over £20,000 (Bone et al., 1992, Table 7.66, p. 160). A third of all retired informants (55–69) said that their savings had decreased since retirement and only 19 per cent reported an increase (Table 7.73, p. 168). This did not augur well for their 'old' old age. There was evidence that two-thirds of this group had invested occupational 'lump sum' benefits, though such capital was also realised for living expenses, purchase of major items and to pay off mortgages (Table 6.51, p. 101). A small minority of men (16 per cent) and women (19 per cent) of all informants (55–69) had insurance/endowment policies yet to mature, though only 19 per cent of men and 5 per cent of women had policies estimated to be worth more than £10,000 (Table 7.83, p. 171). 17 per cent of men and women had inherited property or proceeds from property in unspecified amounts (Table 7.81, p. 171).

For the majority of retirement pensioners investment income is a small component of total income. Estimates for 1989 show that the percentage of couples with investment income has risen since 1979 by 16 per cent to 87 per cent, the average gross weekly income being £38.80. For non-married pensioners the increase was 13 per cent over the same period to 69 per cent, with an average amount of £24.90. Younger couples (65–69) were marginally better off by £2.70 than pensioners in general, while younger non-married people (men 65–69: women 60–64) were better off by £5.60 (DSS, 1993b, Table 6).

The 1988 OPCS retirement survey showed that for all retired people (55–69) the median male net investment income was £6.03 (average £19.23): women £3.30 (£12.30) (Bone et al., 1992, Table 7.16, p. 127). A recent analysis of 1988 GHS data estimates that most 'pensioner units' had some investment income but for only 15 per cent of units (couples/non-married individuals) was it worth over 20 per cent of gross total income and for only 10 per cent was it worth over 30 per cent (Weir, 1992, p. 30). Some wealthier pensioners can afford to invest capital for growth. Most keep their modest capital in building society accounts and in national savings, a fact reflected in the personal financial advice columns of newspapers and Radio 4's 'Money Box' programmes which are besieged by calls from pensioners for advice on appropriate income-producing investment strategies now that interest rates have fallen substantially.

Perspectives on the financial circumstances of elderly people

In the mid 1980s Robert Walker was asked to estimate 'how many pensioners could afford personally to meet the costs of care and how much could they pay?' His answer, after analysis of a wide range of evidence on the financial resources of pensioners, was that perhaps 1 in 10 of the 'very elderly' (75+) pensioners most at risk of needing social care could realistically afford to pay modest charges at around £20 a week in 1982 prices without releasing equity in owner-occupied property (Walker with Hardman, 1988). Weir (1992) after analysis of 1988 GHS data concluded that the number of 'well off' elderly pensioners continues to be small, again with the vast majority needing to realise capital to afford residential care which, for most, would mean the sale of a house. Gibbs (1992), examining the role of housing wealth as a means of paying for residential care, analysed the potential of 'very elderly' households (75+) to pay for care out of income or housing wealth, again using 1988 GHS data. He found that only 4 per cent of households could have met residential care fees out of income: this represented 10 per cent of all homeowners and virtually nil renters. Allowing for one partner to remain in the joint home, only 7 per cent of couples had sufficient income to pay for residential care out of income.

McKay (1992) completed a wide-ranging survey of pensioners' assets which clearly indicates the limitations of available evidence. He presents data on pensioners' incomes which show that in 1988, around 60 per cent of pensioners were almost entirely reliant on some form of state social security payments. The fourth pensioner income quintile were still mainly reliant on state pensions or social security. Even in the top quintile, social security payments represented roughly (a by no means negligible) 22 per cent of total gross income, the other components being occupational pension income (37 per cent), savings (28 per cent) and earnings (13 per cent), (McKay, 1992, Figure 2, p. 8). It is only in this top quintile that elderly people who can 'pay for care' are likely to be found and for reasons already stated, they are likely to be found among those typically younger pensioners whose continuing earnings lift them into the top quintile.

Johnson and Falkingham (1992) examined a number of sanguine statements on pensioners' assets and the likelihood of these increasing substantially in the fairly near future. They gave as their opinion that 'it is not possible to conclude that the elderly as a whole have become a relatively more affluent group' (p. 58) and point to the existence of a small, highly visible, affluent minority (p. 65). Johnson and Falkingham (1992, p. 66) conclude that few others could 'survive without state benefits or make a sufficient contribution to the cost of any substantial form of care'. In pointing up this really small minority of 'affluent' pensioners they cite research by Atkinson and Sutherland (1988) which showed that were means-testing of state pensions to be applied to all tax units (couples and non-married persons) at the top of the then threshold for the 'age allowance' for people over 65, only 230,000 pensioner units (3 per cent of the total) would be targeted and around 5 per cent if means-tests were applied to all units lying within the 'taper' (Johnson and Falkingham, 1992, p. 78). Women, of course, have since become entitled to independent taxation.

Falkingham and Victor (1991) went in search of the 'woopie' and analysed the socio-economic status of the most affluent pensioners, revealing the archetypal woopie as male, under 75 and from the professional classes, with income from assets and a good occupational pension. Evidence from the 1974–85 GHS data files showed that while the proportion of pensioners over 65 had increased from 14 per cent to 15 per cent of the total population, the proportion in the top income quintile had remained static at nearly 5 per cent. However 10 per cent of 'young' (65–69) pensioners were in the top income quintile of the total GB income distribution as compared with around 4 per cent of the 'over 75's' (Falkingham and Victor, 1991, Table 4, p. 11). Women greatly outnumber men in this age group. Arber and Ginn (1991) have documented why elderly women are poorer than men, raising issues as to the extent to which household income is fairly shared between elderly couples.

Falkingham and Victor (1991, p. 15, Table 5) having pinpointed their woopies as affluent pensioners with a high level of car, phone and outright home ownership, typically married and living in small centrally heated households, argue strenuously that most pensioners, by contrast, are living on or just above the poverty line, with only 3 per cent having income worth at least twice the average weekly net income of the whole population. They conclude that 'woopies' are a highly visible, tiny minority, whose financial status may well decline with age (Falkingham and Victor, 1991, p. 30). These authors present interesting evidence in the context of 'personalising' payments for care, in that the top quintile of pensioners are least likely to be incapacitated and make less use than other pensioners over 65 of publicly provided personal social services (Table 11, p. 29). This is consonant with 'woopies' being younger, married men.

The OPCS 1988 retirement study found that 52 per cent of men 65–69 had a net income from all sources of under £80 a week. A further 12 per cent had £80–£100, 12 per cent had £100–£125 and a further 15 per cent had £125–£175. Only 10 per cent had more than that amount, including 1 per cent with an income in excess of £375 a week. Women in that age group were less well off, with 74 per cent having an individual income under £80. Only 9 per cent of all women had an income over £100 weekly, the top 1 per cent having £225–£275 (Bone et al., 1992, Table 7.2, p. 113). Among all retired people 55–69, retired divorced/separated women recorded the lowest median net income at £48.28 and were worse off than retired widows (£56.71) (Table 7.44b, p. 147).

Finally, the 1991 Family Expenditure Survey results show a weekly disposable income of just under £72 for retired one-adult households mainly dependent on state pension and around £164 for other retired one-person households. For couples the equivalent figures were £126 and £267 (CSO, 1992, Table 20, p. 44). The average weekly disposable income where the head of household was 65–74 was £200 and if 75+, £151 (Table 20, p. 45). Retired households mainly dependent on state pensions spent an average £70 weekly and other retired households spent £146 (Table 9, p. 28). The Joseph Rowntree Foundation (1992) estimated a 'low-cost' budget for a 'lone' pensioner in April 1992 as £53 (local authority tenant excluding rent) and £67 (owner occupier). A 'modest but adequate' budget was £119 (tenant) and £112 (owner/occupier). It was estimated that only about half of all 'lone' pensioners met the 'low cost' living standard including that 30 per cent who were at least 'modest but adequate'. Again, this evidence suggests that it is only a small minority of 'lone' pensioners, a category typical of the 'over 75s', would have any potential capacity to pay towards care charges out of income, even allowing for receipt of attendance allowance.

Will future generations of pensioners be better off?

The outlook is not good for pensioners who have to rely mainly on state social security. Since 1980, state retirement pensions have been linked only to the Retail Price Index, rather than, as previously, to whichever was the greater annual increase in prices or earnings. Oppenheim (1993, pp. 68–69) states that had pensions been uprated in line with the rise in earnings, the basic retirement pension would be £19.35 higher for a single person and £30.65 higher for a couple. Whereas a single pension was worth 20.4 per cent of male average earnings in 1979, it was worth 17.8 per cent in 1992. The basic state retirement pension is, in point of fact, being allowed to wither away, with means-tested 'pensioner premiums' being targeted at the very poorest pensioners. If pensionable age for women is in fact raised to 65, women will have to wait five years longer for benefits in their own right. Single and divorced women are likely to be particularly disadvantaged by such a move. Given current trends in labour force participation and an absence of age discrimination legislation, it is hard to see how large numbers of women can remain economically active to 65. They are less likely than men to have good occupational pensions to fall back on (Groves, 1993b).

As noted, the value of SERPS is to be severely down-graded from the turn of the century. Not only will the pension be calculated from a reduction in accrual rate but on a lengthy national working life (16–60/65), with home responsibility credits allowed, rather than the previous best twenty years of earnings. Women who work part-time, thus reducing the total value of their life time earnings, will be heavily penalised. Widows' benefits will be reduced. In future there are likely to be greater inequalities among pensioners, mainly related to differential access to occupational pensions. The proportion of full-time employees in occupational pension schemes remained steady between 1975–90 at around 60 per cent. The GHS 1990 showed 63 per cent of men and 55 per cent of women enrolled, but only 16 per cent of part-time women (OPCS, 1992, Table 4.1, p. 77). The Social Security Act 1986 improved employee rights to 'preserved' pensions, including possibilities of transferring rights from one scheme to another when changing jobs, if the new employer allows it. However, there can be problems over such pension assets losing value when preserved or transferred (Ward, 1990, Ch.16). Of late, many non-manual employees in good final salary schemes have prejudiced the long-term value of their pension benefits by taking early retirement. Even the best occupational pensions, fully linked to the RPI, erode in value over time, like state pensions. In addition, mothers, carers and others with substantial periods of absence from the labour force will continue to find it difficult to notch up a really substantial number of 'pensionable years'. Hence for many occupational pensioners the actual benefits will be modest and some people may well end up in 'old' old age in the 'occupational pension trap' – not quite poor enough to qualify for means-tested benefits, but no better off than pensioners receiving such benefits (Walker, Hardman and Hutton, 1989).

The Social Security Act 1986 made it illegal for employers to insist on membership of an occupational pension scheme as a condition of service. The government has had considerable success in persuading young people to opt out of SERPS into the new approved 'personal pensions' or to take out an APP in preference to joining an employer's scheme. By 1990 over 4 million people (a third women) were in such schemes (Johnson *et al.*, 1992, pp. 51–52). National insurance contributions from employer/employee are diverted into a 'portable' money purchase scheme for eventual purchase of an annuity (incorporating a half-rate survivor's benefit) to be drawn at pensionable age. The annuity will increase annually by the lesser of 3 per cent or the RPI, since an APP offers 'protected rights' analogous to the guaranteed component of an occupational pension. Experts believe that men up to their mid-forties will do better in an APP than SERPS (Johnson *et al*, 1992, p. 55). Women, with their typically fragmented employment patterns, are unlikely to be better off in an APP than SERPS: at the very time they should be maximising their contributions their earning capacities are liable to be subordinated to the demands of child care (Davis and Ward, 1992).

It is an open question whether employers will themselves move towards providing 'money purchase' rather than 'final salary' schemes as a cost-cutting exercise, especially for categories of employee where staff 'retention' is not an issue. To the extent to which employees themselves expect to change jobs, work on contracts etc. in an increasingly fragmented labour market, opting out of any employer's scheme (or not opting in, in the first place) may become a more popular option, especially if inflation remains low, possibly to the eventual hazard of occupational pension provision in general. However, in order to provide anything like adequately for old age, employees will need to take out one or more personal pensions over and above the APP. Employers do not contribute to these though they qualify for age-related tax relief. People will need to pay in consistently and increase the annual value of such contributions, while there will be no guarantees as to the performance of the accrued fund. Women will be required to pay much higher contributions than men (Keighley, 1992). The end result will depend on the economic situation at the point where the capital is realised. People need really good advice when purchasing personal pensions: some current advice is dubious (Carnegie UK Trust, 1993, pp. 47–48.) Recent surveys by the accountants KPMG Peat Marwick and the Department of Social Security illustrate the extent to which millions of employees, including many women, have wrongly opted out of SERPS or occupational pension schemes (Rutherford, 1994)

Adequacy of contribution is a key issue since people of working age already have other major demands on their income such as housing costs. In future many more will be paying off substantial loans incurred towards the costs of tertiary education, helping to fund their own children's education and possibly subsidising the care needs of their elderly parents. (See Walker Chapter 10, this volume.) Another issue is that there are no requirements to make provision for survivors from personal pensions taken out in addition to the APP which replaces SERPS, nor will husbands or wives necessarily know what pension arrangements their spouses have made. It is possible that widows will be less well provided for in future. Increasing divorce compounds women's risk to inadequate provision for old age since, to date, no way has been found to compensate ex-wives for loss of potential widows' benefits on divorce, though the issues are under discussion (Joshi and Davies, 1991). Finally, people in PPs (other than APPs) will be entitled to take their personal pensions from the age of 50. If pensionable age goes up to 65 and current trends towards early departure from the labour market continue, it is possible that in the future there will be a sizeable group of pensioners whose incomes are inadequate because they realised their personal pensions too early.

With regard to capital assets, it seems likely that the pensioner-owner-occupation rate will increase given the greater proportion of home owners among the current generation of younger people, but it remains to be seen where owner occupation will 'peak' and what will happen to property values. It is possible that more 'younger' elderly people will still be paying off mortgages after retirement and with less tax-relief than was originally the case. It is also impossible to predict rates of savings and investments and the likely returns on investment, but it must be noted that many young people, including graduates, are currently finding it difficult to get employment or avoid 'under employment' which, again, may have long-term effects on the ability of this, and any other similarly affected, generation's ability to defer earnings for old age.

In future, with declining state pension income and the possibility that some personal pension contracts may disappoint, it seems likely that most pensioners will continue to live on poor-to-modest incomes, with an owner occupied home as the only possible major capital asset. Divorced and single women will continue to be at particular risk of poverty in old age, as will people disabled before reaching pensionable age. Anecdotal evidence suggests that wives may be at risk to poverty where local authority means tests apply a husband's occupational pension income towards the costs of residential care. In future (Jones, 1993) there are likely to be greater inequalities of income and wealth among people from ethnic minorities, with knock-on effects for old age. That small minority of very affluent pensioners is likely to increase, not least because in future there will be more couples where both parties end up with substantial income and assets, but these will be the exception (see Bosanquet and Propper, 1991). Cohabiting women of the non-affluent variety will be particularly vulnerable to poverty in old age, since cohabitees in Britain do not have rights to derived benefits in the same way as married women, nor relief from payment of inheritance tax on widowhood. Obviously the levels of charges for social care in the future are unknown. Whatever the cost, it is to be hoped that politicians and policy-makers are not persuaded by the 'high visibility' of some very affluent pensioners that most pensioners are well off: it is unlikely that they will be. In future we need to hear a lot more about median pensioner incomes and less about averages: more about individual women's incomes and assets and less about 'couples'.

Conclusion

It is patently clear that only a very small minority of elderly people could fund an indefinite stay in residential or nursing home care out of income. Given that the average stay is about 3 years (Hamnett, Chapter 8 this volume) it would be possible for some home owners in a position to release the capital value of their home to fully fund their care in this way, though the psychological effects of actually 'selling up' can be devastating (Tinker, Chapter 9 this volume). Only a minority of pensioners could make a substantial contribution towards the cost of domiciliary care from income alone, even with a higher rate of attendance allowance at £44.90 (1993–4): most would need to dip into savings or release equity on their owner-occupied home (Hamnett, Chapter 8 this volume).

There has recently been publicity around the economic viability of current public funding mechanisms for state pension provision (Carnegie UK Trust, 1993, Ch.5: Johnson and Falkingham, 1992, pp. 49–51). If basic state pensions were to be means-tested and wholly or partly withdrawn from elderly people not wholly reliant on state benefits, then given the modest value of most occupational pensions and investment incomes, even fewer pensioners would have the means to pay towards care out of income than is now the case. They might be under more pressure to release equity from their homes (if any) and at an earlier stage (see Hamnett, Chapter 8 this volume).

Oldman (1991, pp. 26–29) has reviewed recent attempts to explore the notion of long-term care insurance, noting that elderly people seeking to insure against the risk of chronic ill health are not an attractive proposition to commercial insurance companies. Early schemes marketed in the US were highly restrictive and take-up was poor. Spero (1992) gives details of a number of schemes recently introduced in the UK but points out that this is an immature market as yet. Wittenberg (1989) has modelled a scheme which would require weekly payments of £12.10 (1986 prices) to insure with a non-profit-making company for up to three years' domiciliary or residential care. He estimated that were elderly couples/individuals (not mainly dependent on state benefits) to pay 20 per cent of their weekly disposable income to such an insurance plan, 2.77 million households would be covered: at 10 per cent coverage would be 680,000 and at 5 per cent – 175,000.

Davies (1988) has outlined a 'social care maintenance organisation' which would link insurance to care management and offer financial advice, though Oldman (1991, p. 28) cites Schlesinger (1986, Milbanke Quarterly 64:2, pp. 189–215) as being sceptical that pre-paid social care is a viable proposition. Spero (1992) notes the prohibitive cost of current long-term care insurance plans in the UK. The Commercial Union (1991) estimates the cost of a single premium insurance purchased at 60 for £18,000 annual, permanent (escalating) coverage at £21,571 for a man and £40,597 for a woman. Women, who live longer than men, are more at risk of needing such care, but actuarial calculations make insurance cover far more expensive for women to buy (Keighley, 1992). Few women would have such free capital at their disposal. Annual premiums commenced at 70 would cost £2484 (men) and £3648 (women). Oldman (1991, pp. 28–29) cites Benjamin (1989) as favouring the concept of long-term care funded by payment of a single premium and linked to residence in a 'continuing care community' which combines housing, social and medical care in one location. Johnson and Falkingham (1992, pp. 79–80) argue that such long-term care insurance schemes might simply serve to increase inequality among elderly people.

Such insurance depends on ability to pay and as Oldman (1991, p. 29) states, 'very few of the current generation of the 'old' old have 'surplus' or 'discretionary' income'. Among those most at risk of having inadequate incomes in old age are people who depressed their earning power when of 'working age' by substantial front line caring in a household without other earners and who have no spouse from whom eventually to derive rights to pension benefits (Glendinning, 1992).

Possible financial complications in the context of releasing capital assets to pay for care include situations where property is in some form of joint ownership, as with husbands/wives, cohabitees or same-sex partners and one partner is deemed to need permanent residential care. There is also the position of adult children or other carers co-resident with an elderly parent, sibling or other person needing such care. Obviously there can be very knotty problems where a dwelling or equity from a house, which otherwise might constitute an inheritance, is targeted as a source of funding for care. As Allen *et al.* (1992,

Ch.8) illustrate, many admissions to residential care take place as a 'crisis move' and not necessarily as an active choice made by elderly people themselves.

Another set of issues surrounds the situation of frail, elderly people who are unable to take responsibility for their own finances and/or who are vulnerable to financial exploitation. In some cases the elderly person may have conferred an enduring power of attorney on someone else (Farrand, 1989) or may be under the jurisdiction of the Court of Protection. Hoggett (1989, pp. 523–4) points out that this court controls incapacitated people's property and financial affairs but has no jurisdiction over care. 'Paying for care' can mean conflicts of interest over stewardship of assets and the provision of care, including any 'care package' devised by a local authority. Again, there are local authority or 'agency' staff who may be in a position of trust regarding cash, possessions or financial assets belonging to frail, elderly people. It would appear that the new community care regime will need to embody viable safeguards against financial abuse (see Tinker, Chapter 9 this volume). Likewise, issues will arise around the local authority's powers to require contributions towards payment for care and mechanisms to deal with grievances on the part of clients or their representatives. One likely issue relates to the extent to which elderly people may legally divest themselves of assets so as to avoid 'paying for care', perhaps to pass on an inheritance.

A number of commentators have addressed potential conflicts of interest between adults of 'working age' and pensioners (Thane, 1989; Johnson *et al.*, 1989; Walker, 1990; Phillipson, 1991). From one standpoint elderly people are defined as a burden on society, draining financial resources from the state and from the younger generation which subsidises pensioners' income. Others emphasise the extent to which pensioners are 'productive' in that they perform substantial amounts of voluntary and unpaid work. They also vote. Some policy analysts affirm pensioners' rights and needs: other critics argue that inter-generational justice demands that individuals should be much more self-reliant in funding their own retirement pensions and making financial provision for the contingencies of old age. This viewpoint has made some political headway in the UK, as illustrated by the passage of the Social Security Act 1986.

As previously outlined, such people as do accumulate financial assets over a lifetime can potentially contribute towards the costs of chronic ill health in old age by using up capital, notably when property is sold to pay for care. Finch (1989, Chs 1 and 2) has outlined the traditional role played by inheritance in passing wealth down to the next generations. 'Paying for care' by realisation and, in some cases, exhaustion of capital raises smaller scale issues of 'inter-generational equity' around the circumstances under which property is appropriately 'used up' as opposed to being 'passed on'. To what extent will people become more fearful of the eventualities of living on into 'old' old age and anxious to make contingency plans?

This chapter has pointed up the need for both men and women to have access to good, unbiased financial and legal advice and 'pension education' so as to be aware of the possible strategies available to maximise income and financial resources for old age. That said, there will continue to be many people, especially women, who are not in a position to undertake substantial financial planning and others, more affluent, who may prefer to let 'old' old age take care of itself, since it may never come or life may end not in chronic illness but in a 'terminal drop' (Wilson, 1991). It could well be that the prohibitive costs of providing adequate individual funding against the risks of needing substantial care in 'old' old age may fuel enthusiasm for the development of new forms of collective insurance against such risks.

Acknowledgements

Dulcie Groves would like to thank Raphael Wittenberg (Department of Health), Peter Searle (DSS), Ann Netten (PSSRU, University of Kent), Mavis Maclean (Fellow, Wolfson College, University of Oxford) and the Commercial Union Life Assurance Company for advice, information and gift/loan of materials.

References

Allen, I., Hogg, D. and Peace, S. (1992) *Elderly People: Choice, Participation and Satisfaction*, Policy Studies Institute, London

Arber, S. and Ginn, J. (1991) *Gender and Later Life: A Sociological Analysis of Resources and Constraints*, Sage, London

Atkinson, A. B. and Sutherland, H. (eds.) *Tax Benefit Models*. Occasional Paper 10, Suntory-Toyota International Centre for Economics and Related Disciplines, London School of Economics, London

Baldwin, S., Parker, G. and Walker, R. (1988) *Social Security and Community Care*, Avebury, Aldershot

Benjamin, S. (1989) *Private funding of long-term care: an actuarial perspective*. Paper presented at 'Care of elderly people' conference organised by Laing and Bulsson and Health Care Information Services, and sponsored by Peat Marwick McLintock.

Bone, M., Gregory, J., Baljit, G. and Lader, D. (1992) *Retirement and Retirement Plans*, a survey carried out by Social Survey Division of OPCS on behalf of the Department of Social Security, HMSO, London

Bornat, J., Perera, C., Pilgrim, D. and Williams, F. (1993) *Community Care: a reader*, Macmillan, Open University, London

Bosanquet, N. and Propper, C. (1991) 'Charting the Gray Economy in the 1990s', *Policy and Politics*, 19:4, pp. 269–281

Carnegie UK Trust (1993) *Life, Work and Livelihood in the Third Age*, The Carnegie Inquiry into the Third Age: Final Report, Carnegie UK Trust, Dunfermline, Fife

Central Statistical Office (1993) *Social Trends 23*, HMSO, London

Central Statistical Office (1992) *Family Spending: a report on the 1991 Family Expenditure Survey*, HMSO, London

Commercial Union (1991) *Third Age Initiative: Well Being Insurance: Assuring your peace of mind*, Commercial Union Life Assurance, London

Corden, A. (1992) 'Setting fees in private homes: some reasons why they vary so much', pp. 22–28 in Morton, J. (ed.)

Davies, Bleddyn. (1988) 'Financing long-term social care', *Social Policy and Administration*, 22:2, pp. 97–114

Davies, Bryn and Ward, S., (1992) *Women and Personal Pensions*. Equal Opportunities Commission, Manchester.

Department of Health (1993) *Community Care Charges in April 1993*, leaflet, Department of Health, London

Department of Health (1989) *Caring for People: Community Care in the Next Decade and Beyond*, Cm 849, HMSO, London

Department of Health and Social Security (1985) *Green Paper: Reform of Social Security, Vol. 2, Programme for Change*, Cmnd. 9518, HMSO, London

Department of Health and Social Security (1984) *Population, Pension Costs and Pensioners' Incomes: a Background Paper for the Inquiry into Provision for Retirement*, HMSO, London

Department of Social Security (1993a) *Equality in State Pension Age*, Cm. 2420, HMSO, London.

Department of Social Security (1993b) *Pensioner Income Results 1979–89*, Tables 1, 6–8, personal communication, DSS, London

Department of Social Security (1992) *Social Security Statistics 1992*, HMSO, London

Drabble, R. (1977) *CPAG Rights Guide 3: Contributory Benefits*, HMSO, London

Eekelaar, J. and Pearl, D. (1989) *An Aging World: Dilemmas and Challenges for Law and Social Policy*, Clarenden Press, Oxford

Employment Gazette (1993) Vol.101:1

Equal Opportunities Commission (1992) *A Question of Fairness: Response by the EOC*, EOC, Manchester

Falkingham, J. and Victor, C. (1991) *The Myth of the Woopee? Incomes, the Elderly and Targeting Welfare*, Discussion Paper WSP/55, Suntory-Toyota International Centre for Economics and Related Disciplines, London School of Economics, London

Finch, J. (1989) *Family Obligations and Social Change*, Polity Press, Cambridge

Farrand, J. T. (1989) 'Enduring Powers of Attorney', pp. 637–49 in Eekelaar, J. and Pearl, D. (eds.)

Gibbs, I. (1992) 'A substantial but limited asset: the role of housing wealth in paying for residential care', pp. 35–42 in Morton, J. (ed.)

Glendinning, C. (1992) *The Costs of Informal Care: Looking inside the Household*, HMSO, London

Glendinning, C. and Millar, J. (1992) *Women and Poverty in Britain: the 1990s*, Harvester Wheatsheaf, London

Groves, D. (1993a) '*Onward, Spinsters, Onward!' The National Spinsters Pensions Association 1935–58*. Paper presented at the Centennial Suffrage Conference, Victoria University, Wellington, New Zealand, August 27–29

Groves, D. (1993b) 'Work, Poverty and Older Women' in Bernard, M. and Meade, K. (eds.) *Women Come of Age: Perspectives on the Lives of Older Women*, Edward Arnold, London

Groves, D. (1992) 'Occupational pensions and women's poverty in old age' in Glendinning, C. and Millar, J., *Women and Poverty in Britain: the 1990s*, Harvester Wheatsheaf, London

Groves, D. (1991) 'Women and financial provision for old age' in Maclean, M. and Groves, D. (eds.), *Women's Issues in Social Policy*, Routledge, London

Groves, D. (1983) 'Members and Survivors: women and retirement pensions legislation' in Lewis, J. (ed.), *Women's Welfare: Women's Rights*, Croom Helm, London

Hannah, L. (1986) *Inventing Retirement*, Cambridge University Press, Cambridge

Hoggett, B. (1989) 'The Elderly Mentally-Ill and Infirm: Procedures for Civil Commitment and Guardianship', pp. 517–29 in Eekelaar, J. and Pearl, D. (eds.)

Johnson, P. with Dilnot, A., Disney, R. and Whitehouse, E. (1992) *Income: Pensions, Earnings and Savings in the Third Age, Research Paper 2*, The Carnegie Inquiry into the Third Age, Carnegie UK Trust, Dunfermline, Fife

Johnson, P. and Falkingham, J. (1992) *Ageing and Economic Welfare*, Sage, London

Johnson, P., Conrad, C., and Thomson, D. (eds.) 1989) *Workers Versus Pensioners: Intergenerational Justice in an Ageing World*. Manchester University Press, Manchester.

Johnson, P. and Webb, S., (1990) *Poverty in Official Statistics: Two Reports*. Institute for Fiscal Studies, commentary no. 24, IFS, London.

Jones, T. (1993) *Britain's Ethnic Minorities*, Policy Studies Institute, London

Joseph Rowntree Foundation (1992) Social Policy Research Findings 31, November, 1992, Joseph Rowntree Foundation, York

Joshi, H. (ed.) (1989) *The Changing Population of Britain*, Basil Blackwell, Oxford.

Joshi, H. and Davies H. B. (1991) *The Pension Consequence of Divorce*, CEPR Discussion Paper 550

Keighley, J. (1992) 'Sex Discrimination and Private Insurance: should sex differences make a difference?', *Policy and Politics*, 20:2, pp. 99–110

Kestenbaum, A. (1993) *Taking Care in the Market: a study of agency homecare*, Independent Living Fund, Nottingham

Lewis, J. (ed.) (1983) *Women's Welfare, Women's Rights*, Croom Helm, London

Maclean, M. and Groves, D. (eds.) (1991) *Women's Issues in Social Policy*, Routledge, London.

Matthewman, J. (1992) *Tolley's Social Security and State Benefits 1992–3*, Tolley, Croydon, Surrey

McKay, S. (1992) *Pensioners' Assets*, Policy Studies Institute, London

Morton, J. (ed) (1992) *Financing Elderly People in Independent Sector Homes: the Future*, Age Concern Institute of Gerontology, King's College, London

Netten, A. (1994) *Unit Costs of Community Care 1994*, PSSRU, University of Kent, Canterbury

OPCS (1992) *General Household Survey 1990*, HMSO, London

Oldfield, S. (1984) *Spinsters of this Parish: the Life and Times of F.M. Mayor and Mary Sheepshanks*, Virago, London

Oldman, C. (1991) *Paying for Care: Personal Sources of Funding Care*, Joseph Rowntree Foundation, York

Oppenheim, C. (1993) *Poverty: the Facts*, Child Poverty Action Group, London

Phillipson, C. (1991) 'Inter-generational relations: conflict or consensus in the 21st century', *Policy and Politics*, 19:1, pp. 27–36.

Poynter, R. and Martin, C. (1992) *Rights Guide to Non-Means-Tested Benefits 1992/3*, 15th edition, Child Poverty Action Group, London

Rutherford, J. (1994) 'Keep it simple to avoid more costly pension mistakes' *The Guardian*, 3.1.1994, p. 10.

Spero, R. (1992) 'Long-Term Care', *Money Management Survey*, December 1992.

Thane, P. (1989) 'Old Age: Burden or Benefit?' in Joshi, H. (ed.) *The Changing Population of Britain*, Basil Blackwell, Oxford.

Trinder, C., Hulme, G. and McCarthy, U. (1992) *Employment: the Role of Work in the Third Age*, The Carnegie Inquiry into the Third Age, Carnegie UK Trust, Dunfermline, Scotland

Walker, A. (1993) 'Community care policy: from consensus to conflict', Ch.23 in Bornat, J., *Community Care: a Reader*, Macmillan/Open University Press, London

Walker, A. (1992) 'The poor relation: poverty among older women', in Glendinning, C., *Women and Poverty in Britain: the 1990s*, Harvester Wheatsheaf and Millar, J. (eds.), London

Walker, A. (1990) 'The Economic "Burden" of Ageing and the Prospect of Intergenerational Conflict', *Ageing and Society 10*, pp. 377–396

Walker, R., Hardman, G. and Hutton, S. (1989) 'The Occupational Pension Trap: Towards a Preliminary Empirical Specification', *Journal of Social Policy*, 18:4, pp. 575–93

Walker, R. with Hardman, G. (1988) 'The Financial Resources of the Elderly or Paying Your Own Way in Old Age' in Baldwin, S., Parker, G. and Walker, R. (eds.), *Social Security and Community Care*, Avebury, Aldershot

Ward, S. (1990) *The Essential Guide to Pensions: A Worker's Handbook*, 3rd edition, Pluto Press, London

Weir, P. (1992) 'Paying for care: the adequacy of current and future pensioners' incomes' in Morton, J. (ed.)

Whitaker's (1993) *Whitaker's Almanac*, 125th edition, Whitaker, London

Wilson, G. (1991) 'Models of ageing and their relation to policy formation and service provision', *Policy and Politics*, 19:1, pp. 37–47

Wittenberg, R. (1989) *Prototype Insurance Policy for Long Term Care*, Government Service Working Paper 105, Department of Health, London

Chapter 8
HOUSING EQUITY RELEASE AND INHERITANCE

CHRIS HAMNETT

Introduction: a nation of inheritors?

Inheritance has long been the principal mechanism by which wealth is transmitted from one generation to another, and many of Trollope or Galsworthy's novels display a concern with inheritance. But, given the marked concentration of wealth in Britain until the post war period, significant inheritance was limited to a relatively small number of wealthy people. The rise of home ownership has both widened the distribution of wealth and fostered the view that housing inheritance is of growing importance.

The late 1980s saw a surge of interest in housing wealth and inheritance in Britain. There has been a rapid expansion of home ownership post war and rising levels of home ownership among the over 65's in conjunction with rapid house price inflation during the 1970's and 1980's. It has been suggested that Britain was about to become a nation of house inheritors as older home owners began to die in large numbers and leave their homes to their children or other beneficiaries. As one research report commented:

> *The higher ownership rate for the over 65's, approaching one half, means that inheritance, which until recently affected a minority of the population is becoming increasingly common. A large proportion of the population, and particularly existing property owners, will inherit previously owner occupied property which they will be at liberty to sell. (Morgan Grenfell, 1987, p. 13).*

The flows of money involved were said to be substantial and Morgan Grenfell (1987) suggested that they;

> *could be equivalent to as much as 3 per cent of household disposable income, larger than the PSBR and almost as large as the personal sectors' entire net financial surplus (p. 13).*

The Morgan Grenfell report led to considerable interest in the financial services industry about the possible destinations of sale proceeds and the implications for financial investment. The house building industry were interested in the implications for the growth of home ownership and moves up market. There was also some interest from politicians and commentators, who anticipated the coming of Anthony Eden's 'property-owning democracy'.

Thus, Professor Peter Saunders (1986) declared that:

> *With 60 per cent of households now in the owner occupied sector in Britain ... not only is a majority of the population now in a position to accumulate such capital gains as may accrue through the housing market, but for the*

first time in human history, we are approaching the point where millions of working people stand at some time in their lives to inherit capital sums far in excess of anything they could hope to save through earnings from employment.

Brian Walden (1986) wrote in the Sunday Times that:

For the first time a large number of people are going to get their hands on valuable property. It is difficult not to overstress the importance of this change both socially and politically.

The Economist (1988) argues in an editorial 'Growing Rich Again' that:

Britain's middle classes, so long demoralised and impoverished (sic), are about to grow rich again. Two main mechanisms are changing the way money is distributed in Britain. One is inheritance; the other is tax reform. The generation of Britons now reaching retirement age was the first to put a big proportion of its savings into home ownership. Houses have proved a wonderful investment and those pensioners, often caricatured as poor, are really growing rich, but their riches are tied up in the roofs over their heads. Only when they die, bequeathing their property to their children, can this most popular form of British investment be cashed in. So the bequest, a staple of Victorian melodrama, is about to make a come-back.

Finally, Nigel Lawson, then Chancellor of the Exchequer, argued that:

We are about to become a nation of inheritors. Inheritance, which used to be the preserve of the few, will become a fact of life for the many. People will be inheriting houses, and stocks and shares.

These are radical statements which suggest that we are about to enter a brave new world of mass inheritance. If they are part true they could have major implications for the distribution of household wealth in the future. Thus Morgan Grenfell (1987) suggested that:

Higher household wealth from first generation property inheritance will ultimately result in a larger inheritance of financial and physical assets bequeathed to successive generations. As such, it may be appropriate to term this process as one of 'familial accumulation' (p. 20).

But while these views have become the conventional wisdom on housing inheritance, they have overlooked a number of other significant trends which are serving to reduce both the amount of property available for inheritance and the value of some property inheritances. In particular, little attention has been paid to the role of equity extraction from the owner occupied housing market prior to death and its impact on housing inheritance. Equity extraction can take a number of different forms including extraction on moving house, sales to pay for residential care or to buy annuities or raise capital. The importance of these forms of equity extraction lies in the fact that, at any point in time, the amount of equity tied up in housing is fixed. It can either be transmitted via inheritance or extracted prior to death, but not both. Put simply, the greater the level of equity extraction, the less the amount available for inheritance. The more of one, the less of the other.

The structure of the chapter is as follows. First it looks at the growth of home ownership and house price inflation, and the age structure of home owners. Second, it looks at predictions of the future scale of housing inheritance and third it examines Inland Revenue figures on the scale and value of housing inheritance over the last 20 years. Fourth, it looks at the importance of forms of equity extraction, particularly the growth of residential care for elderly, and finally it assesses the future of housing inheritance.

Home ownership and housing wealth in Britain

The 1970s and 1980s were a period in which housing wealth became much more important in Britain. There are two main reasons. First, Britain witnessed a very rapid expansion of home ownership post-war. In 1951 3.9 million households (31 per cent) owned their own home. By 1991 this had risen to 15.5 million and 67 per cent of households. Not only has the proportion of owners more than doubled, but the absolute number of home owners has risen fourfold. It is not too much of an exaggeration to say that the last 40 years have seen the transformation of Britain from a nation of tenants into a nation of home owners.

In addition, the 1970s and 1980s saw three major periods of house price inflation. National average house prices rose from £5,000 in 1969 to £60,000 in 1989 according to the Building Societies Association (1992). This represents an increase of 1,100 per cent at current prices and about 2.5 times in real terms (Holmans, 1990). As a result of these trends housing now accounts for a much larger share of personal net wealth than it did in the early post-war years. The Royal Commission on the Distribution of Income and Wealth (1977) estimated that in 1960 housing accounted for 17 per cent of net personal wealth. By 1975 this had risen to 35 per cent and by 1988 it had risen to over half (52 per cent) (Inland Revenue, 1990). This proportion will now have fallen back as a result of the marked house price falls in the early 1990s, but it will not significantly erode the gains of the previous 30 years.

As the relative importance of housing in personal wealth has grown, and the importance of other, more unequally distributed, assets has declined, there has been a small, but significant, redistribution of wealth away from the top 10 per cent of wealth holders towards the next 40 per cent. The share of the top 1 per cent of wealth holders fell from 55 per cent in 1938 to 31 per cent in 1971 and 17 per cent in 1988. The share of the top 10 per cent of wealth holders fell from 85 per cent in 1938 to 65 per cent in 1971 and 52 per cent in 1988. The share of the bottom 50 per cent rose considerably (from 3 per cent in 1966 to 10 per cent in 1986) before falling back to 6 per cent in 1988 (see Table 1). These changes are not solely the result of the expansion of home ownership but there is a strong argument that the combination of wider home ownership, which is particularly important in the middle wealth owning bands, from £25–100,000, and house price inflation from 1971 onwards has helped to reduce the degree of wealth inequality in Britain (Atkinson, 1989).

Home ownership and age

The impact of these changes has varied by age group. The rapid growth of home ownership in the 1950s and 1960s was primarily concentrated among the 25 to

TABLE 1
Distribution of wealth in England and Wales, 1923–88

	Top 1%	Top 5%	Top 10%	Top 20%	Top 50%
1923	61	82	89	94	nd
1938	55	77	85	91	nd
1950	47	74	nd	nd	nd
1960	34	59	71	83	nd
1970	30	54	69	84	97
1980	23	42	59	79	94
1985	20	40	54	73*	93
1988	17	38	53	75*	94

Source: Figures for 1923–1980; Atkinson *et al.* (1989); figures for 1985 and top 50 per cent from Social Trends, CSO.

45 age groups: the prime house buying age groups. In 1960 approximately 42 per cent of household heads aged 25–40 were home owners compared to 25 per cent of the over 65s. This reflects the fact that home ownership was much less common in the interwar years when the older generation entered the housing market. Older householders are much more likely to be renters than owners. But, as ownership rates increase and younger age cohorts age, so the home ownership rate among older people has risen. GHS data shows that the ownership rate among the 65 and over age group has risen from 44 per cent in 1975 to 54 per cent in 1990, and irrespective of whether home ownership rises further it should rise to over 60 per cent by 2000 as existing home owners age.

As a result, housing wealth is now quite widespread in the 65+ age group. Data from the English House Condition Survey (Leather, 1990) shows that more than 80 per cent of owner occupied households headed by a person aged between 65 and 74 years, and nearly 70 per cent of those headed by a person aged 75 years or older, had equity worth at least £25,000 in 1986. Average levels of equity were higher than this, and almost all households had equity of more than £10,000. These figures will be higher today as a result of house price inflation (McKay, 1992). The impact of these trends led to a growing belief in the 1980s that housing inheritance could potentially be of considerable significance in Britain. As Morgan Grenfell (1987) observed:

> *The effect of increased property ownership in the 25–40 age group during the fifties and sixties is now being reflected in high owner occupation rates for the retired population. Half of heads of households in the UK over 65 years of age are now owner-occupiers; this is likely to approach two-thirds by 2000. As a result there will be a majority of households over the coming years. (Morgan Grenfell, 1987;8)*

Projections of the future scale of housing inheritance

Two projections of the scale of housing inheritance flows have been undertaken. Both involve indirect estimation of the number of dying home owners each year. Current age specific death rates are applied to home ownership rates by age

TABLE 2
Property transfer and release, 1986–2031 (000's)

	Properties transferred	Properties released pa	Transfers (av) pa	Release (av)
1986–91	1723	841	344	168
1991–96	1892	938	379	188
1996–2001	2062	1036	412	207
2001–2006	2244	1134	449	227
2006–2011	2420	1230	485	246
2011–2016	2612	1343	523	269
2016–2012	2816	1455	563	291
2021–2026	3032	1588	606	318
2026–2031	3217	1715	643	343

Source: Hamnett, Harmer and Williams (1991).

group. The estimates are then reduced to allow for the proportion of two person households in the age group where the survivor assumes ownership and continues to live in the property. This yields a figure of the number of finally dissolving owner occupied households and hence of the number of inherited properties. These figures are multiplied by estimated average house prices to estimate figures for the future value of housing inheritance. Both projections assume that the number of housing inheritances is a direct function of the level of home ownership among the dying population. Possible countervailing factors were not taken into account in the projections.

The Morgan Grenfell (1987) projection of housing inheritances was methodologically imprecise, but estimated a total of 155,000 properties available for inheritance in 1986 rising to 160,000 per annum by 1990, 178,000 by 1995 and 202,000 by the year 2000. I shall not discuss their estimates of housing inheritance values as these are largely dependent on the level of house prices which, as the experience of the early 1990s has shown, are notoriously fickle.

The second projection (Hamnett, Harmer and Williams, 1991) was more detailed and explicit about the methodology but arrived at similar figures. We projected a figure of 168,000 finally dissolving owner occupied households per annum in the 5 year period 1986–91, rising to 188,000 in 1991–6, 207,000 in 1996–2001, 227,000 in 2001–6 and 343,000 by 2026–31. This is double the current level, and given that there are three main beneficiaries per estate on average, this suggests that about 2 per cent of the adult population and 4 per cent of households could benefit from housing inheritance every year within 40 years other things being equal (Table 2).

The projections support the views advanced by those who suggest that Britain is becoming a nation of inheritors. But the validity of their assumptions and some of these are very questionable, particularly the view that house inheritance is a direct, unmediated, outcome of home ownership rates of the dying population. It will be argued that there are strong reasons for thinking that projected increases will not occur, and that much of the equity tied up in housing will leak out prior to death. The number of cases of house inheritance is likely to remain stable at current levels and may even fall. Britain is unlikely to become a nation of inheritors, now or in the future. The first step in the argument is to look at the published Inland Revenue statistics on the scale and value of housing inheritance.

The Inland Revenues statistics on estates passing at death

The Inland Revenue have, for many years, produced annual figures on the number, value and asset composition of 'estates passing at death'. Since 1968/9 the Inland Revenue Statistics (IRS) figures have included figures on UK residential property as a separate category. This information is collected for the purposes of taxation rather than analysis of inheritance, and the figures are based on a stratified sample of applications by executors for grants of representation or probate for deceased persons estates. This source has advantages and disadvantages. On the positive side, it is consistent and comprehensive in terms of the categories it collects data for. As estates of over a certain minimum value require a grant of representation, a grant of probate or letters of administration before they can be legally administered or distributed to beneficiaries, evasion is limited and the figures are comprehensive. No probate, no inheritance.

The value of estates may be depressed by the transfer of assets prior to death to avoid inheritance tax, but this is more likely to result in a reduction in the value of assets rather than failure to enter the statistics at all. The cuts in inheritance taxation rates and the increase in thresholds in recent years have reduced the incentives to avoid inheritance tax for all but a minority of wealthy individuals and few estates escape the Inland Revenue net. From 1977 to March 1980, inheritance tax began at £25,000 at a rate of 10 per cent. It then rose progressively on slices of the estate to 75 per cent tax over £2.01 million. In 1980 minimum thresholds were raised to £50,000 with a 25 per cent rate of tax, and in 1984, the top rate of tax was cut to 60 per cent on values over £258,000. This system remained stable until 1989 when the graduated system was replaced with a flat rate of tax of 40 per cent over £110,000. This was subsequently raised to the current threshold of £150,000. As a result, the proportion of recorded estates liable for tax has fallen from 11.1 per cent in 1985–6 to 8.5 per cent in 1988–9 and the amount raised by tax has remained stable at about £1 billion per year. This is only a tiny proportion (6 per cent) of the total value of estates. This interpretation is supported by Inland Revenue data on discretionary trusts which wealthy individuals establish in order to avoid inheritance tax. Accounts for these are provided to the Inland Revenue on the 10 year anniversary of the foundation of the trust and they show the number of trusts has fallen from a peak of 686 in 1983–4 to 323 in 1989–90. This suggests that few individuals are using trusts to avoid inheritance tax.

The problems with the Inland Revenue statistics concern exclusions not avoidance. There are two major exclusions from the Inland Revenue statistics. *First*, joint property passing between spouses is exempt from tax and a formal account is not always submitted for property which is exempt. *Second*, orders made the Administration of Estates (Small Payments) Act 1965 permits small estates containing certain assets up to a value of £1,500 (raised in 1984 to £5,000) to be dealt with without production of a grant. As many people, particularly tenants, have little in the way of assets, these two exclusions together

168

account for the fact that the Inland Revenue statistics on 'estates passing at death' average about 270,000 per annum or only 40 per cent of the 660,000 deaths a year.

This may seem a significant omission, but as the excluded estates are either (a) small estates with assets under £5,000 or, (b) where joint property passes between spouses, the exclusions are unlikely to have a significant effect on housing as they do not involve any significant inter-generational transfer of assets. As the IRS (1991) notes:

> *The main assets which can be transferred without a grant of representation are National Savings, cash, some bank and building society accounts, consumer durables and insurance policies. Between 1976 and 10th May 1984, the amounts in any individual asset could not exceed £1,500 and, in practice, the estate would rarely exceed £10,000; for deaths on or after 11 May 1984, the upper limit per asset has been £5,000 with few estates above £25,000 administered under these provisions. An excluded estate can therefore include a dwelling only if it is owned jointly in such a way that the deceased's share passes automatically to the surviving joint owner* (p. 100).

As it is now more common for property, particularly house property, to be owned jointly by a husband and wife rather than just by the husband, it is likely that there are now more excluded estates involving house property than there were 20 or 30 years ago. This will delay but not eliminate entry of property into recorded statistics as surviving joint owners eventually die. The next section examines the evidence from the Inland Revenue statistics.

Inland Revenue data on the scale of housing inheritance

The prophets of an 'inheritance economy' suggest that the scale of housing inheritance is likely to grow rapidly in the future. And, because home ownership and the proportion of older home owners has been growing rapidly since the 1950s, there is an implication that the scale of housing inheritance should have increased over the last 20 years. But Inland Revenue statistics show no evidence for a long term increase in the number of 'estates passing at death' including housing. On the contrary, the number of estates containing house property has been broadly stable through the 1970s and 1980s at around 15,000 per annum (Table 3). These figures include estates with privately rented as well as owner-occupied property, but the proportion of privately rented property is now very small and almost all landlords will be home owners. The existence of private rented property in estates is thus very unlikely to increase the number of estates containing house property although it will increase the value of house property in estates by around 10 per cent.

The figures were lower in 1968–69 (the first year for which data was available) and 1987–88. In both years there were 125,000 estates with UK house property (Table 3). In 1988–89 there were 140,561 estates with house property: a rise of just 12 per cent over 20 years. Excluding 1968–69 on grounds of its atypicality, there has been *no increase* in numbers of recorded estates containing

TABLE 3
The number and value of estates passing at death

	No of estates with UK dwellings	Total No. estates	% of total	Value of housing (£m)	Total value (£m)	%
1068–69	125,085	271,238	46.1	465	1,923	24.2
1969–70	149,592	287,239	52.1	501	1.948	25.7
1970–71	142,473	267,718	53.2	530	1.967	26.9
1971–72	149,052	288,796	51.6	638	2,275	28.0
1980–81	143,343	294,841	48.6	3,057	6,883	44.4
1981–82	147,894	295,236	50.1	3,280	7,628	43.0
1982–83	143,980	288,199	50.0	3,383	8,211	41.2
1983–84	148,800	296,890	50.1	3,683	9,195	40.0
1984–85	147,717	273,762	53.9	4,163	10,372	40.1
1985–86	137,486	245,071	56.1	4,567	11,482	39.8
1986–87	149,265	270,947	55.1	5,398	12,738	42.2
1987–88	125,532	234,688	53.5	6,020	14,310	42.1
1988–89	140,561	249,233	56.4	8,439	17,320	48.7

Source: Inland Revenue Statistics, various years.

house property although the proportion of estates containing house property rose from 46 per cent in 1968–69 to 53 per cent in 1987–88 and 56 per cent in 1988–89. On the basis of these figures Britain has shown no signs of becoming a nation of inheritors over the last 20 years.

The stability in the number of estates containing house property raise two major questions. *First,* are the Inland Revenue recording all estates containing house property which require a grant of representation? The answer is yes because, as we have seen, only estates containing certain assets worth under £5,000 are exempt from the statistics and they exclude housing unless jointly owned (IRS, 1991).

Second, given that the Inland Revenue figures include all estates with house property where it does not pass to the surviving spouse, why has there been no increase in the number of recorded estates containing house property given the rapid growth of home ownership postwar? This question is taken up later in the chapter. First it is important to look at the extent to which transfers to spouses reduce the number of houses available for intergenerational inheritance.

Housing inheritance and spouse beneficiaries

The figures in Table 3 include all estates containing house property. But some of these will pass to surviving spouses even though they do not own the property jointly. It is thus important to exclude these properties as they are not available for inheritance as commonly defined. The published Inland Revenue data on assets by sex, age and marital status does not identify house property as a separate category. It does however, identify a category of 'net land and buildings' which can be taken as broadly comparable and used as a surrogate.

170

In 1986–87 there were 149,265 estates which contained house property worth a total of £5.4 bn. The 'net land and buildings' category contains 154,049 estates worth £5.61 bn. The differences between the two sets of figures are largely accounted for by the value of land. The match between the figures for other years is also very similar.

The Inland Revenue identify 62,218 estates containing land and buildings (40.4 per cent of the total) which belonged to married persons. Of these some 50,335 belonged to married males (59 per cent of male estates) and 11,883 belonged to married females (17 per cent of female estates). The discrepancy between males and females is simply a result of the fact that men tend to die before women. It therefore appears that about 40 per cent of estates containing house property are inherited by spouses even though they are not joint owners. The number of estates containing house property which are available for inheritance to non-spouses should therefore be reduced by about 40 per cent. In 1986–87 this reduces the 140,561 estates to 84,500: far fewer than commonly supposed. In 1988–89 there were 57,637 married persons' estates (41 per cent of the total). The total of other estates was 82,900.

The value of housing inheritance in Britain

The total value of estates passing at death in Britain has risen rapidly from £1.9 bn in 1968–69 to £17.3 bn in 1988–89: an increase of 810 per cent at current prices. But the value of housing inheritance rose far more dramatically from £465m to £8.44 bn: an increase of 1,715 per cent: double the increase in the value of total inheritance (Table 3).

The increase in non-housing inheritance was from £1.458 bn to £8.881 bn an increase of only 509 per cent. The value of housing assets in estates rose by 3.4 times the value of non-housing assets. It is clear that the increase in the value of inheritance over the last 20 years owes a great deal to the increase in the value of housing assets. It is also clear that as the number of estates containing housing has not risen since 1968–69, growth in the value of housing inheritance was entirely the result of house price inflation. This has important implications for the future value of housing inheritance and inheritance in general. The fall in average house prices from 1989 to 1993 will be reflected in a sharp decline in the value of house inheritance.

The average value of residential property in estates passing at death was £60,000. Dividing these figures by the average number of 3 beneficiaries per estate suggests that beneficiaries of estates containing house property inherited £20,000 of house property on average. But the averages are misleading because the value of house property in estates is highly negatively skewed. In other words, there are many estates with a small property component and a few estates with a very large property element. This said, the distribution of property assets in estates is far less unequal than in the case of many other assets.

The value of house property passing to spouses

The value of land and buildings in the estates of married persons in 1988–89 was £3.66 bn, of which the lion's share (£3 bn) was from married males compared

TABLE 4
The distribution of housing inheritance by class

	A	B	C1	C2	D	E	Total
Inheritors(N)	84	342	356	323	145	76	1,326
% distribution	6	26	27	24	11	6	100
Total sample	323	1415	2306	3134	2005	1461	10,644
% incidence	26	24	15	10	7	5	12

Source: NOP Survey for Hamnett and Williams, 1990.

to £660m from married females. Land and building belonging to married persons comprised 41.5 per cent of the total value of land and buildings. The value of house property in inheritance to non-spouses in 1988–89 was approximately £5 bn. This is far less than generally assumed.

A nation of inheritors? Who inherits house property

Peter Saunders (1986) suggested that millions of working people will inherit property. Other commentators have been less sanguine. Both Morgan Grenfell (1987) and the Economist suggested that housing inheritance would tend to accrue to existing home owners, particularly to the middle classes. Evidence from two large national surveys of beneficiaries carried out in 1989 and 1991 (Hamnett, 1991; Hamnett, Harmer and Williams, 1991) show that the great majority (about 80 per cent) of beneficiaries have, in fact, been existing home owners. They also show that, while the majority of beneficiaries are in the intermediate and junior non-manual and skilled manual occupational groups, the incidence of inheritance is far higher among the professional and managerial socio-economic groups than it is amongst other groups (Table 4). Hamnett (1991) has shown this is a result of the parental class and tenure backgrounds of beneficiaries rather than beneficiary characteristics. The current distribution of housing inheritances reflects the characteristics of home owners a generation ago when home ownership was much more restricted to the middle classes than it is today. It can be argued as a corollary to this, that the distribution of housing inheritance will widen considerably over the course of the next 20–30 years as the current generation of home owners leaves property to their beneficiaries.

Why has the scale of housing inheritance not increased?

It has been shown that, to date, Britain has *not* become a nation of housing inheritors. Although the value of house inheritance has risen sharply, this is a result of house price inflation, and the number of housing inheritances recorded by the Inland Revenue has remained stable for 20 years. In addition, about 40 per cent of houses entering into the Inland Revenue statistics pass to spouses and are not available for intergenerational inheritance until the death of the surviving spouse. This does not disprove the argument that Britain is becoming a nation of inheritors, but it certainly raises some crucial questions about why the scale of housing inheritance has not risen, and why the current level of housing inheritance is significantly below the level predicted on the basis of home ownership levels among the dying population.

There are a number of possible reasons why the number of estates containing house property has not increased over the last 20 years. Taking these in order, they are:

1   The Inland Revenue statistics are under-recording the true number of housing inheritances occurring. It has been shown that this is extremely unlikely as estates with a value of over £5,000 require a grant of representation or grant of probate by the executors before the proceeds are able to be released. No probate, no proceeds.

2   The number of estates passing at death containing house property has been reduced by tax avoidance measures such as gifting property 7 years prior to death or establishing trusts. It has been argued that while this is likely to occur for those individuals with large estates, it is unlikely to occur on a significant scale for two reasons. First, increases in the inheritance tax thresholds and the introduction of a flat rate of 40 per cent for estates with a total value of over £150,000, mean that the great majority of estates (over 90 per cent) are not liable for tax and the proportion of estates liable for tax has never exceeded 15 per cent. Second, the growth of home ownership has been in the middle range of estates and is unlikely to significantly increase tax avoidance.

3   Changes in the gender relations of home ownership, and a diminution in the number of sole male owners has led to an increase in the proportion of jointly owned properties passing automatically to the surviving spouse has reduced the number of properties entering into house inheritance statistics. This is extremely likely, but is difficult to quantify and will only delay the release of property till the death of the surviving joint owner. The time lag is unlikely to be more than 10–15 years at the very most.

4   The great expansion of home ownership in the post-war period has not yet percolated down into inheritance.

This is certainly true. There was little or no growth of home ownership between 1939 and the early 1950s, and the majority of new postwar home owners are still alive. A man who bought a house in 1957 aged 30 will only be 67 in 1994. This is taken into account in the projections, and it does suggest that, in the absence of other factors, the number of housing inheritances will increase very rapidly in the next 30 years as the home owners who bought in the 1950s, 60s and 70s gradually die off. But home ownership has been rising rapidly since the 1950s, and it is expected that the growing number of older home owners would have begun to percolate through into inheritance statistics (Table 5).

Why growth in the scale of housing inheritance is unlikely

None of the reasons considered above adequately explain the stability in the number of housing inheritances over the last 20 years. To do so three other

TABLE 5
Home ownership by age, 1984, 1990

	% outright owners	% mortgage owners %	% 1984 owners	% 2001 level 2001
Under 25	1	27	28	34
25–29	2	55	57	63
30–34	7	64	71	75
45–59	23	43	66	72
60–64	43	13	56	66
65–69	46	3	49	56
70–79	46	2	48	50
80 plus	45	1	46	48

Source: 1984 GHS.

factors need to be taken into account. These factors also suggest that levels of housing inheritance in the future may be far less than the simple projections would indicate.

1   Home owners are extracting more equity in life through moving, remortgaging, further advances etc.

2   A growing number of elderly owners may be passing on their houses to their children prior to death in order to avoid paying for residential or nursing home care.

3   A growing number of elderly home owners are using the capital from their house, either to pay for residential care or to increase income as part of an equity release scheme. These factors are considered in detail below.

Equity extraction from the home ownership market

Equity extraction from the housing market has occurred at death for generations. Davis and Saville (1982) comment that 'this is inevitable; every chain in the second hand housing market has an end; the final house comes onto the market because its owner occupier has died, or ceased to own his own house for other reasons, or because it is put on the market by its landlord after the tenant has left' (p. 395).

But during the early 1980s concern first surfaced that an increasing number of home owners were using the greater availability of mortgage finance to prematurely extract equity via moves and remortgages during life rather than on death. This, it was argued, was increasing consumer spending power and leading to an increase in inflation. The most definitive work on equity extraction by owners has been done by Holmans (1986, 1991). His comprehensive second study covering the period 1970–1990 is used here. He distinguishes four separate categories of withdrawal. These are: (1) last time sales where the seller does not use the proceeds to buy another house, (2) trading down by moving owners to a smaller house or cheaper area, (3) moves involving a larger mortgage

174

than necessary to buy the new house, and (4) borrowing on the security of a house without purchase, sale or move.

The *first* category of 'last-time sellers' includes sales by beneficiaries or executors, sales by (or on behalf of) home owners who have gone into residential care or moved in with relatives, sales by emigrants, sales by divorced couples who do not buy other houses or flats, and sales by couples where both previously owned homes. Holmans notes that : 'a defining characteristic of this form of equity withdrawal is that it takes place through sales of houses, so that the amount is likely to vary strongly with the volume of sales and purchases' (p. 3).

The *second* category, of 'trading down' by moving owner occupiers is self-explanatory and involves buying a house for less than the sum received for the house being sold. Mortgage finance is not always necessary for such moves. The *third* category, which Holmans terms 'over-mortgaging' involves taking out a larger mortgage than is required if all the proceeds from the sale of the previous home were used to help finance the purchase. Holmans notes that the defining characteristic of this type of equity extraction are that: 'it can only take place in the course of a move of house in which the previous residence is sold and a fresh one is bought; and . . . it requires mortgage finance'. The *fourth* category, borrowing on the securing of a house without a purchase, sale or move taking place is termed 'further advances, remortgages' by Holmans (1991) and can involve a further advance on an existing house, replacing existing mortgages by new and larger ones, or raising a fresh loan alongside an existing one or on an unmortgaged house. The crucial distinction, according to Holmans, is that whereas the first three categories depend on the purchase and sale of dwellings and are related to house prices and volume of transactions, the final category is independent of the volume of sales. It should be noted that, owing to the paucity of statistics, it is estimated as a residual with all the consequent problems of measurement error.

The four categories of housing equity withdrawal (HEW) identified by Holmans comprise total *gross* housing equity withdrawal. *Net* housing equity withdrawal comprises gross HEW net of injections of equity which add to the value of the owner occupied housing stock without a corresponding increase in debt secured on it or reduce the indebtedness secured on the stock.

What do his findings show? The *first* point is that *net* housing equity withdrawal has tended to be cyclical with peaks at the peak of each housing market boom but with a rising long term trend. Thus net HEW (which was negative in 1970) rose to £163 million in current prices 1971 and £608 million in 1972 before falling back to £174 million in 1973 and -£37 million in 1974. It then rose steadily from 1975 to 1977, reaching a peak of £1.1 billion in 1978 and falling back in 1979 and 1980. It then began to grow rapidly, particularly in 1982 when it rose to £4 bn rising to a peak of £16.2 bn in 1988 and falling back to £11 bn in 1989 and 1990.

The *second* point to note is that housing equity withdrawal really began to expand in 1982 when the banks entered the mortgage market in a major way and mortgage rationing was replaced by lender competition. Measured in current prices, net equity withdrawal had its biggest proportionate rise between 1980 and 1982 when it rose tenfold from £407m to £4,039m. Although the absolute increase was much greater in later years, the proportionate rise was much smaller. The *third* point to note is that equity extraction has not completely dried up since the housing market slump. It has merely fallen back in real terms to the level prevailing in 1986–7 before the peak of the boom. Holmans attributes this partly to the fact that the scale of housing equity extraction by last time sellers and owners trading down is partly related to the overall level of home ownership and higher house prices as well as market conditions.

The *fourth*, and most important, point is that there has been a very marked shift in the internal composition of equity extraction during the twenty year period 1970–1990. The proportion of gross equity accounted for by elderly last time sellers fell from 52 per cent in 1970 to 42 per cent in 1979, to 30 per cent in 1985 and an all time low of 21 per cent in 1990. This may be an anomaly, but even excluding 1990, the proportion has fallen to under 30 per cent in the late 1980s. The proportion of gross HEW accounted for by other last time sellers has been more variable, but it shows a secular decline from an average of about 18 per cent between 1970 and 1981 to between 10 and 15 per cent, with a downward trend to 10 per cent, in the 1980s. Taken together, the importance of last time sellers in HEW has fallen from around 67 per cent in 1970 to 1973 to 40 per cent in the late 1980s and 30 per cent in 1990. The importance of trading down has also fallen consistently, but from only 6 per cent to about 2.5 per cent.

As these three 'traditional' forms of HEW have declined in importance, so the importance of over-mortgaging and remortgaging has grown in importance. The importance of over mortgaging can be seen to be highly cyclical, with a peak in each of the three housing booms. It rose from 15 per cent in 1970 to 32 per cent in 1972, before falling once again to 19 per cent in 1973 and 13 per cent in 1974. It then rose through the 1980s from 20 per cent in 1979 and 1980, to a peak of 41 per cent in 1988. This form of HEW thus appears to be very strongly correlated with housing booms. It is important to stress that although the absolute value of last time sales has risen greatly over the 20 year period, its proportionate share of total equity extraction has fallen as other forms have grown in importance. Although the late 1980s may be seen as an exceptional period in the ownership market, marked by the rapid growth of 'non-traditional' forms of equity extraction consequent on the growth of mortgage finance, the overall level of equity extraction has grown rapidly over the last twenty years. This will reduce the housing equity available for inheritance in the future.

Equity extraction by elderly home owners

In the past elderly home owners had little option but to leave their property to beneficiaries. This is no longer true. The last 10 years have seen the rapid expansion of private residential care for the elderly and of a variety of equity extraction schemes which enable elderly owners to exchange housing equity for income. There was a marked increase in both the number and variety of equity release schemes on offer to elderly home owners during the 1980s and in the number of elderly home owners taking up such schemes. The main types of scheme are mortgage annuities, investment bonds, rolled up interest loans and reversions. The characteristics of these schemes and the value of the equity involved are noted by Mullings and Hamnett (1992). It is impossible to estimate the number of elderly home owners taking out investment bond schemes as no records are kept. This type of scheme mushroomed rapidly in the late 1980s but collapsed spectacularly in the late 1980s as interest rates rose. They are now effectively banned, but it is suggested that up to 20,000 owners are affected.

Estimates by Mullings and Hamnett (1992) suggest that, excluding investment bond schemes, the number of equity release transactions rose slowly from some 660 per annum in 1980 to 1,800 in 1985. The number then rose to 12,700 in 1989 largely as a result of a massive increase in interest roll-up schemes. The number of such transactions then collapsed dramatically in 1990 as a result of very high interest rates. The number of transactions in 1990 fell back to 4,900. This is not a large number and very few of these transactions involved the extraction of all the equity in a house.

Latent demand may be strong for equity extraction schemes but it is difficult to predict the likely number of equity extraction transactions in the future, given the turmoil in the home ownership market in Britain. Confidence in the home equity extraction market has been badly damaged in the last few years, and may take many years to return. We estimate that the number of equity extraction schemes is unlikely to increase significantly until the mid 1990s and it may double by the end of the decade to 10,000 per annum. This is not large, but it will depress growth of housing inheritance in the future.

The growth of private residential care for the elderly

The number of elderly persons in residential care in England and Wales has risen dramatically in recent years: from 143,000 in 1975 to 232,000 in 1988. All the increase has taken place in private residential care. The numbers of elderly persons in this sector increased from 19,000 in 1975 to 30,000 in 1980 and 102,000 in 1988. From 1980 to 1988 the number of persons in private homes rose 242 per cent, and from 1970 to 1988 the increase was over 450 per cent.

The number in local authority homes fell slightly from 110,000 in 1980 to 104,000 in 1988 and are likely to fall further as cash limited local authorities dispose of their homes to the private sector. The number of elderly persons in voluntary sector homes remained stable at some 26,000. The number of private nursing home places in the UK also increased rapidly from 37,000 in 1986 to 129,000 in 1991. Taking the UK as a whole, Laing and Buisson estimate the number of private residential and nursing home places in 1991 was 296,400 compared to 54,000 voluntary places and 120,000 local authority places. The 1980s have, in effect, been characterised by privatisation of residential care for the elderly. This care has to be paid for and it eats into housing equity (Hamnett and Mullings, 1992).

As has been noted in previous chapters, private residential care is expensive. Laing and Buisson estimate that in 1991 average weekly nursing home fees ranged from £272 in Northern England to £350 in the Home Counties and £434 in Greater London. The national average is about £300. Residential home fees are somewhat less but averaged about £250 pw. Costs have risen rapidly as a result of the high labour inputs and interest servicing. Given that 54 per cent of retired single persons (the group most likely to enter care) in the UK in 1990 had a gross weekly income of under £80, 69 per cent under £100 and 85 per cent under £150 it is very clear that the overwhelming majority of elderly persons cannot afford private care out of income. Laing and Buisson estimate that only

15 per cent of elderly people are able to pay for residential care and only 9 per cent are able to pay for nursing care out of income (McKay, 1992).

Under current arrangements, local authorities are responsible for assessing an individual's need for residential care and their ability to pay for it. 'Ability to pay' is determined by an individual's resources both capital and income. Although under certain circumstances the value of a house or property may be disregarded, it is likely that the sale of property will increasingly be necessary in order to fund the costs of residential care. It is unlikely that people not assessed as needing residential care but who may nevertheless wish to go into a home would have sufficient resources to fund their place without selling their property.

Although there is no direct evidence, there is clearly an incentive for elderly people likely to go into care to transfer their assets to their family to ensure that they are not eaten away be care costs. Although this may not be very common, there is no doubt that many elderly home owners are forced to sell their homes to pay for care. The average length of stay in care homes is approximately 2.5 years. This suggests an average turnover of residents of about 40 per cent. There are 470,000 nursing and residential places in total. This suggests 190,000 new entrants a year on average. Even a conservative estimate of 25 per cent turnover would indicate 125,000 entrants a year. The proportion of these who are home owners is not known with certainty, but if the tenure background of residents reflects the tenure composition of the elderly population as a whole some 44 per cent or 55,000 may be home owners (Hamnett and Mullings, 1992b).

On the assumption that two-thirds of residents are forced to sell their homes to pay for care, about 36,000 elderly home owners sell their homes each year. The actual figure could be higher, depending on the turnover rate and the proportion who have to sell. Holmans (1991) has estimated that 30,000 older owner occupied households were dissolved in 1990 through moves to live with relatives or into care. This figure would account for the difference between the projected number of properties inherited 168,000, 1986–91 and the numbers recorded by the Inland Revenue (145,000).

Summary and conclusions

The rapid expansion of home ownership post war combined with the rapid rise in house prices in the 1970s and 80s led to the sudden realisation that a large number of older home owners now owned considerable housing assets. This realisation led to frequent suggestions that Britain is set to become a nation of inheritors. These suggestions appear to be supported by the projections made of future levels of housing inheritance. But an examination of the Inland Revenue data shows that, rather surprisingly, there was no increase in the number of recorded estates passing at death which contain house property. The number has been remarkably stable for the last 20 years and there is a shortfall of some 20–30,000 between projected 'releases' in 1986–90 and the number of cases recorded by the Inland Revenue. When the estates of married persons are excluded from the Inland Revenue statistics (some 40 per cent of cases), the shortfall is even more dramatic. This poses considerable problems for the proponents of the nation of inheritors. Even though the value of housing inheritance has rapidly increased over the 20 years 1968/9–88/9, this is entirely a product of house price inflation.

The projections assume that the principal factor which influences the scale of housing inheritance is the level of home ownership among the elderly population. This has steadily increased in recent years and is set to increase further as high home ownership levels among the 30 to 35 year olds work through to older households. But the scale of housing inheritance is not just a result of ownership levels among the elderly. There are a variety of factors which may reduce or eliminate home equity prior to death. The significance of these other factors is clearly shown by the fact that the number of estates containing house property has not increased over the last 20 years on the basis of the IRS statistics. This evidence is counter to the suggestion of steadily rising home ownership amongst the elderly population. The projections overestimate the current number of housing inheritances by 20–30 per annum.

Although the Inland Revenue statistics are problematic because of their exclusions (particularly joint property passing between spouses), and the possibility of transfer of assets prior to death, it is clear that the number of property inheritances recorded has not increased. A number of possibilities were suggested to account for this. They included an increase in numbers of joint property passing to spouses, the growth of inheritance tax avoidance (which is very unlikely) and a time lag effect before the growth of home ownership post-war percolates into inheritances. This is very likely and will have had some effect, but it would still be expected that some increase in the number of estates containing house property would have occurred.

It was argued that there has been a secular increase in the scale and volume of equity extraction prior to death, and that more older owners were likely to transfer their properties prior to death either to pay for residential care or, in some cases, to avoid payment. This is likely, but impossible to document. What is certain is that there has been a remarkable expansion of residential care for the elderly during the 1980s, and given the cost of such care, it is likely that many (but not all) residents have had to sell their houses to pay for the costs care.

It is estimated that some 36,000 homes a year may be sold to pay for care, and that a further 2,000 per year may be lost to inheritance via equity extraction schemes. Also an unknown number of houses may be transferred by elderly owners to their children prior to residential care. These figures suggest that the number of houses actually passed on for inheritance is likely to remain stable at 145,000 per year for some years to come. If the number of houses transferred prior to death or sold prior to death to pay for care increases, the number of houses passing at death will fall rather than rise. The notion of a vast wave of housing inheritances in the 1990s is highly improbable.

References

Atkinson, A. (1978) *Distribution of Personal Wealth in Britain*. Clarendon: Oxford

Davis and Saville (1982) 'Mortgage lending and the housing market'. *Bank of England Quarterly Bulletin*, 390–8 Sept 1982

The Economist (1988) 'Growing Rich Again'. *The Economist*, 19 April 1988

Forrest, R. and Murie, A. (1989) 'Differential accumulation: wealth inheritance and housing policy'. *Policy and Politics*, 17, 1 pp25–39

Hamnett, C. (1991). 'A Nation of Inheritors? Housing Inheritance, Wealth and Inequality in Britain'. *Journal of Social Policy*, 20, 4, 509–536.

Hamnett, C., Harmer, M. and Williams, P. (1991). *Safe as Houses: Housing Inheritance in Britain*. Paul Chapman.

Hamnett, C. and Mullings, B. (1992a). 'The distribution of public and private residential homes for elderly persons in England and Wales'. *Area*, 24, 2, 130–144.

Hamnett, C. and Mullings, B. (1992b) 'A New Consumption Cleavage? The case of residential care for the elderly'. *Environment and Planning*, 24, pp807–820

Holmans, A. (1986) 'Flows of Funds associated with House Purchase for Owner-occupation in the United Kingdom, 1977–1984, and Equity Withdrawal from House Purchase Finance'. *Government Economic Service Working Paper*, No 92

Holmans, A. (1991) 'House Prices: Changes through Time at the National and Subnational Level'. *Government Economic Service Working Paper*, No 110, December

Holmans, A. (1991) 'Estimates of Housing Equity withdrawal by Owner Occupiers in the United Kingdom 1970 to 1990'. *Government Economic Service Working Paper*, No 116, November

Inland Revenue (1991) *Inland Revenue Statistics*. HMSO: London

Leather, P. (1990) 'The potential and implications of home equity release in old age'. *Housing Studies*, 5, 1 pp3–13

McKay, S. (1992). *Pensioners' Assets*. Policy Studies Institute: London.

Morgan Grenfell (1987). 'Housing inheritance and wealth'. *Morgan Grenfell Economic Review*, 45, November.

Mullings, B. and Hamnett, C. (1992). 'Equity Release Schemes and Equity Extraction by Elderly Households in Britain'. *Ageing and Society*, 12, 413–442.

Murie, A. and Forrest, R. (1980). 'Wealth, inheritance and housing policy'. *Policy and Politics*, 8, 1, 1–19.

Royal Commission on the Distribution of Income and Wealth (1977) *Third Report on the Standing Reference. Report no 5*, Cmnd. 6999, HMSO: London

Saunders, P. (1986) 'Comment on Dunleavy and Preteceille'. *Society and Space*, 4, pp155–63

Chapter 9
HOUSING AND OLDER PEOPLE

ANTHEA TINKER

Introduction

The objective of this chapter is to examine the role that housing plays in the lives of older people, with specific reference to family links and the provision of family care. While the focus of the book is on the family care of older people, it must be emphasised that care by older people of younger family members is far from uncommon. The impact of housing on such arrangements will be mentioned where it is relevant.

The context is the changing demographic picture brought out in previous chapters. Particularly significant for the future will be the expected continued rise in the number and proportion of older people who live alone. This increase in solitary living has implications for the amount and type of housing which must be provided for small households. As this trend to solitary living is especially pronounced among very elderly people, and mainly women, this has to be related to health status. As is well known, very elderly people, especially women, are more likely to have long-standing illnesses and disabilities than younger age groups. This has implications for the kind of housing and support which needs to be provided.

A central argument is the danger of generalising about older people. Important differences concern age, gender, ethnicity and cohorts. Examples of these will be given in the chapter. They all illustrate the value of looking ahead when thinking about the future of family care. For example, elderly people from black and ethnic minority groups are more likely to live in extended families than their white counterparts, but it is not known whether this will continue. The tendency for people from black and ethnic minority groups to conform to a norm in this country can be seen in the falling fertility rates for women born outside the United Kingdom (UK). Despite these falls, rates for mothers born in India, Pakistan, Bangladesh and Africa remain higher than rates for mothers born in the UK (Central Statistical Office [CSO] 1993, p. 17).

Housing in the context of community care

While there may be argument about the exact meaning of community care, there is no doubt that one element is care by the family. If families are to care, housing may help or hinder. For those who wish to share their home the availability of a home of sufficient size and appropriate design is crucial. For others the important element may be in housing policies which help families and older people to move closer. For those who want independence for both the younger and older households, yet wish to be near, planning, legal and financial constraints may hinder the provision of one solution – a granny flat.

A greatly neglected area of research is the place that housing plays in community care and how it can be taken into account when designing packages of care. Little is known, for example, about the relative importance of housing as opposed to other forms of support such as financial help, or services such as home care. What is becoming increasingly evident is the significance of home to older people. The positive features of familiarity and the disorienting effects of moving are matched by evidence about the psychological benefits that home plays in personal identity (Howell, 1980).

What is also self-evident is the desire of older people for independence and a self-determined lifestyle. Research both in this country and in others shows that most elderly people, even the frailest, wish to remain in homes of their own. Policies to implement this are variously known as 'staying at home', 'staying put', 'ageing in place' and 'maintien domicile' (see Tinker, forthcoming).

Despite the emphasis on these policies by ministers and local authorities in Britain, they have not been emphasised to the same degree in community care policies. In the Griffiths report on community care, for example, housing was relegated to a few sentences (Griffiths, 1988). The subsequent White Paper was more explicit (Secretaries of State for Health *et al.*, 1989). It stated 'The Government believes that housing is a vital component of community care and is often the key to independent living' (ibid, p. 25). The National Federation of Housing Associations (NFHA) entitled their report in an even more forceful way: *Housing: the Foundation of Community Care* (NFHA/MIND, 1987).

The National Health Service and Community Care Act 1990 contains a number of important sections which stress the part that housing authorities – local authorities and housing associations – should play in community care. They include the requirement to consult these bodies when community care plans are drawn up for that area. At the level of individual assessment of the person the local authority must notify the District Health Authority or local housing authority '. . . and invite them to assist, to such extent as is reasonable in the circumstances, in the making of the assessment; and, in making their decision as to the provision of the services needed for the person in question, the local authority shall take into account any services which are likely to be made available for him by that District Health Authority or local housing authority' (Section 47(3)). This is a clear acknowledgement of the role of housing in community care policies.

It remains to be seen whether housing *will* be brought in to community care policies. Early signs are not encouraging. Research has shown that few housing authorities had been involved in the preparation of community care plans and there is widespread scepticism about the capacity of the joint planning system to address housing issues (Arnold & Page, 1992). The same research found that housing authorities attributed their marginalisation to the failure of health and social services authorities to recognise or understand the key role of housing. Whether detailed guidance from the Department of the Environment (DOE) and the Department of Health (DOH) will have much effect remains to be seen (DOE/DOH circular *Housing and Community Care*, 24.9.92).

TABLE 1

Changes in tenure* between 1979 and 1989 by gender and age groups 60–74 and 75+(in percentages)

| Tenure: | 1979 | | | | 1989 | | | |
| | 60–74 | | 75+ years | | 60–74 years | | 75+ years | |
	Women	Men	Women	Men	Women	Men	Women	Men
Owned outright	41.9	41.1	38.6	42.1	48.3	50.8	43.2	51.4
Owned mortgage	4.8	6.6	4.4	2.6	11.2	13.6	5.4	4.1
Rented LA	37.7	36.2	38.0	36.2	31.2	27.2	36.6	32.7
Rented HA	1.7	1.2	2.3	1.5	2.8	2.2	4.5	3.1
Rented private	13.4	14.3	16.4	17.5	5.1	4.5	9.5	7.8
Total Base N	2445	1924	1040	542	1947	1614	1031	588

*Tenure is tenure of the household as a whole, i.e. it does not necessarily imply, for example, that the individual pensioner is an owner occupier. He/she could be living with a younger person who was an owner-occupier.

Source: General Household Surveys 1979 and 1989 analysed by the Gerontology Data Service

A discussion of housing tenure in old age

There are a number of aspects of housing related to tenure which have an impact on family care. One of the most striking features of recent years has been the increase among the general population of owner occupation. Elderly people have shared in this increase but proportions who are owner–occupiers are not as large as among middle–aged people. Taking the ten years between 1979 and 1989, the increase in owner–occupation has been higher amongst older men; in particular amongst those men aged 60–74. The growth in owner–occupation amongst men is very little different for the under and over 75s. The growth rates for women, particularly the over 75s, are considerably lower than for older age groups for men, thereby increasing the difference in the percentage of men and women who are owners (Table 1). At the same time there has been a decline in the proportion of both men and women aged 60–74 and 75+ renting in the local authority and private sectors. There has been a slight increase in renting from housing associations over this period.

The increase in owner–occupation reflects the preferred tenure of elderly people. In 1988 respondents to the *General Household Survey* (GHS) were asked, 'If you were considering moving somewhere else would you prefer to rent or to buy your house?' Actual tenure was reflected in preferred tenure patterns (Askham *et al.* 1992).

The next sections will consider the tenure pattern and discuss some of the implications for family care of elderly people.

The rise in owner occupation

It has been seen that the present cohort of very elderly people is less likely to be owner-occupiers than the cohort below them. If trends continue there will be a

TABLE 2
Owner-occupation by birth cohort 1979–1989

Born	Age in 1989	Percentages living in owner-occupied housing	
		1979	1989
1930–39	50–59	61	76
1920–29	60–69	51	64
1910–19	70–79	47	54
1900–09	80–89	45	50

Source: General Household Surveys 1979 and 1989 analysed by the Gerontology Data Service

higher rate of owner-occupation in the future among the very elderly. It is interesting to compare birth cohorts and note the increase in owner-occupation between 1979 and 1989 of all cohorts. It is also significant to note that there is still a large difference between the proportions who were owner-occupiers in 1989; whereas 76 per cent of 50–59 year olds were in this tenure, only 50 per cent of the 80–89 year olds were (Table 2).

Very little is known, however, about changes in tenure in old age and so a degree of caution has to be exercised when thinking about the future. Nor is it known how many families help their elderly relatives to buy their own homes, for example under the right to buy. There is evidence from inquiries to Age Concern England (ACE) that this does take place and that there are sometimes subsequent problems (ACE, personal communication).

Owner-occupation brings responsibilities for maintenance and it is this that sometimes brings problems in old age. The problem may be one of not knowing about grants and procedures, it may be the lack of finance, or it may be an inability to supervise and check the work or find a builder. It is here that family support may be vital. The 41 per cent of over 75 year olds who were owner-occupiers in 1989 may need someone to turn to. However, there is little research on how many do ask for, or are offered, help from families.

What is known, however, is that the older age groups have dwellings with the highest rates of disrepair but on average the least financial resources. This is usually known as 'asset rich and income poor'. As a study of housing in the Third Age (people aged 50–74) commented, 'It is likely that keeping frail and solitary older people in their own homes will give issues of repair and condition increased prominence during the 1990s . . . . more general and generous help may be required' (Warnes, 1992;51). If this help is not forthcoming from statutory sources, which looks increasingly likely, older people may be forced to turn to their families.

Although housing equity and housing inheritance are the subjects of a separate chapter, it is important to note that any discussion of owner-occupation has to consider the relevance of both. Using the equity in a home can enable older people to raise money to pay for repairs and other things. The issue of housing inheritance is important in that it may affect the behaviour of both the older person and the family. The older person may not want to become involved in raising equity because they wish to leave their home intact to their relatives. Sons and daughters too may exert pressure on their parents not to sell their home or remortgage it so that they can inherit it. Most of the evidence about this is anecdotal but there is concern among those who help older people who wish to move into residential care that younger relatives do not want the house sold to pay for this care (*see, for example*, the correspondence in The Times 10.2.93, and Social Work Today 3.9.92). The literature on abuse of older people is increasingly taking a wider view of abuse than physical abuse and includes financial abuse of this kind (McCreadie, 1991). The 'disappearing pension' is not the only kind of financial abuse that can occur.

A further point which must be mentioned about owner-occupation is that it has always been thought of as being preferable to renting for older people who wish to move near relatives. It is argued that they can sell up and buy somewhere near the younger family, rather than throw themselves on the mercy of a local authority or housing association in another part of the country. At a time when the property market is sluggish, older people are likely to find it increasingly difficult to sell their homes. This is the case whether the reason is to move nearer relatives or to some other form of accommodation such as private sheltered housing.

Renting

It has been seen (Table 1) that renting by older people from local authorities and privately has declined. Nevertheless, in 1989 substantial numbers and proportions were in this tenure. Approximately one-third of men and women over the age of 75 rented from local authorities. While they currently share many of the advantages and disadvantages of other local authority tenants, those who are in sheltered housing or purpose-built accommodation are likely to be in a home which is of a higher standard than, for example, some owner-occupiers or those who rent privately.

Particular features of being a local authority tenant which are likely to affect family care include specially designed housing, the right to occupy the accommodation after the death of the older person and policies over moving.

The best known form of specially designed housing is granny flats. Some local authorities, mainly in the 1950s and 1960s, built special housing for families and older people in the form of granny flats. These were self-contained homes attached to family homes. Some were bungalows, others were ground or first floor flats. Research showed that although they were originally planned so that a family could have their own Granny next door, only about one-fifth were used by relatives (Tinker, 1976). And 'Granny' was a misnomer as one-quarter of the tenants were men and others were unmarried or had no children. The majority for various reasons had never contained a relative. Schemes were very successful when a relative did live next door (see Type of Housing) but local authorities did not find these schemes easy to operate after the first let. Practical problems with the schemes included what happens when:

- the elderly related person dies?
- the family moves?
- the relative or old person comes from a different local authority and does not qualify for housing?
- one unit is sold by the local authority and not the other?

Most local authorities felt that the schemes had a 'limited' or 'qualified' success. The general consensus seemed to be that when the units were let to relatives that was very successful but that the whole thing got out of step very quickly when there was a death or move (Tinker, 1976). Authorities felt frustrated that the arrangement seemed a once and for all one and after the first let they could not use the units for their original purpose.

For all local authority tenants the right to occupy the accommodation after the death of the older person is important for a carer who may have given up their home and moved in. This right is now secured for a close relative, but only one succession is allowed. There is no right for any subsequent relative to inherit the tenancy.

Elderly people who want to move to be near their relatives or vice versa to gain or give support may find problems if they are local authority tenants. The two groups who have been found to have problems are:

- owner–occupiers who want to move into council housing in their own area,
- people from any tenure who want to rent in another local authority area (Tinker, 1980).

The decline in the amount of council housing, because much has been sold under right to buy and because of the decline in council house building, have meant that the amount of housing available has diminished. Most local authorities have long waiting lists and may not be able to offer anything in the desired area, if at all. Exchanges are possible but often difficult to arrange if the chosen area is a popular one. Moving to another area is likely to pose even more problems. Exchanges are again possible and there is an official Tenants Exchange Scheme, but it is '...not usually a realistic option for tenants living in poor housing' (Bookbinder, 1992;39). There is also a National Mobility Scheme where some councils make available a small proportion of their annual vacancies for letting, but again this is a very limited scheme.

Tenants in privately rented homes are in a form of housing which is declining despite Government attempts to revive it. For many people it is a good option and it may be that this sector expands if given sufficient incentives by the Government. Although on the whole elderly people in this tenure occupy some of the worst housing, it gives another option to both elderly people and their relatives who wish to remain in an area or to live near one another.

Housing Association tenancies are the only form of rented housing which is expanding. Much of the accommodation for elderly people is purpose–built, often sheltered housing, and there is great demand for it. In 1988, 34 per cent of all new lettings were to elderly people aged 60 and over (Randolph & Levison, 1988). Some associations require the applicant to live in the area but others do take people from other areas. It may be easier for an elderly person to move nearer a family to get a housing association tenancy than one in the local authority sector. It seems that this form of housing is still continuing to grow, in contrast to the council sector. Housing associations also participate in mobility schemes.

In all forms of renting there may be problems over rent levels as they rise to higher levels. In the private sector there may also be problems over security of tenure.

Tenants in tied accommodation

People who live in accommodation provided by their employers generally lose their right to their home when they stop working. The home is usually needed by the employer for the next employee. Some elderly people in this situation may have saved enough to buy a home or have already bought one, but others will depend on the local authority or housing association. The 1990 GHS showed that 2 per cent of the population lived in tied accommodation (OPCS, 1992;56). This figure dropped to 1 per cent for the age group 65–69 (OPCS, 1992;65). The kinds of people who live in this type of accommodation include the clergy, agricultural workers and the police.

Because the older worker has to move, family links may be broken if younger members of the family remain in the locality. When a single person loses his or her home this way homelessness may result.

Homelessness

Two types of homelessness must be distinguished. The first is that of families and the other is single people. It is the last category which is relevant here. There are also two kinds of homelessness. The first is technically homeless, that is accepted as homeless by the local authority. Under the Housing (Homeless Persons) Act 1977, later consolidated in the Housing Act 1985, with minor amendments in the Housing and Planning Act 1986, local authorities in Great Britain were given a statutory duty to secure accommodation for applicants who are homeless and who are in priority need. In 1991, 4 per cent of homeless households found accommodation by local authorities were in the category of vulnerable because of old age (CSO, 1993;117). The other kind of homelessness occurs among people who either do not present themselves to the local authority or who are not accepted. They are the ones who will often be found sleeping rough or in squats.

Little is known about elderly people who are homeless but interest and research in this topic is growing in both the United States and Great Britain. One of the findings is the effect of family breakdown, especially a marriage break-up, and how this can cause homelessness. For some the onset of homelessness is connected with the loss of family or death of a spouse (Crane, 1990 and 1992). Family care is likely to be non-existent if people have lost touch with one another.

It may, however, be the carer who becomes homeless. A study of older homeless people in London reported:

> *Many people caring for an elderly dependent relative will find themselves homeless when the dependent person dies. On a practical level, the carer may not inherit the tenancy or right to the home which means that they literally have nowhere to live. On a more emotional level, the carer's reasons for staying in the home may disappear with the death of the dependent. Many carers themselves are elderly and a combination of grief, loss of purpose and lack of knowledge about what to do may lead them to lose interest in the upkeep of the home, or simply to walk out.*

'Some people never leave the parental home and live with their parents into their own old age. On the death of their parents, these 'elderly orphans' are vulnerable to homelessness. They may not inherit the tenancy which belonged to their parents; they may lose the will to carry on living in the parental home; or they may lack the will to carry on living in the parental home; or they may lack the life skills needed to maintain a home of their own after a lifetime of dependency.' (Kelling, 1991;6).

TABLE 3

Preferred type of housing by actual type occupied 1988 (GB) (in percentages)

| | 60–74 years | | 75+ years | |
	Actual	Preferred	Actual	Preferred
Detached house	21	11	16	5
Semi-detached house	31	5	30	3
Terraced house	28	2	27	2
House – other or type not specified	–	2	–	2
Bungalow	#	64	#	56
Flat	19	11	26	20
Other/Don't know	1	5	1	12

bungalows included in relevant category of house for actual accommodation
Source: General Household Survey 1988 analysed by the Gerontology Data Service

Type of housing

Older people, like people of other age groups, may live in many different kinds of housing. This section is concerned with various types of housing, from a family home to sheltered housing. The question to be posed is: What effect, if any, does the type of housing have on family care? Are relationships, or the lack of them, to do with the design or are they more a result of household composition? In attempting to answer these questions the following issues will be discussed:

- the type of housing currently occupied by elderly people and preferred options,
- features that may help or hinder the independence of the old person and the nature and extent of family care (design, condition of the home, support available and affordability).
- the special case of families and older people who live in one household.

Much of what follows has been drawn from various pieces of research. There is very little research which directly answers the questions posed. This is part of the neglect of housing referred to at the beginning of this chapter.

Type of Housing Occupied by Elderly People and Preferred Options

In 1988 respondents to the GHS were asked what kind of accommodation they would prefer to live in if they moved. Table 3 shows the type of housing that elderly people currently occupy compared with their stated preferences.

A bungalow is the most preferred option being given by 64 per cent of those between the ages of 60–74, declining to 56 per cent for those over the age of 75, with flats becoming slightly more popular with age.

When thinking about future provision it is interesting to note the desire for separate accommodation, and therefore a measure of independence, by the cohorts of people who are now younger. In a study of the circumstances and preferences of sharing households, concealed families and unmarried people aged 18–59, a strong preference emerged overall for self-contained accommodation (Rauta, 1986). Self-contained accommodation enables elderly people to have their own front door and be able to cook for themselves. It is interesting that in Denmark, where '...the legislation abolishing residential homes is more correctly described as legislation abolishing incomplete accommodation: the minimum standard is defined as two rooms, kitchen and bathroom. This does not prevent dwellings being grouped together' (Potter & Zill, 1992;126).

Features that may Help or Hinder the Independence of the Elderly Person and the Nature and Extent of Family Care

Design

The only kind of accommodation that is specifically designed for families and elderly people, as was noted earlier in this chapter, is the granny flat. Because it is the only kind of housing planned to encourage family links, it is worth exploring the potential in greater detail. The theory of granny flats sounds ideal.

> 'The older person can be independent in his or her daily life, while the younger members of the family can keep in touch and help when required. The separate lives and interests of the generations can be maintained and the security and safety of the older one assured. In an emergency, there is someone at hand to cope, and if the older parent becomes ill or housebound, the family will be able to care for him or her without the inconvenience of distance or journey' (Rudinger, 1977;91).

It was seen that it had not proved to be a very flexible form of housing for local authorities to provide. A comparison between those elderly people who were related in the family home and the granny flat showed that links were, as would be expected, much closer than where there was no relationship (Tinker, 1976). While the relationship varied with non–related linked neighbours from no contact to a very close one, that between related households was one where there was nearly always a good deal of contact and mutual support. What the research also showed was that the major source of help for both related and unrelated elderly people was their own families. Those elderly people with relatives next door got nearly all their help from them. Those elderly people who were not related to their linked neighbours received a good deal of help from their families. In addition, there was some support between elderly neighbours, and some of the elderly people were themselves giving some help to their own families.

Where there seems more interest now in this country is the private sector (Tinker, 1991). A small exploratory study of estate agents found that approximately 5 per cent of accommodation for sale in two areas of the country contained granny flats (Morton, forthcoming). There are, however, problems over the design of the property, the need to get planning permission, legal issues and difficulties over insurance. In a comparison of granny flats in different countries, Lazarowich favours rented granny flats which can be installed and then removed when the need has passed (Lazarowich, 1991). When this was suggested in this country in the 1970s it was not met with great enthusiasm.

In the study of local authority granny flats the type was examined, i.e. whether the elderly person was living next door in a bungalow, or in a ground floor flat underneath the linked neighbours, or living above the latter and related to the level of interaction. It was difficult to draw firm conclusions because the older people in the three groups were dissimilar. However, it would appear that the house/bungalow or adjacent homes is more conducive to links.

A form of design which would help older people, both in their own homes and when they visit others, is some kind of 'barrier-free' housing. This can be loosely defined as housing which is accessible to people with wheelchairs but not to the complete 'wheelchair' standard (Goldsmith, 1975).

Conditions of the Home

It is becoming increasingly realised that shortcomings in the condition of the home can lead to an enforced move (Potter & Zill, 1992). There are many ways in which this can be manifested. An inability to manage a garden is sometimes a reason, though often combined with other factors, for people giving up their independence and moving. The lack of an inside lavatory or dangerous wiring and floors may lead to accidents, which again may lead to a move. One percent of elderly people in 1989 over the age of 75 had only an outside lavatory (special analysis of the 1989 GHS by the GDS). Although this had improved from 1979 when the figure was 7 per cent, it is still too high.

Elderly owner-occupiers are likely to face particular problems. These include physical inability to cope with maintenance and improvements. Some specific problems faced by this group are lack of knowledge about the grant system, lack of money, difficulty in finding builders to carry out the work and dislike of having workmen in the house. A number of schemes have developed to help with these problems in the last ten years. The biggest development has been the setting up of home improvement agencies, usually called agency services. Local authorities, housing associations and the private sector can provide them. They provide advice and practical assistance for householders seeking to repair and maintain the fabric of their homes. Their help is both technical and financial and can include advice on raising money to pay for the work. Research has confirmed the value of these agencies (Leather & Mackintosh, 1990).

Support available

If support is available for elderly people, either on a short- or long-term basis, they may be prevented from going into residential care. Sometimes this support may be needed in the person's own home. The presence of a spare room in a house or granny flat may mean that a relative or someone else can stay and give help.

190

In other cases a move may be to the kind of environment where support is provided. Abbeyfield Society, for example, provides small homely accommodation where 8–10 older people live together in bedsitters. A housekeeper lives there too and provides meals. Schemes which give more independence are sheltered housing where the elderly person has their own flat with communal facilities and a warden on hand to give neighbourly help. Research shows that many elderly people like this form of housing and it often gives peace of mind to relatives. There is no evidence that family links are destroyed by a move into this kind of environment. The large national survey of local authority and housing association schemes found no evidence that elderly people were neglected by their families (Butler et al. 1983). They found that 95 per cent of tenants claimed to have existing relatives and that contact was maintained in 94 per cent of cases. In their follow-up study they found that nearly 20 per cent of tenants said that the frequency of visiting by relatives had increased since the move, as opposed to 10 per cent who felt that it had declined (Butler et al., 1983).

The authors of this national study said,

> 'What does clearly emerge from our work is the amount of practical assistance provided by relatives with regard to help with shopping, housework, cooking and laundry duties. In each case this exceeds that of the warden and is only matched, with regard to meals, by the meals-on-wheels service' (Butler et al., 1983;192).

A rather different picture is presented in a national study of very sheltered, or extra care, housing (Tinker, 1989b). These were defined as schemes which had more provision, or a greater level of care than ordinary sheltered housing, for example, provision of meals, extra wardens, domiciliary assistants or additional communal facilities. This research showed that the majority of household and personal tasks in very sheltered housing were carried out by staff in the scheme. For tenants of a similar level of dependency in sheltered housing these tasks were mainly performed by families (Tinker, 1989b).

Affordability

Another issue which must be addressed is whether elderly people have the means to remain in their home, or to move, with some degree of comfort. If they cannot, they may be tempted to move in with relatives or into residential care. While we know that the savings of elderly local authority and housing association tenants are very small (MacLennan et al., 1990), rents are likely to rise.

For elderly home owners, too, finance may present problems and narrow choices. Property values vary so much from one area to another and between different groups of elderly people that it is difficult to generalise. It is, however, possible to say that for some the amount of money they would raise from the sale of their home would be very small (Gibbs 1992). Lack of capital and income will act as a restriction to the choices open to elderly people. On the other hand, some elderly people will receive some housing inheritance from relatives. Recent research revealed that 63 per cent of beneficiaries were aged 50 and over (Hamnett & Williams, 1992). This research, however, also found that the average value of inheritances for the period 1985–89 was not large. It was £32,700. This varied from £48,500 in Greater London to £13,000 in the North.

The special case of families and old people who live in one household

Families and elderly people who live in one household may have particular advantages when it comes to family care, but they may also have stresses which others who live at a distance do not have. Research is lacking on household dynamics and, in particular, on the effect that housing has on the situation. This is probably because of the difficulty in researching such a sensitive topic. Most studies of intergenerational living are based on very small samples. Nevertheless there some conclusions that can be pieced together from the limited research available.

Only a small proportion of people – mainly the old and the young – live respectively with their sons or daughters or their children. Families and elderly people may move in together for a variety of reasons. The older person may go to live with a younger household when it is felt that they need more care. However, caution must be exercised in assuming that the move is necessarily for care. Studies by Wenger (1984) and Qureshi & Walker (1989), both of which contained some co-resident families, showed that few households were formed in response to the elderly person's need for care. Another kind of movement is when younger family members move back into the family home after a relationship breakdown. Some households have never split for a number of reasons. A daughter may have never left home, and younger couple may not have been able to move out because of housing shortages or an elderly couple may be left with a disabled son or daughter. Little is known about the effect of housing on moves of elderly people to younger families and vice versa.

Co-residence between elderly married couples and their married children has never been a usual situation (Grundy, 1992). What has had an effect has been the availability, quality and type of housing (Wall, 1989). Wall maintains that

> '...at the end of the Second World War ... many young couples had to commence their married life in the parental household. This may well explain both the peak in the number of relatives noted in English households at this time (married offspring were certainly a more important element within the kin group than they were earlier or later) and, more generally, the strong ties between mothers and their married daughters that surfaced in the wave of post-war studies of working class communities' (Wall, 1989;371–372).

What needs to be emphasised is the evidence that support is often mutual and that there may be reciprocal relationships.

In this book the emphasis is on care of elderly people. A number of questions need to be addressed:

● is there evidence of a greater level of care in a co-resident household?
● is there evidence of a lack of care?
● is more or less help given to co-resident carers than non co-residents?
● do older people and families want this form of living?

The answers need to be placed in the context of the form of housing and how this affects the position.

A greater level of care?

Common sense dictates that it is in theory easier for help to be given to an older person when they are in the same household. Long journeys do not have to be undertaken and this can be particularly important at night. One of the few studies of co-resident carers, that of 41 daughters who cared for their mothers at home, shows the extent of care given was much greater than if they had lived apart (Lewis & Meredith, 1988).

However a lot may depend on the design of the home. If, for example, the co-resident family does not have a suitable bathroom or downstairs lavatory, it is possible that the older person may receive a lower standard of care than if they had remained in their own home or moved to a purpose-built flat where a professional, other relative or neighbour could have helped. It is also possible that the younger family may be out at work or school all day and the older person may be left unattended for long periods of time.

Evidence from some studies, however, does show that co-residents do give a good deal of personal and financial help to the older person living with them and are likely to suffer later in their own lives because of lost opportunities to work and have social lives (Askham et al., 1992).

A lack of care?

Because it is so difficult to see what is going on in people's own homes, the level and possible lack of care is not easy to assess. What is known, however, is that there is growing evidence of abuse to elderly people in their own homes (McCreadie, 1992). The nature of the home and its privacy makes this very difficult to uncover. When family care is considered in the home with a co-resident the private nature of the home must always be taken into account, especially if there are difficult relationships. The abuse may be physical, financial, psychological, emotional or neglect. This is not to say that abuse cannot and does not take place in institutions but it may be more difficult to hide unless there is a conspiracy to do so among staff.

More or less help from outside?

There is a good deal of evidence that families who have an older person in their household are less likely to receive help from domiciliary services. Early small qualitative studies, such as those undertaken by Nissel & Bonnerjea (1982), Charlesworth et al. (1984) and Lewis & Meredith (1988), showed the lack of statutory services (especially home helps) for carers. These findings about discrimination against co-resident carers were confirmed in analyses of large national surveys (Evandrou et al., 1986; Arber et al., 1988).

Do older people and families want co-resident care?

We know little about the preferences of older people for co-resident care. There is some evidence from Scandinavia of a possible shift towards professional care

(Sundstrom, *forthcoming*). Sundstrom noted a marked shift away from family care and towards public care between 1969 and 1981 in Norway (Sundstrom, forthcoming). He also noted that in New Zealand one study showed that elderly people saw receiving care from co-resident children as the worst of all possible solutions. If institutions improve and can provide the high level of privacy and care that some very sheltered housing and nursing homes do, it is not difficult to imagine that older people may choose this rather than the perhaps reluctant care by their family. This may be especially the case if they see the strain that this imposes on the younger generation.

From the point-of-view of families, it is clear that some do want this kind of living arrangement. For example, the study of co-resident mothers and daughters found that most daughters cared willingly and there was a sense of reciprocity in what they did. Nevertheless the authors conclude that '. . . it would be hard to over-estimate the emotional and material costs of caring' (Lewis & Meredith, 1988;153). It was also evident in this study that many of the husbands and children suffered from the caring role of the woman. In another study of older people living in the same household as a family, 'Several teenage children were said to be threatening to leave home and school at least partly because the house was overcrowded and tense' (Nissel & Bonnerjea, 1982;36). Here is an example where a larger house or granny flat might have helped.

In this book the focus is on older people and care, but younger people must also be considered, as the example above shows. A recent study of younger people when they leave home concluded that they express a desire for independent housing (Darke *et al.*, 1992, pp 3–4). The study showed that the supply of accommodation, especially rented, has declined and some young people are being denied the right to independent housing on the grounds that they are satisfactorily housed with their parents (Darke *et al.*, 1992). The possible tensions when an older person is in the household, as well as the parents, must be taken into account.

Moving in old age

As has been seen in Chapter 4, a proportion of elderly people move in old age. Some of them move reluctantly and some wish to do so. In both categories are people who move to gain support from relatives. In a national survey of people aged 75 and over, carried out in the mid-1970s, it was found that the major reason given by all movers (40 per cent) was to be near relatives (Hunt, 1978). In a national study of local authorities and housing associations in England and Wales, *Housing the Elderly near Relatives*, it was found that many elderly people already lived near their families (Tinker, 1980). However, there was demand from some of those who did not to move closer. Two groups of elderly people who faced particular problems over moving were owner-occupiers who wanted to move into council accommodation in their own area and people from any tenure who wanted to rent in another local authority area. There are a number of schemes sponsored by central government to help local authority and housing association tenants move, and wanting to give or receive support from relatives is one criterion.

There are problems for owner-occupiers, especially when they cannot sell their homes. It is interesting though that there is some evidence that when

TABLE 4

Percentage of elderly people living alone aged 60–74 and over 75 with access to a telephone, by tenure, 1989

Tenure	60–74 years	75+ years
Owned outright	92	91
Owned with mortgage	98	94
Rented – local authority	68	65
Rented – housing association	69	77
Rented – private	80	78
TOTAL Base N	849	775

Source: General Household Survey 1989 analysed by the Gerontology Data Service

owner-occupiers trade down, that is sell their home for a cheaper one, this may result in money being available to spend on their current needs. For example, a study of private sheltered housing found that some of the money realised from the sale of the previous home was used to buy in domiciliary help (Fleiss, 1985). This may be a case where independence had been enhanced by a move.

The role of telephones and alarms

Telephones and alarms fulfil an important role in the family care of elderly people. They enable families to keep in touch and they make it possible for elderly people to call for help in an emergency. In some alarm systems the alarm will go through to a central point which may alert relatives. In other cases it may go through to a professional – often a warden. Possession of telephones has grown in the last decade and there is little difference between the over 60s and people aged 15–59 – 87 per cent and 88 per cent respectively in 1988 (Askham *et al.*, 1992). However this masks the differences among elderly people. The 1988 General Household Survey showed that whereas 90 per cent of people aged 60–69 owned a telephone, only 80 per cent of those aged over 80 did (Askham *et al.*, 1992). The lowest level of telephone ownership among the over 60s was among those living alone (Askham *et al.*, 1992). An analysis of the 1989 General Household Survey showed that elderly people who rented were much less likely to own a telephone than those who owned their own home (Table 4). This must be a matter of concern.

In a study of the telephone needs of elderly and disabled people it was found that most telephone calls were made to relatives (Tinker, 1989a). Of equal importance was the role of the telephone for other people to talk to them. There appeared to be an understanding, within families at least, that the cost of phoning long distance would be met by the younger generation.

Alarms may play a similar role in giving reassurance to both the family and the elderly person. Research in 1984 and 1986 found that although the main use was for emergencies (often falls) and at night, they were also used for non-emergencies (Tinker, 1984; Research Institute for Consumer Affairs [RICA] 1986). Alarm systems in this country were first introduced in public sector housing but manufacturers have extended their marketing to private households. Marketing is often aimed at relatives and there is some evidence that they are buying alarms. This appears to be for their older relatives. The research both on alarms and telephones has found a reluctance on the part of older people to use them, for the latter often on the grounds of cost.

An interesting development is that of passive alarms, that is alarms which monitor a person without their active intervention. Other technological developments include systems to operate doors, control central heating etc. These may all increase the independence of elderly people and also put relatives' minds at rest.

Matters of concern for family care include the numbers of elderly people who do not have access to a telephone and the reluctance of older people to use both them and alarms.

Conclusions

When considering the future of family care for elderly people there are many parts of a jigsaw to put together. This chapter has shown that housing is an important element. This concluding section will suggest that:

- policies must be flexible to cover many possible options for the future,
- attention must be paid to the housing needs of different groups of people,
- a variety of strategies need to be employed,
- housing strategies must be integrated with those of other organisations.

Before looking at these issues, however, it must be stressed that there may be cases when frail older people are themselves acting as carers. Often this is for a spouse but there are also cases where elderly parent are caring for a disabled older child or a grandchild. The home of the elderly person may also on occasions become the home of an adult child whose marriage has broken up. It is for reasons like these that there is need to consider seriously issues of underoccupation. Although logic may suggest that an older person has more room than they 'need' the fact that they may need to give as well as receive care means that a longer term view has to be taken.

Flexible options for an uncertain future

This chapter has pointed to some directions in which provision and policies are going. However, it should not be assumed that they will continue in these directions. It is by no means certain, for example, that owner occupation will continue to be the favoured option. If renting becomes more fashionable, for whatever reasons, numbers entering old age in this tenure may have different problems. In the foreseeable future it is true that cohorts which have to be planned for will probably consist of a majority of homeowners but this may not always be the case.

Nor should there be assumptions about the pattern of family living. Increasing numbers of families are becoming fractured. It may be that some in the future find themselves caring for ex parents in laws, step parents in laws as well as their own parents possibly at the same time. There may be a need for houses with a number of granny flats for example. On the other hand extended families, which are more a feature of people from black and ethnic minorities, may in the future become a number of small households. In the absence of research on future needs and wishes by these groups it is difficult to plan.

Another area of uncertainty is to what extent older people will choose family care. If they choose professional help then the case for more sheltered, or very sheltered, housing or nursing homes may be forceful.

All of these unknown factors mean that caution must be adopted when planning for the housing needs of older people. It also points to the need for research on the needs of future generations. It is not enough to ask the present generation of elderly people what they would choose.

Another imponderable which has to be taken into account is future technology. Alarms are relatively commonplace now and their role for both emergencies and as reassurance for elderly people and their carers is well established. The extension of surveillance systems, sometimes built into the home, for the monitoring of behaviour and health is likely to occur as it has for disabled and other people. This raises ethical issues.

The needs of different people

Although the focus of this book is on the care of elderly people it is not suggested that theirs are the only ones whose views and wishes must be taken into account. The needs of the family also need to be listened to as well. Nor may the family be the conventional one of parents and children. Previous chapters have reminded us that families have changed and so have patterns of work. For example the growth of numbers of women in paid employment has not necessarily led to a decline in their care of others. But the patterns of caring may have become different. For example the adult, man or woman, who goes out to work leaving an elderly person in a home may need a variety of gadgets to enable them to operate switches to turn on machines, such as dishwashers, in their absence. The concept of the smart house, which has a high degree of automation may be what is needed.

The needs of the primary carers also have to be balanced by those of others who may be affected, For example if an elderly person occupies a granny flat or lives with the family the need for privacy of the children has to be provided for as well as that of the older person. The importance of design is crucial here.

Moving on from the older person and the family the needs of professional carers should be considered. A well designed home can aid the task of those who come in to bath, toilet and nurse a frail older person.

The need for a variety of strategies

Some of the examples given in the previous section have been concerned with design. This is very important. If all homes were designed with disability in mind a great deal of trouble could be saved in the future. If every home, for example, had doors wide enough to accommodate a walking frame, all houses had a downstairs lavatory and waist high sockets that would make a good start.

The financial aspects of housing are often neglected. Future strategies need to take into account that some elderly people and some carers are likely to be in low income groups. Subsidised housing, targeted grants for repairs and insulation etc are crucial if money is to be saved on expensive residential care.

Training of staff is also important. This involves many professionals in housing, in health and all other relevant staff being aware of the housing needs of older people. Training needs to cover the wider issues such as the psychological meaning of home to the very practical knowledge of welfare benefits.

Practical help is another element. Schemes such as Care and Repair need to be developed more widely and to cover more older people. Small scale jobs such as help with wiring and decorating may be just as important as larger ones such as reroofing.

The provision of more small housing and policies which allow those elderly people who wish to move to do so are also crucial.

The integration of strategies

As has already been shown there is still a tendency to neglect housing by other organisations concerned with helping families and older people. Although much good co-ordination depends on individuals there is still room for mechanisms. Co-ordinating machinery needs to take into account all the many agencies concerned, This is one of the problems when there are a great variety of agencies. It is difficult enough to get statutory bodies to work together but now there are many more private and voluntary ones who need to be involved the position is becoming even more complicated. This is not the place to suggest detailed solutions but the issue must be addressed. For too long lip service has been paid to co-operation among agencies and too little to actual action.

Acknowledgements

Ruth Hancock and Christine Barry of the Gerontology Data Service (GDS) contributed to this chapter and provided the tables.

Material from the General Household Surveys, made available through the Office of Population Censuses and Surveys, and the ESRC Data Archive have been used by permission of the Controller of HMSO. Analyses of the GHS were carried out by The Gerontology Data Service, Age Concern Institute of Gerontology, King's College London.

References

Archer, S., Gilbert, N. and Evandrou, M. (1988) 'Gender, household composition and receipt of domiciliary services', *Journal of Social Policy* 17(2), pp 153–176.

Arnold, P. and Page, D. (1992) *Housing and Community Care: bricks and mortar or foundation for action?* School of Social and Professional Studies, Humberside Polytechnic.

Askham, J., Barry, C., Grundy, E., Hancock, R. and Tinker, A. (1992) *Life after 60*, ACIOG.

Bookbinder, D. (1991) *Housing Options for Older People*, Age Concern England.

Butler, A., Oldman, C. and Greve, J. (1983) *Sheltered Housing for the Elderly*, Allen & Unwin.

Central Statistical Office (1993) *Social Trends* 23, HMSO.

Charlesworth, A., Wilkins, D. and Durie, A. (1984) *Carers and Services*, Equal Opportunities Commission.

Crane, M. (1990) *Elderly Homeless People in Central London*, Age Concern England and Age Concern Greater London.

Crane, M. (1992) 'Elderly, homeless and mentally ill: a study.' *Nursing Standard*, 7(13), pp 35–38.

Darke, J., Conway, J., Holman, C. and Buckley, K. (1992) *Homes for Our Children*, National Housing Forum.

DOE/DOH (1992) *Housing and Community Care*, DOE 10/92 and DOH LAC (92)12, HMSO.

Evandrou, M., Arber, S., Dale, A. and Gilbert, N. (1986) 'Who cares for the elderly? Family care and receipt of Statutory Services', in Phillipson, C., Bernard, M. and Strang, P. (eds), *Dependency and Interdependency in Old Age*, Croom Helm.

Fleiss, A. (1985) *Home Ownership Alternatives for the Elderly*, HMSO.

Gibbs, I. (1992) 'A substantial but limited asset: the role of housing wealth in paying for residential care', in Morton J (ed.), *Financing Elderly People in Independent Sector Homes: the future*, ACIOG.

Goldsmith, S. (1975) *Wheelchair Housing*, Department of the Environment.

Griffiths, R. (1988) *Community Care: an agenda for action*, HMSO.

Grundy, E. (1992) 'The living arrangements of elderly people', *Reviews in Clinical Gerontology* 2, 353–361.

Hamnett, C. and Williams, P. (1992) *Housing Inheritance in Britain*, Joseph Rowntree Foundation Findings Series.

Howell, S. (1980) *Designing for Ageing – Patterns of Use*, The MIT Press.

Kelling, K. (1991) *Older Homeless People in London*, Age Concern Greater London.

Lazarowich, M. (ed.), (1991) *Granny Flats as Housing for the Elderly: International Perspectives*, The Haworth Press.

Leather, P. and Mackintosh, S. (1990) *Monitoring Assisted Agency Services*, HMSO.

Lewis, J. and Meredith, B. (1988) *Daughters Who Care*, Routledge.

Maclennan, O., Gibb, K. and More, A. (1990) *Paying for Britain's Housing*, Joseph Rowntree Foundation.

McCreadie, C. (1991) *Elder Abuse: an exploratory study*, ACIOG.

Morton, J. (1993) *Planning a Granny Flat: pitfalls and procedures.* ACIOG, 1993.

NFHA/MIND (1987) *Housing: the Foundation of Community Care*, NFHA/ MIND.

Nissell, M. and Bonnerjea, L. (1982) *Family Care of the Elderly: Who Pays?* Policy Studies Institute.

OPCS (1981) *General Household Survey 1979*, HMSO.

OPCS (1990) *General Household Survey 1988*, HMSO.

OPCS (1991) *General Household Survey 1989*, HMSO.

OPCS (1992) *General Household Survey 1990*, HMSO.

Potter, P. and Zill, G. (1992) 'Older households and their housing situation', in Age Concern England, *The Coming of Age in Europe*, ACE.

Qureshi, H. and Walker, A. (1989) *The Caring Relationship*, Macmillan.

Randolph, B. and Levison, D. (1988) *A Profile of New Tenancies*, National Federation of Housing Associations.

Rauta, I. (1986) *Who Would Prefer Separate Accommodation?* HMSO.

RICA (1986) *Dispersed Alarms*, RICA.

Rudinger, E. (1977) *Where to Live After Retirement*, Consumers' Association.

Secretaries of State for Health, Wales, Northern Ireland and Scotland (1989) *Caring for People: community care in the next decade and beyond*, HMSO.

Sundstrom, G. (forthcoming), 'Family care for frail elderly people in OECD countries: an overview of trends', in OECD, *Providing for the Long-Term Care of Frail Elderly People.*

Tinker, A. (1976) *Housing the Elderly: How successful are Granny Annexes?* Department of the Environment. (reprinted HMSO, 1980)

Tinker, A. (1980) *Housing the Elderly near Relatives*, HMSO.

Tinker, A. (1989a) *The Telecommunication Needs of Disabled and Elderly People*, Office of Telecommunications.

Tinker, A. (1989b) *An Evaluation of Very Sheltered Housing*, HMSO.

Tinker, A. (1991) 'Granny flats – the British experience' in Lazarowich (ed.).

Tinker, A. (forthcoming). 'The role of housing policies in the care of elderly people', in OECD, *Providing for the Long-Term Care of Frail Elderly People.*

Wall, R. (1989) 'Leaving home and living alone: an historical perspective'. *Population Studies*, 43, pp 369–389.

Warnes, T. (ed.) (1992) *Homes and Travel: local life in the Third Age*, The Carnegie United Kingdom Trust.

Wenger, C. (1984) *The Supportive Network*, Allen & Unwin.

Chapter 10
THE FAMILY AND THE MIXED ECONOMY OF CARE – CAN THEY BE INTEGRATED?

ALAN WALKER

The main purpose of this chapter is to explore the possible impact of the changes underway in the management and delivery of care services – changes that are commonly described as the move towards a 'more mixed economy of care' – on the provision of informal support to older people by their families. It is likely that the various other factors discussed in this book, especially socio-demographic change and growing female labour force participation, will have a profound impact on the supply of informal care. But policy is important too, in determining the context in which family care takes place and in the assumptions it makes, implicitly or explicitly, about the availability and supply of such care. Thus policy is influential on both the demand and supply sides of the family care equation.

The core of this chapter focuses on the changing relationships between the health and personal social services and families that are implied by the current attempt to develop a new mix in care provision, and on the policy issues that still remain to be resolved. This section is followed by a discussion of the sorts of changes necessary over the next decade in order to support the family system of care more effectively by ensuring that care is shared between the family and other providers. This discussion includes references to the factors that are inhibiting the extension of choice and the effective empowerment of older people and their family carers in decisions concerning care. My starting point is a discussion of the nature of the mixed economy of care and the policy context in which family care is provided.

The mixed economy of care

Discussion of the care of older people and other groups has been bedevilled by the use and misuse of value-laden terminology for at least the past 45 years. This is inevitable in such a politically sensitive field but it sometimes inhibits effective policy development and open public discussion. The obvious example is that much abused term 'community care', full of symbolic meaning and idealistic connotations but only a partial reality at the best of post-war times (Titmuss, 1968; Walker, 1982; Edelman, 1977). The term 'mixed economy of care' suffers from many of the same limitations, including lack of clarity. Rather than, as is sometimes suggested, occupying a monopoly or near monopoly position in the provision of care to older people, the public health and personal social services are, in fact, junior partners. They may still dominate the delivery of formal services, at least as far as home care is concerned, but with regard to the totality of care, the vast bulk of which is informal – from friends, neighbours and especially kin – their role is comparatively small. This fact has been amply

Diagram 1
The Welfare Triangle

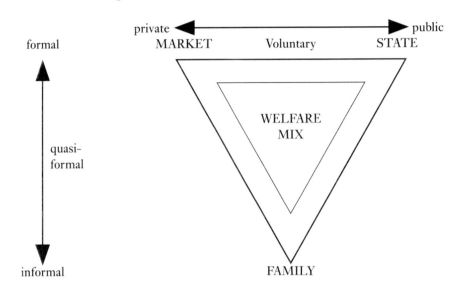

demonstrated elsewhere in this book. Even among confused older people, the group which places particularly heavy strains on carers, some four-fifths are cared for in private households (Levin, Sinclair and Gorbach, 1986). Thus, in so far as care is associated with any economy, it is largely a domestic one. It is necessary, therefore, to exercise extreme caution in using the term 'mixed economy'. (Similar cautions may also be made concerning the term 'independent sector' on the grounds that it is grossly misleading, since the providers it refers to are neither independent nor a homogeneous sector.)

Recent evidence may also be adduced to show that this applies not only to the UK but to virtually all European Union (EU) countries. Looking at the EU as a whole, the 1992 Eurobarometer survey found that the primary supporters of older people in need of care are adult children, followed by spouses; in all, two-thirds of the care received by older people comes from within their own families. Furthermore, these statistics ignore the fact that a large amount of care by disabled older people is unrecorded because it is self-care. The public social services are responsible for only 13 per cent of the care provided to older EU citizens, private paid help 11 per cent and voluntary assistance only 3 per cent (Walker, 1993, p. 28).

This mix of welfare provision – formal, quasi-formal and informal; public and private – has been helpfully represented diagramatically as a 'welfare triangle' (Evers and Wintersberger, 1986). As with all such simplifications caution must be exercised in interpreting the meaning of the so-called mixed economy from the diagram. What it shows is the *potential* sources of welfare not the actual provision. Diagram 1 suggests that the welfare mix consists of a balance between different providers, but in reality the 'mix' may be dominated by one provider. Looking at the welfare triangle as a whole we have already seen that the family is the leading provider, by a long way. Secondly, when viewed from the perspective of the family, the mixed economy is virtually non-existent.

This point was forcefully underlined by some recent research by Allen and her colleagues:

> *There was little evidence in this research of extensive packages of care being provided to help elderly people stay at home rather than enter residential care. Most help for the elderly people interviewed, whether they were still living in the community or had entered residential care, was being provided or had been provided by relatives, with the bulk of the care being provided by only one person. This was particularly true of personal care, which required help with intimate tasks such as bathing, washing, dressing, getting to bed and so on. Other members of the family might give help with more functional tasks, such as shopping, cleaning, cooking, laundry, transport and so on. Help from friends and neighbours was limited and rarely took the form of personal care. (Allen, Hogg and Peace, 1992, p. 300)*

These researchers go on to show that for many older people, there was virtually no help from *either* informal or formal sources: 'one third of those living in the community had little or no help from anyone with either personal or functional tasks, even though some of them were very old and becoming increasingly frail' (Allen, Hogg and Peace, 1992, p. 300).

Thus, the 'mixed economy' takes its least useful form as a macro-level policy concept, where it is one-dimensional. While it certainly has resonant meaning for politicians and policy makers, often as an ideologically endowed prescription rather than a description, from the bottom up perspective of older people in need of care, it is very rarely encountered and has little practical relevance.

The post-war 'equilibrium' in the British welfare mix, whereby community care was largely a matter of family care with substitute care in the community or residential care provided by local authority social services departments, was disturbed in the early 1980s as a result of a policy aimed explicitly at reducing the social services department's role and boosting that of other providers, especially the private sector. There is not space here to discuss the reasons for this change of policy and the departure from consensus it represented (see Walker, 1989). However, it is important to note that, although there are unique aspects of the policy being pursued in the UK, including its pace and scale, similar developments are taking place in most other advanced industrial societies. The key constituents of the policy being pursued currently in this country, such as the diminution of the role of the state and enhancement of the roles of the private, voluntary and informal sectors; the separation of provider and funding roles; care-packaging; case management and the tailoring of services to users (Friedmann, Gilbert and Sherer, 1987; Evers, 1991); may be found in other countries, although they are only rarely being implemented all at the same time. The pressures for change are common to all advanced industrial societies – socio-demographic, political, economic, the reassertion of individualism, grassroots and professional pressures – and the different weight given to each of them by policy makers goes a long way towards explaining the variations in policies between countries.

Thus in most comparable industrial countries the welfare mix is being reconstituted in a variety of different ways. In the UK this change is still underway and the outcome remains unclear. Certainly it cannot be assumed that the current changes will be permanent. But any slight shift in the welfare mix has implications for informal support and care for older people, because it is this sector that forms the bedrock of all contemporary mixed economies of care.

The policy context of family care

This brings us to the relationship between the formal and informal sectors of care or, more specifically, between the family and the state. Of course it is an *inter*-relationship, a two-way street, since any diminution in the caring capacity of the family has implications for the demand for formal care, as discussed at length in previous chapters. But the focus of this chapter is directed the other way and, seen from the perspective of policy makers, there are three main ways in which the provision of family care may be influenced. First, the state may attempt a variety of direct forms of intervention, from outright coercion (for example, prosecution for neglect) through to the provision of incentives, such as tax allowances or special benefits for those caring for older people and other dependents. Secondly, family help may be influenced, less directly, by the way that services are organised and provided to those in need of care and by the assumptions made about the nature and availability of such informal assistance in the rationing of formal care. There is an extensive literature, particularly in this country, on the considerable degree to which policy makers and prac- titioners have not only taken family care for granted but have made value judgements about who should provide care *within* the family (Moroney, 1976; Land, 1978; Walker, 1981; Finch and Groves, 1982; Dalley, 1988; Qureshi and Walker, 1989; Twigg, 1991). Thirdly, the government's general economic and social policies set the framework of material and social conditions within which individual families find themselves. Thus macro-level policies may increase or reduce strains in and around the caring relationship by, for example, influencing the levels of poverty and unemployment. In other words care *by* the community depends, in part, on care *for* the community (Walker, 1982).

These various factors impinging on the need for care may be represented in another triangular form (Diagram 2). Excluded, for the sake of simplicity, are those crucial societal-wide influences on the ability and propensity of the family to care, such as women's labour force participation rates, geographical mobility, family size and divorce rates, factors that are discussed at length in earlier chapters in this book.

With regard to the care of older people visible coercion has rarely proved a successful policy. Some countries, such as Canada (some Provinces) and Israel, place a legislative obligation on adult children to support their parents, but these are not enforced strictly. Such provisions echo those found in the English Poor Law. But even the Poor Law administrators gave little credence to the idea that the state could compel families to care for older parents:

> If the deficiencies of parental and filial affection are to be supplied by the
> parish, and the natural motives to the exercise of those virtues are thus to
> be withdrawn, it may be proper to endeavour to replace them, however
> imperfectly, by artificial stimulants, and to make fines, distress warrants,

or imprisonment act as substitutes for gratitude and love. The attempt however is hardly ever made. (Checkland and Checkland, 1974, p. 115)

Diagram 2
The Care Triangle

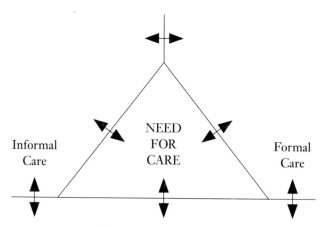

Socio-Economic Policies

This emphasises the fact that if informal care is given unwillingly it may lose its special qualities – particularly the *intrinsic* benefits such as emotional warmth, affection and interest – and could no longer claim to be a superior form of care. Indeed in this situation it can become destructive of relationships, inducing resentment and guilt in both giver and receiver (Qureshi and Walker, 1989).

As noted earlier, the formal sector, including the state as a direct provider or funder of other providers, is but a junior partner in care provision. Indeed for the past 45 years formal care has been primarily concerned with crisis intervention or long-term residential care. One important reason for the maintenance of this casualty orientation and the norm of non-intervention underpinning it is the flood-gate scenario. From the late sixteenth century to the nineteenth century, the primacy of family responsibility was enshrined in the Poor Laws, and the fear that state help, if too easy to obtain, would undermine family relationships has been present ever since. The words of an Assistant Poor Law Commissioner in 1834 have a familiar ring today, 'social ties... (are) now in the course of rapid extinction by the Poor Law'. From his study of the evidence Anderson (1977) reached the opposite conclusion:

The (legal obligation) to assist was often a source of tension between parents and children throughout the nineteenth century. The 'quality' of relationships was thus clearly worsened in these cases.

Contemporary research also provides no support for the assumption that official intervention would undermine family care. Indeed there are clear indications that *non*-intervention is more likely to put caring relationships under strain. Today it is still assumed by policy makers and service providers that state help, once offered, would inevitably be preferred. But in practice, those older people receiving services from their families do *not* seem to be anxious to apply for financial or other formal assistance instead (unless, that is, they want to relieve a perceived burden on their relatives – see below and Chapter 6).

In the Sheffield survey of older people and their families, although there was considerable unmet demand from those not receiving care, less than 10 per cent of those in receipt of weekly practical assistance from relatives or (in a few cases) neighbours, said that they would prefer such tasks to be performed by a home help (Qureshi and Walker, 1989). Most people preferred their existing family help even if a home help would have been available. What of those few who would have preferred a home help? Most frequently these older people did not exactly prefer formal help but wished to relieve a perceived burden upon their family carer. Most older people felt (and their carers agreed) that family members were the right people to help them (see also Finch, 1989).

This research also demonstrated that seeking formal help is only the final stage of a dynamic process in which the available sources of informal assistance have all been considered, and the costs associated with them evaluated, before any approach is made to statutory services for assistance. Moreover, judgements about the quality of informal help available are made by those with the most detailed and exhaustive knowledge of the informal network: that is, the members of the network themselves.

Current allocation practices in the social services show little respect for, or insight into, these prior processes in the informal sector. Statutory services are often delivered, and to some extent rationed, on the assumption that other family members, particularly daughters, should help in preference to formal carers, especially in tasks where no recognised professional expertise is required. Such services as home help and auxiliaries to assist with bathing have been denied to, reduced or withdrawn from older people who have local relatives, particularly daughters, available (Qureshi and Walker, 1989). Also it has been clearly shown that older people living with relatives are less likely to receive statutory help, no matter what their level of dependency (Charlesworth, Wilkin and Durie, 1984; Levin, Sinclair and Gorbach, 1986).

In the face of the pervasive expectation of non-intervention on the part of policy makers and formal providers, it is important not to lose sight of the fact that the provision of services can strengthen family ties. It is also important to remember that statutory services are often highly valued by recipients, a point I return to later. Additionally, it should be noted that the impersonal nature of help delivered through a bureaucratic structure may be seen as an advantage by some of those receiving help. Agents of an outside organisation are detached from past family quarrels or disputes, and have no future expectations of a return for services rendered. Equally, from the point of view of carers, there are sometimes situations in which an older person behaves less reasonably towards family members than towards formal or quasi-formal care staff. A number of family carers in the Sheffield study indicated occasions on which their elderly relative 'put on a different face', generally a more cooperative face, for people from outside agencies. Other evidence (Boyd and Woodman, 1978) suggests that this can be carried to the extreme in situations in which an older person's capacity for, or willingness to display, independence drops dramatically as soon as they are returned from a hospital or residential home to the care of their relative.

The myth of declining family commitment to care

There is no research evidence to support the idea of a bulging floodgate of demands waiting to burst forth from the family system of care. This is because, in most families, individual feelings of affect and reciprocity and normative values concerning the obligations of family members to provide care are mutually reinforcing. The provision of such care is regarded by all of those involved as being both right and unremarkable (Qureshi and Walker, 1989; Finch, 1989). Thus the main challenges to the family as a source of care will come from social, demographic and economic changes rather than from the provision of support from other sectors of the mixed economy, causing informal carers to 'down tools' and desert their older relatives. In fact, as I indicate below, formal care is more likely to help than to hinder family care.

Rather than formal, particularly public, services taking over the care functions of the family, it appears that these services substitute to some extent for the loss of family care. Recent research covering the EU as a whole shows that, in successively older age groups of pensioners, the proportion receiving regular help from spouses declines: from 54 per cent among those aged 60–64 to 16 per cent among those aged 80 and over. Conversely the role of the public services increases with age group, from 8 per cent to 20 per cent respectively (Walker, 1993, p. 28).

Despite the weight of contrary research however, it must be reported that the results of a recent Eurobarometer survey in the UK and other EU countries indicates that older people themselves think that the family system of care is weakening. Nearly three out of five older people in the UK believe that families are less willing to care for older relatives than they used to be, with 26 per cent being strongly of that opinion and 32 per cent slightly. The average for the EU as a whole is 67 per cent and it is interesting to note that only Ireland has a lower proportion than the UK of older people who think that families are now less willing to care than they used to be (Walker, 1993, p. 29). Such statistics are of great importance because they point to a worrying perception on the part of older people, but they must be treated with caution. As other chapters have shown, it is not so much a lack of willingness but growing constraints on the ability of families to care that are the main problems.

Changing the balance of care provision

The NHS and Community Care Act (1990) represented the culmination of the previous decade of community care policy developments and established a new framework for services. The Act and its antecedents *Caring for People* (Department of Health, 1989) and the Griffiths Report (1988) were intended primarily to change the mix of formal sector providers, in order to try to enhance cost efficiency by creating a quasi-market, and to increase the choice of care available to older people and others in need. The White Paper defined four key components of community care which together reflected the emphasis on promoting choice by expanding the alternatives to local authority provision. They are: services that respond flexibly and sensitively to the needs of individuals and their carers; services that intervene no more than is necessary to foster independence; services that allow a range of options for consumers; and services that concentrate on those with the greatest needs (Department of Health, 1989, p. 5). In the White Paper 'choice' is defined as 'giving people a greater individual say in how they live their lives and the services they need to help them' (Department of Health, 1989, p. 4). This is to be achieved in two main ways: a comprehensive process of assessment and care (or case) management, which 'where possible should induce [the] active participation of the individual and his or her carer', and a more diverse range of non-statutory providers among whose benefits is held to be 'a wider range of choice of services for the consumer' (Department of Health, 1989, pp. 19, 22).

The policy changes associated with these goals are currently taking effect and local authority social services departments are learning to become facilitators and regulators rather than straightforward providers. The outcome of the whole policy rests on the successful achievement of this 'cultural revolution' in the role of local authorities but, since this new role is still being realised, it is possible only to speculate about the implications of this change for the future of family care. This speculation takes the form of a series of seven questions, the answers to which will determine the precise nature of the relationship between the family and to her providers in the mixed economy.

First of all, to what extent will the intended shift in the formal welfare mix – from public to for-profit and non-profit providers – maintain the existing relationship between the formal and informal sectors? The obvious danger is that the same 'taken-for-granted' assumptions that have helped to maintain the primacy of the family over the past four decades will be sustained in an unmodified form, despite the fact that the nature of both the family and the care it provides is changing (see chapters 1, 2, 6 and 7). Most importantly, increasing longevity means that new intergenerational caring relationships are emerging – new in terms of both their duration and intensity – which require the adoption of longer term supportive strategies rather than short term casualty ones. Unless services adapt to this changing need for support on the part of informal carers, the demand for long term formal care is likely to increase as caring relationships are pushed to the limit. Thus the key question about the future interface between the formal and informal sectors concerns the ability of services to act in a supportive role to the family, a question which the debate about a mixed economy of care has so far signally failed to address.

Secondly, will it be assumed that more care can be squeezed out of the family? The danger here is that, faced with a severe shortage of resources, care managers may expect the informal sector to play a larger role in the provision of care. This would be a great mistake since all the available evidence shows that the family is as fully committed as it can be to the task of caring and that there is no spare capacity. Indeed for the reasons outlined above, any attempt to push the family into providing more care may be counter-productive.

These first two questions indicate that policy makers and service providers require a more sophisticated understanding of the dynamics of family care than they have at present. Such an understanding would form the basis for the more effective support of the family by services. An important part of this new approach is the recognition of diverse family types, depending, for example on kinship network structures, family history and ethnic or racial background (Wenger, 1989; Finch, 1989, Twigg and Atkin, 1991). In other words the family itself is heterogeneous – a mixed economy if you like – and this requires flexible responses from services providers.

An important element of this flexibility is the provision of direct funding to people with disabilities in order that they can organise their own care. The independent living fund (ILF) is a prime example of such flexible provision. Even though there is no statutory right to payments from the ILF and no right of appeal if requests are refused, people with disabilities seem to prefer having control over the money which pays for their services rather than have local authorities arrange help for them (Lakey, 1993). Also social services departments have long provided direct payments to enable people with disabilities to buy in their own services, such as home helps or occupational therapists. A study conducted in 1990 found that 59 per cent of social services departments made such payments either directly or through intermediaries such as housing associations (Hatchett, 1991). These payments represent a model of a truly flexible service – taking welfare pluralism beyond a narrow focus on the choice between different formal and quasi-formal providers towards genuine user power. But such payments are actually illegal under the 1948 National Assistance Act which forbids local authorities to make cash payment in lieu of services, and it is unfortunate that the government chose not to use the opportunity of the House of Lords amendment to the NHS and Community Care Bill to legalise them.

This raises a third question: to what extent will the local authority, as purchaser, be able to determine the way diverse providers interact with the family? The main problem here is that there are conflicting pressures on local authorities: on the one hand they have to stimulate quickly the non-governmental sector of domiciliary care, with the immediate imposition of the requirement to spend 85 per cent of Department of Social Security transfer money in this sector, while on the other they have to ensure the maintenance of standards of care and equity between different users. But new domiciliary services will take time to emerge in all parts of the country and, in the rush to contract new providers, social services departments may be tempted to compromise on the expectations that should properly be made of such services. With regard to the private sector there is always a conflict between the requirements of a contract and the need to ensure a commercial return on capital. Thus case managers' stipulations concerning the operation of services may be regarded by private providers as unreasonable encumbrances on their ability to make a profit. In the absence of any on-going system of regulation and inspection of domiciliary care, once contracts are awarded the quality of provision may be compromised.

This points to a fundamental weakness in the principle of diversification underlying the particular variant of the mixed economy of care currently being implemented. If diversity is seen as its greatest strength, then the downside to diversity is the difficulty of ensuring certain standardised methods, approaches and quality levels on the ground when services are operating to different management rules and provider motivations. Any failure by new or existing domiciliary care providers to offer high quality support to family carers and to respond flexibly to the changes underway in the family is likely to have a severe impact on the supply of family care in the future.

Fourthly, therefore, will local authorities be able to encourage the growth of new domiciliary care providers? Obviously this will differ considerably from one part of the country to another depending on the existing service infrastructure (just as the initial spread of private residential and nursing homes was uneven territorially). And there is a supplementary question concerning the extent to which the process of pluralistic service innovation will result in widely different services being available to older people with similar needs in different parts of the country. This speculation can be answered to some extent by reference to the impact of innovations in the social services over the last decade or so.

While there are several very positive features of the many experiments in community care that have taken place in recent years; by definition the process of pluralistic service innovation has been haphazard and confined to very small local areas and, therefore, it has tended to reinforce territorial disparities in social services. The process of innovation has also reflected the political colour of local authorities and the desire of the government to sponsor particular kinds of change. The result of this fragmentary innovation is that people with similar needs in different parts of the country, or sometimes local area, are experiencing very different forms of care, based on different assumptions, different sorts of providers and, crucially, different rights of access. Incidentally this also raises a fundamental issue of human rights. In general, these sorts of innovations were not sought by the older people concerned, nor did they have an equal voice to that of the service providers in the process of innovation – they were top-down innovations – although, of course, the honourable motives of those responsible for the new developments are not in doubt. But older people and other groups of people with disabilities have, in effect, been used as guinea pigs in the testing of service innovations.

This is an issue that those who argue against the standardisation associated with universalism must confront. At the same time it must be acknowledged that the universalism associated with the UK model of personal social services is a very minimal one indeed and moreover – in contrast to, say, provision in Scandinavian countries – one that is characterised by territorial injustice in the formal sector (Bebbington, *et al*, 1990). Thus long-term underfunding has created a growing 'care gap' with the result that most older (and younger) people with disabilities in receipt of care do not get sufficient assistance to cover all of their care needs, and many receive none at all. Moreover there is no evidence of a wide dissemination of innovatory approaches, such as paid neighbours, which instead remain largely confined to the 'demonstration projects'. Yet these projects are sometimes quoted as examples of how the welfare mix has changed. In the research on older people living in the community and in residential care, Allen and her colleagues (1992, p. 302) found that:

> *There was little evidence of use by either sample of elderly people of private or voluntary sector community services. The organised use of 'paid neighbours' or of a recognised variety of helpers aiming to maintain elderly people at home, as found in the Kent Community Care Scheme and other*

schemes, was not found at all. Perhaps this indicates how difficult such schemes are to replicate without the resources of a 'demonstration' model.

In the short term the outlook does not seem to be very favourable because it will take time to establish new domiciliary providers and, therefore, many local authorities will be forced to comply with the '85 per cent rule' by using the bulk of the money to purchase private residential care. The remaining 15 per cent is unlikely to be sufficient for social services departments to set up demonstration projects. If the outcome is indeed an increase in private institutional care, even in the short term, this would be perverse, since everyone agrees that what families require is more support within the community. (This pessimistic prediction may be confounded by rapid diversification in the private residential care home sector, though whether this could generate sufficient high quality services in every locality is an open question.)

Fifthly, how will the conflict between choice and rationing be resolved? The professed aim of increasing choice and sensitivity to user requirements is likely to be compromised by the process of assessment which is inevitably required to ration resources. The process of assessment is bound to limit individual choice and user influence while, conversely, enhancing the power of bureau-professionals acting as case managers. Moreover while users do not have a right to elect to be assessed and while there are no safeguards – such as an appeals procedure – for those who disagree with professional assessments, choice will come a poor second place to rationing.

The distribution of the personal social services has never been based on legally enforceable rights. The only rights in this field have been granted through the social security system – for example, the attendance allowance and payments for those entering private homes. But even the limited right to social security board and lodging payments that older people had in order to enter private residential homes has been replaced by care management discretion. Since April 1993 financial assessments for residential and nursing home support have come under the National Assistance Act. This gives local authorities the discretion to increase personal allowances or to delay selling an older person's property. The Act also makes local authorities responsible for care costs. Thus it is likely that payments for care will become a bureaucratised transaction between local authorities and proprietors. This does not have to be the outcome, but past performance suggests that residents will be expected to part with their benefit books and money and, with them, the dignity that accompanies the right to make payments themselves.

When coupled with the parallel changes taking place within the National Health Service, there is a clear danger that hospital care which is free at the point of use will be replaced to some extent by discretionary social care which will have charges levied on it. Thus alongside the expansion in private residential and nursing homes there has been a decline in the average length of stay for older people in geriatric wards (from 77.5 days in 1979 to 44.8 days in 1986), and it is now very common for older people to move directly from hospital to nursing homes. Moreover the NHS has already radically reduced its continuing care facilities for older people in anticipation of the implementation of the NHS and Community Care Act (1990).

These developments serve to remind us that the welfare mix is not necessarily one-dimensional even with regard to the formal sector. It is not a simple matter of a state/non-state or 'dependent'/'independent' dichotomy because care may derive from different sources *within* the state. Thus, in the past, professionals in the health service and personal social services have often vied competitively for control over the welfare of older people. During the 1980s, because the private sector was the only one expanding in line with or ahead of need, medical consultants were able to by-pass social services staff and arrange a direct transfer from hospital to private home. The new community care system will put a brake on this exercise of professional power and, therefore, may result in a new source of conflict between the health and social services.

The shift within the welfare mix from public to private and voluntary provision also affects citizenship rights in other ways. For example, lines of accountability become less straightforward. Who is responsible: the service provider, the case manager or the local councillor? The increasing prominence given to equal opportunities policies by social services departments will be diminished in significance by the atomisation of care provision under a cost-effectiveness imperative. Similarly the option of choosing public provision instead of private or voluntary care will be closed off.

Sixthly, what financial contribution will the family be expected to make to the formal care of its older relatives? I have already mentioned the potential loss of income rights associated with the new system. In addition, increasing financial contributions are being expected of older people and their families, both of which may create resentment and, thereby, contribute to a weakening of the family care system. Successive generations have built up an expectation of financial and property inheritance, an expectation that was enhanced by the housing policies of the 1980s. Although the research evidence shows that such transfers are relatively small (Hamnett, 1992), the expectation continues to be present (see chapter 8). Thus inheritance is part of the complex matrix of intergenerational relations and obligations on which the family care system is founded and policy-makers tinkering with it should exercise extreme caution. But caution does not seem to have been the guiding principle, and the expectation of contributions from older people and, either directly or indirectly, from other relatives, may be counter-productive in creating resentment on the part of family members.

In a similar vein it is important for the policy makers to recognise that increases in family poverty over the last decade have weakened the domestic economies of many families. If this continues it will affect the ability of some families to provide support, for example by constraining their opportunities to visit older relatives. Also continuing poverty among a significant minority of older people is an important factor in limiting their ability to care for themselves. This harks back to the discussion earlier about the need to care *for* the community, or the family, if it is to be expected to go on being the primary source of care.

Finally, the $64,000 question is, will the needs of older people and their family carers be taken fully into account in determining what *level* of service is needed and what *type* of provision is appropriate? The guidance accompanying the Act emphasises the importance of values based on user choice shaping service specifications, contracts and quality control. However, apart from the important legal right to a choice of a residential home (providing it is not a public one), there are no concrete proposals for empowering or, at least, involving older users and carers. In the absence of clear guidelines for such involvement it is likely that professional opinions will continue to dominate. This is signalled to some extent in the language employed in the White Paper: 'managers of care packages', 'case managers' and 'caring *for* people'. Thus, rather than determining their own packages of care, the impression is given that service users will continue to be seen as passive receivers of care. Similar signals are given by the prominence allocated to care (or case) management. This can be either administration centred or user centred. In the context of the pre-eminence given to the goals of value for money and economic efficiency the clear danger is that care management is likely to prove to be primarily an administrative tool for rationing and cost containment. If this happens it will constrain the potential of the care management role to orchestrate a truly supportive network for older people and will result in the perpetuation of the present situation of over-reliance on family carers.

There is a further contradiction between the goal of extending choice and other motivations behind the present policy of community care. The problem is not the desire to stimulate a range of providers but the premium placed on non-state or 'independent' forms of care and the mechanism chosen to encourage them. Thus local authorities are expected to employ competitive tendering or other means of 'testing the market' for the production of care. This gives a rather slanted meaning to the mixed economy of care. For example, the White Paper suggested that one of the ways in which social services departments could promote a mixed economy of care is by 'determining clear specifications of service requirements, and arrangements for tenders and contracts' (DoH, 1989, p. 23). But evidence from the US indicates that competitive tendering may actually *reduce* the choice available by driving small producers out of contention (Demone and Gibelman, 1989). This is likely to affect specialist provision for some minority group needs, such as those for older ethnic minorities and particular disability groups.

These are the key questions concerning the policy that is currently evolving and the future relationship between the formal and informal sectors of care and the viability of the new mixed economy of care rests on the answers to them. It must be emphasised that the commentary in this section of the chapter is speculative and, as such, awaits the emergence of some hard evidence in the implementation of the NHS and Community Care Act (1990). The shift in the welfare mix that is underway currently could have a very beneficial impact on the ability of the family to care for the next generation of older people, but only if the new system does not overburden the family with expectations and if traditional service provider assumptions about the nature and availability of family care are adapted to changed circumstances. If it fails to make this transition in thinking and approach, the new system is likely to have a deleterious effect on the caring capacity of the family.

Towards shared care and user empowerment

The surest way in which a mixed economy of care can enhance the ability of the family to meet the needs of future generations of older people with disabilities is for formal and quasi-formal service providers to work in partnership with families: in short, to share care. How might care be shared more effectively between the various providers in the mixed economy?

In the first place, older service users or potential users and their family carers must be centrally involved in decisions concerning the need for and supply of care services. This chimes in unison with the emphases on user choice and involvement in the White Paper and policy guidelines. Unfortunately neither went far enough in developing concrete proposals for user involvement or empowerment. Thus, when viewed from the perspective of service users, the conception of user involvement underlying the present changes is a very restricted one based on a simplistic market analogy (Walker, 1991a, 1992). The Griffiths Report, White Paper and NHS and Community Care Act all derive from what is, in essence, a limited form of supermarket-style consumerism which assumes that, if there is a choice between 'products', service users will automatically have the power of 'exit' from a particular product or market. Of course, even if this is true in markets for consumer goods, in the field of social care many older people are mentally disabled, frail and vulnerable, they are not in a position to 'shop around' and have no realistic prospect of exit. In other words the concept of 'active consumers' is not entirely appropriate with regard to the great majority of older people in need of care, whose voices are often too quiet to be heard in the market place.

The only way that frail and vulnerable service users can be assured of influence and power over service provision is if they, or their advocates, are guaranteed a 'voice' in the organisation and delivery of services. This would, in turn, ensure that services actually reflected their needs. In practice, the weaker form of consumer consultation being pursued currently consists of no more than an occasional survey among users together with minimal individual consultation at the point of assessment. Despite official acceptance of the central principle of making services more responsive to users, in practice the DoH policy and guidelines are silent on how user involvement can become a reality.

In contrast to the consumer orientated model of care, the user-centred or empowerment approach would aim to involve users in the development, management and operation of services as well as in the assessment of need. The intention would be to provide users and potential users with a range of realisable opportunities to define their own needs and the sort of services they require to meet them. Both carers and cared for would be regarded as potential service users. Where necessary the interests of older people with mental disabilities would be represented by independent advocates. Services would be organised to respect users' rights to self-determination, normalisation and dignity. They would be distributed as a matter of right rather than discretion, with independent inspection and appeals procedures, and would be subject to democratic oversight and accountability.

In order to realise the goal of user involvement local authorities and direct care providers must develop explicit strategies to achieve it. The essential ingredients of such a strategy are positive action – to provide users and potential users with support, skills training, advocacy and resources – so that they can make informed choices, and access – the structures of both the facilitating and the providing agency must afford opportunities for genuine involvement. According to Croft and Beresford (1990, p. 24):

Unless both are present people may either lack the confidence, expectations or abilities to get involved, or be discouraged by the difficulties entailed. Without them, participatory initiatives are likely to reinforce rather than overcome existing race, class, gender and other inequalities.

Thus user involvement must be built into the structure and operations of services and not bolted-on.

Secondly, change is necessary in the organisation and operation of formal services. The concept of social support networks is particularly helpful in emphasising the need for formal and informal helpers to cooperate, share tasks and decision-making and 'interweave' with each other (Whittaker and Garbarino, 1983). This means that care would take the form of coordinated 'packages' in which both formal and informal carers would act as parts of a team. This purposive integration of informal carer and formal provider(s) has also been referred to as a 'care partnership' (Allen, 1983) and 'sensitive interweaving' (Bayley, 1980). According to Wenger (1984, p. 192): 'This approach calls for a more integrated perspective of service provision where the personnel of different agencies adopt a cooperative stance, sharing tasks and information in order to provide a cohesive support package.' As indicated earlier it is as important for providers *within* the public sector to cooperate as it is for cooperation to exist between the public sector and non-public providers.

Thirdly, there has to be an open policy of supporting informal carers and regarding their needs as having the same priority as those of users (recognising, of course, the frequent conflicts of interest involved). In the typology developed by Twigg and Atkin (1991) this would mean agencies shifting from regarding carers as 'resources', as part of the taken-for-granted context of care with only a marginal concern for the carers' well-being, to seeing them as 'co-workers' or 'co-clients'.

The most important method of supporting the carer is by providing the user with an appropriate level and quality of service (Twigg, Atkin and Perring, 1990). If it is possible to maximise the well-being and independence of the user this will relieve both the physical strain and the mental anxiety of the informal carer. This calls for increased domiciliary care provision, in which there are currently considerable 'care gaps', rather than residential care which is in excess supply.

Research by Levin and her colleagues (1983, 1985) indicates the enormous potential significance of domiciliary care in supporting the carers of older people with mental infirmity. As well as showing the inverse relationship between the burdens borne by carers and home care services received by their older relatives, this research demonstrated the high relevance of these services to the needs of carers. Home care is the most appropriate form of service to address the problems carers face – such as the need for relief from household tasks, providing carers with a break and a chance for an ordinary conversation with the person they are caring for. Carers wanted more home care support. Most importantly though, this research illustrated the beneficial impact of the home care service on the well-being of informal carers. Home helps considerably reduced strain among carers and improved their psychological health. Thus by listening to the needs of carers, domiciliary care services can contribute enormously to enhancing the quality of the relationship between these carers and frail older people. This emphasises the importance of the role of local authorities as stimulators of more domiciliary care provision and the risk that, under pressure from the '85 per cent rule', resources will continue to flow either directly into private sector homes or half-hearted diversifications into the domiciliary sector.

Fourthly, change must be initiated in professional values and attitudes within the formal sector so that cooperation and partnership with users is regarded as a normal activity. This does not mean that service provision must be deprofessionalised if shared care based around user involvement is to flourish, but rather that the role of professionals and para-professionals must change in order to share power with users.

Fifthly, the previous two points suggest a major transformation in training and re-training for service personnel. Thus the emphasis in training would shift away from autonomous expertise and individual diagnosis towards skills for working in partnership with users and encouraging community participation. The research by Allen et al., (1992) on service provision and receipt by older people shows that social workers and home carers often lack the skills to operate in a more flexible, open and empowering way. It is questionable, to say the least, whether hurriedly put together domiciliary services, driven primarily by cost efficiency, will be able to train workers in empowerment.

Sixthly, a new approach to the provision of community care services is required. It is important to reorientate policy makers and formal service providers away from a short-term, casualty perception of need towards a longer-term strategy of prevention, for example the prevention of dependency and traumas such as carer breakdown. The function of responsible social care should not be confined to the management of stress, but should also encompass prevention and rehabilitation.

Finally, shared care based on user-involvement is not a cheap option, it is usually time consuming and costly. Therefore there is a need for increased resources in the mixed economy of care not only to improve the choice and quality of services but also to ensure that they provide sufficient space for user-involvement. Again, the recent research by Allen et al., (1992) found that many social workers and home help organisers were 'struggling' with the move from a service-led to a needs-led culture. They wanted to offer a person-centred approach to the delivery of care but this seemed to slip from their grasp as they recognised the overwhelming economic and political pressure to ration and prioritise services. It is also important that resources continue to be allocated to enable older people with disabilities to organise their own services, for example through the attendance allowance and independent living fund.

Thus the key components of an effective policy of shared care and user involvement are: resources, training, information, equal access, clear rights and entitlements, forms of redress, time and, if necessary, advocacy (Croft and Beresford, 1990, p. 42). In addition, if specific local authority initiatives are to contribute to wider policy development, then there must be research and evaluation and the dissemination of good practice.

All of this implies a cultural revolution not just among local authorities but national policy makers and all service providers as well. A sea-change is required to shift from provider-led models of home care to a partnership in which users' needs are uppermost. This would bring benefits to all parties: users, including older people, seem to prefer a more flexible and open approach to service provision (Qureshi, Challis and Davies, 1989); service providers will find their job more rewarding; and policy makers will find that the caring capacity of the family will be fully utilised.

Turning theory into practice

'Empowerment' is an ivory tower academic concept that must be turned into reality by a programme of practical action. This means commitment at all levels and the allocation of resources. The assessment process is crucial: do older people and their carers have a full opportunity to articulate their own needs in their own terms – not service provider categories? Do they feel inferior to service providers/assessors or equal to them? If people cannot articulate their own needs are there advocates to help them? Do staff act like 'experts' or in a way that suggests that they have something to learn from the real experts? Is there scope for self or group assessments? How will we know if a policy of empowerment is working? Most of what I have been discussing concerns processes but, of course, success is judged on the basis of outcomes. Evidence of empowerment may be measured by a simple checklist that can be modified to fit specific circumstances:

- are older users/potential users consulted about what package of services are required to meet their various needs?
- are older people able to exercise any choice about the type of services they receive?
- are they able to make choices about the level of services they receive?
- are family carers consulted independently of older users/potential users?
- where older people are unable to exercise effective choice for reasons of disability or frailty are there independent advocates to speak for them?
- are users, carers, advocates involved in managing agencies, including the setting of goals, and monitoring the operation of services?

It is also essential to have a process of user auditing where older people are asked what they think of a service and what they value about it. Indeed the simple process of asking people helps to make them feel more powerful.

Conclusion

The key message of this chapter is that the mixed economy of welfare is a top-down invention of policy makers intended to prescribe what they believe *should* take place rather than a description of existing reality in which care comes primarily from the informal sector and, seen from the perspective of users, is not a mixed system at all. Moreover, because this present prescription is under-pinned by a strong preference for non-local authority provided care, it under-mines the notion of a 'mixed economy' of care even more. The consequent changes being implemented, via the provisions of the 1990 NHS and Com-munity Care Act, harbour both dangers but also great potential.

The danger resides in the mixed economy being seen by policy makers purely as a mechanism to ensure economic (i.e. least cost) efficiency. The fact is that the family is the most efficient form of care in these narrow terms. But the family is changing at the same time as there are increases in the need for care. Thus, regardless of who provides, the size of the whole mixed economy must grow in order to compensate for the coexistence of these two phenomena. Since the family is already over-providing care to older people, other sources of care must be found. In other words there has to be a redistribution between providers and with it, the realisation of shared care. Furthermore, because the period over which care is provided is getting longer it must be shared over time as well. Thus if a narrow cost efficiency imperative prevails it will constrain the ability of local authority social services departments, as coordinators and stimulators, to encourage new more flexible forms of domiciliary care and will raise and extend the work falling on family carers.

Yet, if the commitments in the White Paper and guidance concerning user involvement are put into practice (which means adequately resourced), thereby allowing the rapid expansion of user-orientated domiciliary services, then current policy developments have enormous potential. In particular they could herald the development of shared care, in which the family is integrated in a mix of other care providers, including public ones. The creation of a genuine mixed economy regulated and coordinated by statutory authorities committed to user empowerment, would help to ensure that the growing care needs of older people into the next century not only will be met, but also in ways that increase the well-being of both older users and their family carers.

References

Allen, I. (1983) *Short Stay Residential Care for the Elderly.* London: Policy Studies Institute.

Allen, I., Hogg, D. and Peace, S. (1992) *Elderly People: Choice, Participation and Satisfaction,* London: Policy Studies Institute.

Bayley, M. (1980) 'Neighbourhood Care and Community Care: A Response to Philip Abrams', *Social Work Service.* No. 26, pp. 4–9.

Bebbington, A., Davies, B., Baines, B., Charnley, H., Ferlie, E., Hughes, M. and Twigg, J. (1990) *Resources, Needs and Outcomes.* Aldershot: Gower.

Checkland, S. G. and Checkland, E. O. A. (eds) (1974) *The Poor Law Report of 1834.* Harmondsworth: Penguin Books.

Croft, S. and Beresford, P. (1990) *From Paternalism to Participation.* London: Open Services Project.

Dalley, G. (1988) *Ideologies of Caring.* London: Macmillan.

Demone, H. and Gibelman, M. (1989) *Services for Sale: Purchasing Health and Human Services.* London: Rutgers University Press.

DoH (1989) *Caring for People.* Cm 849, London, HMSO.

Edelman, M. (1977) *Political Language.* New York: Academic Press.

Evers, A. and Wintersberger, H. (1986) 'Introduction to the Basic Approach of the Project – Main Orientations and Findings', European Comparative Research Project on The Shift in the Welfare Mix, Vienna, European Centre for Social Welfare Research and Development.

Finch, J. (1989) *Family Obligations and Social Change.* Oxford, Polity Press.

Finch, J. and Groves, D. (eds) (1983) *A Labour of Love: Women, Work and Caring.* London: Routledge & Kegal Paul.

Friedmann, R., Gilbert, N. and Sherer, M. (1987) (eds) *Modern Welfare States.* Hemel Hempstead: Wheatsheaf.

Hamnett, C. (1992) *Inheritance in Britain: the disappearing billions.* London: Lifetime PLC.

Lakey, J. (1993) *Paying for Independence.* London, PSI.

Land, H. (1978) 'Who Cares for the Family?', *Journal of Social Policy,* vol.7, no.3, pp. 357–384.

Levin, E., Sinclair, I. and Gorbach, P. (1983) *The Supporters of Confused Elderly Persons at Home.* London: NISW.

Levin, E., Sinclair, I. and Gorbach, P. (1985) 'The Effectiveness of the Home Help Service with Confused Old People and Their Families', *Research, Policy and Planning,* vol. 3, no.2 pp. 1–7.

Levin, E., Sinclair, I. and Gorbach, P. (1986) *Families, Services and Confusion in Old Age.* London: Allen & Unwin.

Moroney, R. M. (1976) *The Family and the State.* London: Longman.

Qureshi, H. and Walker, A. (1989) *The Caring Relationship: Elderly People and their Families,* London: Macmillan.

Qureshi, H., Challis, D. and Davies, B. (1989) *Helpers in Case-Managed Community Care*, Aldershot: Gower.

Titmuss, R. M. (1968) *Commitment to Welfare*. London: Allen & Unwin.

Twigg, J. and Atkin, K. (1991) *Evaluating Support to Informal Carers*. University of York.

Twigg, J., Atkin, K. and Perring, C. (1990) *Carers and Services: A Review of Research*, London: HMSO.

Walker, A. (1981) 'Community Care and the Elderly in Great Britain: Theory and Practice', *International Journal of Health Services*, vol.11, no.4, pp. 541–557.

Walker, A. (1982) 'The Meaning and Social Division of Community Care', in Walker, A. (ed.) *Community Care: The Family, The State and Social Policy*. Oxford: Blackwell/Martin Robertson.

Walker, A. (1982) (ed.) *Community Care: the Family, the State and Social Policy*. Oxford, Basil Blackwell.

Walker, A. (1989) 'Community Care' in M. McCarthy (ed.) *The New Politics of Welfare*. London, Macmillan.

Walker, A. (1991) 'Increasing User Involvement in the Social Services', in T. Arie (ed) *Recent Advances in Psychogeriatrics 2*. London: Churchill Livingstone.

Walker, A. (1992) 'Towards a European Agenda in Home Care for Older People: Convergencies and Controversies', in A. Evers and G. van der Zanden (eds) *Better Care for Dependent People Living at Home: Meeting the New Agenda in Services for the Elderly*. Netherlands Institute of Gerontology (forthcoming).

Walker, A. (1993) *Age and Attitudes*. Brussels, EC Commission.

Wenger, C. (1984) *The Supportive Network*. London: Allen & Unwin.

Wenger, G. C. (1989) 'Support Networks in Old Age: Constructing a Typology', in M. Jefferys (ed.) *Ageing in the 20th Century*. London: Routledge, pp. 166–185.

Whittaker, J. and Garbarino, J. (1983) (eds) *Social Support Networks*. New York: Aldine.

Chapter 11
DISCUSSION OF FINDINGS

ISOBEL ALLEN AND
ELIZABETH PERKINS

The aim of this book was to examine and review what is known about the social and economic factors affecting the future supply of informal support and care for older people, with particular attention to care provided within the family. Although the review was focused primarily on the future *supply* of informal care, it was clear that this had to be placed in the context of the future *demand* for such care. The extent to which the supply and demand for informal care are in balance has important implications for the demand for formal health and social care services. It has been recognised for years that the main source of care for older people comes from family members. If this supply reduces substantially, particularly at a time of increasing demand, there are likely to be major problems in meeting the needs of older people.

The authors of the chapters in this book were asked to review trends in specific areas in which they had particular expertise and knowledge, and to attempt to assess the probable impact of these trends on the extent to which family care would meet the needs of the next generation of older people. We asked authors to use their knowledge and expertise as a basis for forecasting likely trends and to draw out the implications of these trends for policy development.

This was, of course, a daunting task by any standards, and was made more difficult by the fact that no one trend or series of trends can be looked at in isolation from all the other trends which were the subject of other chapters. So many of these factors are interdependent, and changes in one area can have far-reaching and unforeseen effects on other areas.

In addition, as the preceding chapters have shown, crystal ball-gazing is something which does not necessarily come easily to those who know a great deal about the past and present. It is often easier to predict the future with certainty from a position of relative ignorance. A little knowledge can provide a much more comfortable basis for forecasting than a broad and informed view of the world. But even the best-informed pundit can make wildly inaccurate predictions, as history shows. Perhaps the most important lesson to be learnt from the chapters in this book is the extent to which the authors ended up by posing questions to which they did not have the answers rather than by offering solutions.

The context

We asked the authors to look forward to 2025. The task was to look at the future supply of family care within the context of the family as we know it at present and how it was likely to change. But of course the authors had to look at demand

and potential demand for care, which is determined not only by numbers but also by the capacity of older people to look after themselves.

What are the main factors affecting the supply side of family care? First, there are the demographic factors, which can be summarised as depending on fertility and mortality which determine the *numbers* of adult family members relative to the number of elderly people. Secondly, there are the factors affecting *availability* of family care. These depend largely upon the extent to which the potential carers have work commitments, other family commitments such as child care responsibilities, and where they live in relation to the elderly person. Thirdly, there are factors which may affect the *willingness* of potential carers to care. These are subtle and can be divided into four main categories: (i) personal or social feelings of duty, obligation, responsibility and commitment; (ii) other family commitments, for example to spouse or children, or conversely as a result of divorce or separation; (iii) financial costs and expectations; (iv) perceptions or expectations of the role of the welfare state. All these categories have a strong interrelationship which may well affect the willingness of younger family members to care for older people.

But it is important to remember that family care for older people is not always intergenerational. In 1990, 72 per cent of men and 38 per cent of women over the age of 65 were married. Even in the 80–84 age-group 50 per cent of men are living with a spouse compared with 13 per cent of women. In the past the amount of care given by elderly spouses to each other has sometimes tended to be underestimated, but it has enormously important implications for policy, since any diminution in the amount of care from a spouse, however fragile, can often make the difference between an elderly person staying in the community or entering residential or nursing home care.

On the demand side the picture is by no means clear-cut. The future of family care for older people must depend on how much care older people are going to need. On the face of it, it looks as though increasing numbers of very old people are necessarily going to need more care, and, since most care is still given by family members it appears obvious that the supply is the most important factor. But the equation is not quite as straightforward as that, since a simple projection of need and demand as at present constituted may not be appropriate. The future demand for family care is clearly related to the capacity for older people to care for themselves. This capacity for self-care depends of course mainly on their state of health and dependency. But if they are in need of care there are a number of important factors which will affect their demand for care from others: (i) their marital status; (ii) if married, the capacity of their spouse to care for them; (iii) whether they live alone; (iv) their housing arrangements; (v) where they live in relation to relatives; (vi) their income and financial arrangements.

In addition, there is the all-important factor of the availability and accessibility of health and social care services, supplied by or through the health service or by or through local authorities, or, of course, bought in privately. The extent to which family care is needed depends to a large extent on the extent to which older people in need of care can gain access to support services, and conversely, the extent to which older people can gain access to support services usually depends considerably on the availability of family care.

There are a number of other factors which lie somewhat outside the straightforward supply and demand balance, but which have an important bearing on the future care of older people. They have been touched on only in passing in this book, which was designed mainly to look at social care issues, but there are clearly major implications for how older people are going to be looked after in future in terms of technological change, developments in medical and health care, and, not least, changes in economic policy.

Our brief to the authors was to look at supply and demand in relation to family care and to draw out the policy implications. It was a tall order, and this chapter attempts to summarise the findings and to bring them all together.

The future role of family care?

Will family care continue to play as large a role as at present in the care of older people? The authors of the chapters in this book are unsure. They are reluctant to say that it will not, but, on the other hand, most trends indicate that it cannot be assumed that family care for older people will continue at the level which has been fairly constant over the past decades.

In this concluding chapter we draw together these trends in the light of other evidence and examine what the implications might be, both for older people themselves and for government policy. We take as our point of departure the possibility that the supply of family care for older people may be less secure in future than it is at present for reasons which have been outlined in detail in the preceding chapters.

Demographic background

The demographic determinants of the age structure of the population are long-term trends in fertility and mortality. The population of all western countries has been ageing for over a century for a variety of reasons. Fertility rates have been falling but so have infant mortality rates. As Emily Grundy has shown, in 2001 it is expected that the size of the population of 65 and over will be six times greater than in 1901, while the numbers aged 85 and over will have increased twenty-five fold.

The 'demographic timebomb' is always on the horizon, with the 'threat' of increasing numbers of dependent elderly people making increasing demands on the state or family or both. By 2025, present projections indicate that those over 75 will account for 10 per cent and those aged over 85 for 3 per cent of the total population. Not only will the proportion of elderly people to the working population be higher than at present, but the proportion of very old people, potentially with high dependency needs, will be far higher.

But all demographic predictions have to be treated with some caution. Emily Grundy stresses that population projections are always subject to error and makes the important point that most mortality forecasts in the past have consistently underestimated declines in death rates at older ages. For example the size of the elderly population aged 85 and over in 1991 was 30 per cent greater than forecast even as recently as 1976, and the most recent projection of the population aged 75 and over in 2029 is 18 per cent higher than suggested even in 1989-based projections. So it is quite possible that there are going to be even greater numbers of very elderly people than predicted at present.

But who is going to look after these elderly people within the family? The majority of caring other than by spouses is carried out by daughters and, to a lesser extent, sons and daughters-in-law. Present projections assume completed family size of 1.9 for women born in 1965 or later, and these trends have been underway for some time. There are clearly going to be fewer children to look after elderly parents in the next century. But Emily Grundy argues that reducing family size may not matter in itself, since evidence suggests that the difference between having four children as opposed to two or three is minimal compared with the difference between having no children or one or two. In other words, it may not matter how big your family is as long as there is someone around to look after you when you are old.

But she goes on to argue that the most important factor is not so much whether an elderly person has children as whether they are available to look after the older person. And that, as we have seen, depends very much on changes in marriage, family formation, the labour market and physical proximity. It also, of course, depends on the extent to which they are willing to look after their mother and father.

Family and household change

There have been striking changes in the structure of families and households over the past twenty years. The 'nuclear family' with a mother and father who got married in their early twenties and then had two children was a fairly short-lived phenomenon, and was never as widespread as might have been thought. Recent trends have indicated increasing age at first marriage and birth of first child, decreasing marriage rates, increasing divorce rates, increasing remarriage rates and a big increase in cohabiting couples. This has also led to increasing proportions of births outside marriage – from 9 per cent in 1976 to nearly 31 per cent in 1992, over half of which were jointly registered by parents living at the same address. Overall there has been declining fertility and smaller families and an increasing likelihood that recent generations of women will be childless. The family structure has undergone considerable change over the past few years, resulting not only in far more reconstituted families but also in far more families headed by one parent.

The most important changes with implications for the future care of older people are changing marriage and fertility patterns. We have already seen that it looks as though decreasing numbers of elderly women will have ready access to care from family members, not only because increasing numbers of them have never married or had children, but because of increasing divorce rates. There remains a big question-mark over who will look after divorced elderly people who do not remarry, or even those who do remarry. The ever-increasing divorce rate among the children of elderly people also poses many questions about family obligations and responsibilities which may be divided among families and step-families, potentially overlaid with old resentments and lacking the import-ant factor of reciprocity which has such far-reaching implications in inter-generational care.

Responsibilities, obligations and commitments

Janet Finch suggests a move away from the idea that being related to someone brings a series of 'fixed obligations', which include the provision of personal care, to the notion of 'commitments'. She argues that there is little agreement in the population on what should constitute an obligation to look after parents, and indeed she reports that over one third of respondents in her study thought that children did *not* have an obligation to look after their parents when they were old. It was particularly interesting that the older people in the survey were less likely than younger respondents to say that children have a responsibility to care for their parents.

However, she argues that the evidence suggests that people feel that if someone in the family has responsibility for looking after elderly relatives it is the children. In attempting to resolve the seeming paradox, she argues that filial responsibilities evolve out of complex negotiations of commitments over time, through contact, through shared activities and, particularly, through each giving the other help as needed. 'This process of reciprocity – accepting help and then giving something in return – is the engine which drives the process of developing commitments...When people talk about responsibilities to their relatives they mean responsibilities arrived at in this way, through the process of developing commitments over time and between real people, not obligations which flow simply from the genealogical link...'

She makes the important point that the model of 'fixed obligation' may have some reality as the basis for responsibilities which spouses acknowledge towards each other, but argues that for other family relationships we need to see responsibilities as 'commitments' which build up over time between *certain* parents and *certain* children, rather than as obligations which flow simply from being an adult child. She reiterates the feelings of responsibility to provide care for spouses as an intrinsic part of the relationship, whether people have been married once or five times, and argues that spouse care will remain the most reliable form of informal care, as long as both spouses are alive at the point when one of them begins to need personal or nursing care. This, of course, means that men, with their shorter life span, are more likely to benefit from spouse care.

She relates the argument to the specific problem highlighted earlier of changing family structures as a result of divorce and remarriage. Her data suggest that the experience of divorce and/or remarriage is more likely to make relationships with other kin stronger rather than weaker, partly because of the need to 'belong' somewhere and partly because of other factors related to financial and practical support from parents. However, in examining the effect of divorce on the relationship with former in-laws, or even new in-laws, she argues that these links and 'commitments' may become more tenuous when someone has more than one set of in-laws over a lifetime.

Janet Finch's main argument is that filial responsibilities in the abstract cannot be relied upon as the basis for the provision of care, since so much depends on individual relationships and negotiations. 'This concept of family responsibilities as variable and personal is apparently recognised and endorsed as legitimate by the majority of the population...' She argues that this is how it is now and reflects how it has been in the past. The question is how it will be in future.

Will the carers be there to care?

One of the major factors affecting the future of family care is related not only to whether family carers will exist at all but also to whether they will be doing anything which might prevent them from taking on caring responsibilities for their older parents. Traditionally much research has concentrated on whether women 'in the middle' have been torn between caring for their own children and their parents. But in recent years, particularly with the ageing of elderly parents (and their middle-aged children) the emphasis has switched to women's increasing participation in the labour market. It has been recognised that their ability – or willingness – to care may be more and more affected by the extent to which they are in paid work outside the home.

But Heather Joshi's survey of the evidence suggests that caring activity for women has actually grown alongside their increasing participation in the labour market. There is absolutely no evidence to suggest that women cease to care simply because they are in work. All the evidence shows that women with caring responsibilities are almost as likely as others to be in paid employment and that increased employment rates have not affected women's commitment to caring. The main thing that people who work and care give up is leisure.

But there are undoubtedly other problems attached to combining caring and working, particularly for women with low economic resources. Much of the big increase in women's participation in the labour market has been in part-time jobs, mainly in the service or 'caring' occupations, which usually offer poor rates of pay, poor job security, poor promotion prospects and poor pension coverage. The 'two-earner' household is now much more common than the traditional partnership of breadwinner and housewife, but traditional patterns of domestic responsibilities have persisted alongside the expansion in women's responsibilities outside the home, with men taking on only few of the household tasks even where their wives are in full-time employment.

However, women still remain very much the junior partner in terms of pay – usually earning half as much as their husbands on average – and are even more likely to be dependent on their husbands' pensions in old age, meaning that they are particularly financially disadvantaged in this respect if they divorce.

She draws attention to the amount of money a woman who gives up work forgoes, not only in lost earnings but, perhaps more important, in pension contributions, particularly if she is a member of an occupational pension scheme. The importance of keeping at least a foothold in the labour market in order to avoid an impoverished old age is recognised by increasing numbers of women, and policy-makers would be unwise to ignore this.

Like Sally Baldwin, Heather Joshi argues for more flexible working opportunities for carers. She also calls for more flexible domiciliary care services to fit in with the needs and working hours of carers rather than the other way round. She suggests that there could be some form of carers' allowance along the lines of Family Credit and considers it important to give attention to protecting pension rights more adequately than at present. She concludes that so far informal care and the labour market have co-existed in compromise rather than conflict, but that for this to continue needs 'deliberate effort'.

Geographical mobility

Where older people live in relation to their family is clearly of great importance in looking at the future of family care. Tony Warnes and Reuben Ford found, perhaps not surprisingly, that the most important factor in whether families offered personal care was how near they lived to the elderly people. But they stress that living with families is not necessarily the recipe for greater happiness or higher levels of care.

Co-residence between elderly married couples and their married children always seems to have been unusual. What has changed is the extent of co-residence between elderly widows and married children or between elderly couples and unmarried children. There has been a marked decrease in the proportion of elderly people living with a child, from 42 per cent in 1962 to 14 per cent in 1986. Half of all elderly women live alone and the proportion rises to over 60 per cent of those aged 80 and over. All the signs are that the proportion of older people living alone will continue to rise.

Throughout this book we found strong evidence of the determination of older people to retain as much independence as possible, even in advanced old age. Tony Warnes and Reuben Ford suggest that high morale is not dependent upon living with others. They note that recent trends have shown that residential independence can be preserved alongside progressively closer proximity and interaction with children or carers. Around one third of moves made by older people bring them nearer the home of a child, but this does not mean that they want to move in with them. There is plenty of evidence to suggest that moves by older people may often promote family contacts, as long as independence is retained.

Housing

But maintaining independence depends on many factors. One of the main determining factors in a person's capacity to care for themselves is where they live and the conditions in which they live. Perhaps the most important point from Anthea Tinker's chapter is the need to provide more housing of a suitable kind for older people, particularly women with long-standing illnesses and disabilities. It is obvious that it is difficult for disabled people to care for themselves if they live in accommodation which has stairs, steps and inaccessible essential facilities.

The trend in recent years for increasing numbers of older people to live alone is likely to continue, and it is quite clear that much of our present housing stock is unsuitable for elderly frail people living alone. And yet the savings which would accrue in designing or adapting housing specifically for the growing numbers of older people are patently obvious.

One of the most important factors in retaining independence in old age is access to telephones and alarms, and yet again very elderly people, particularly those living alone, have more limited access to telephones than the rest of the population, and often show a reluctance to use both alarms and telephones. Anthea Tinker, among others, points to the important contribution which could be made by developing technology to help both older people and their carers.

Future generations of older people may well be more accustomed to the role of technology in their everyday lives.

Most older people enter residential or nursing home care from hospital or as the result of an illness or fall leading to fears for their safety or well-being at home. The living arrangements of many homes from which elderly people are admitted to residential care are unsuitable, and, in some cases, dangerous. Anthea Tinker concludes that '...if all homes were designed with disability in mind a great deal of trouble could be saved in future.' Perhaps we all need 'smart houses'.

Can older people look after themselves?

To what extent is there a possibility that care for older people can be provided more from their own resources so that their need to rely on family care is reduced? There has been substantial evidence in this book that the majority of older people do not have the resources to pay for their own care in later life, particularly if they need intensive personal health and social care. All the evidence indicates that there is going to be little change in this in the next thirty years since the majority of elderly people, particularly those over the age of 75, will be women who will continue to have much lower incomes in old age than men.

Although there has been much support for the notion that older people will become more independent in future because of the increasing affluence of society over the past fifty years, it is increasingly clear that the picture is skewed by a relatively small proportion of elderly people – mostly men – who have spent a long period in 'final salary' occupational pension schemes, ending up on high salaries which secure them a comfortable standard of living in old age. Dulcie Groves has pointed out that the majority of people, particularly women, reach old age with no income other than the state old age pension and means-tested income support or other benefits. At the moment, very elderly single women are among the poorest in income terms, while, at the same time, being the most likely to be at risk of physical and mental disabilities needing continuing personal care. The evidence suggests that this is going to continue well into the next century.

There are other problems as well. Older women are much less likely than men to have occupational pensions. Even people with occupational pensions may well fall into the 'occupational pension trap' – not quite poor enough to qualify for means-tested benefits but no better off than people receiving such benefits. In addition there is a danger that the trend towards early retirement will lead to a large group of people whose incomes are inadequate because they realised their personal pensions too early.

Dulcie Groves concludes that it is likely that, with declining state pension income and the possibility that some personal pension contracts may prove disappointing, most pensioners will continue to live on poor-to-modest incomes with, in many cases, an owner-occupied home as their only major capital asset. Divorced and single women will continue to be at particular risk of poverty in old age, as will people disabled before reaching pensionable age. Cohabiting women will be particularly vulnerable to poverty in old age since cohabitees in

Britain do not have rights to derived benefits in the same way as married women nor to relief from capital gains tax on widowhood.

There is a danger that policy makers will be misled by a relatively small number of affluent pensioners. Dulcie Groves concludes: 'In future we need to hear a lot more about median pensioner incomes and less about averages: more about individual women's incomes and assets and less about couples'.

A nation of inheritors or paying for care?

So property will remain the most substantial financial asset of elderly people, with owner occupation remaining at a high level. Many elderly owner-occupiers are 'asset rich and income poor'. However, maintenance of property will remain a problem, and there can be little doubt that a generation of middle-aged children are growing old with the realisation that it will be in their own financial interests to be able to inherit property which they can use as a source of income to help provide for their own old age. There are potentially new intergenerational tensions quickly emerging in a system which increasingly assumes that elderly people will contribute to their health or social care in old age by capitalising on their property assets.

To what extent can older people use their capital assets to help pay for their care? Chris Hamnett suggests this is, to some degree, already happening. There has been a rapid rise in the number of owner-occupiers – from 3.9 million (31 per cent of households) in 1951 to 15.5 million in 1991 (67 per cent of households). About half of all over 65-year-olds were in owner-occupied households in 1990.

There was a growing belief in the 1980s that housing inheritance would be of increasing significance, with estimates suggesting the numbers of 'finally dissolving owner occupied households' more than doubling from around 168,000 a year between 1986–91 to over 340,000 between 2026–31. There was widespread talk of Britain becoming a 'nation of inheritors'.

Hamnett stresses, however, that there are strong reasons for thinking that projected increases will not occur and that much of the equity tied up in housing will leak out before death. The number of cases of house inheritance is likely to remain stable at current levels and may even fall for a number of reasons. One of the most obvious reasons is that some 40 per cent of houses pass to spouses and are not available for intergenerational inheritance until after the death of the surviving spouse.

But even so that is only postponing the transaction. However, Chris Hamnett argues that there has been an increase in the scale and volume of equity extraction before death and that increasing numbers of older owner occupiers have been transferring their properties before death either to pay for residential care or, in some cases, to avoid payment. He estimates that this may well continue.

We would argue that there is every sign that it will continue and may even accelerate. There is little doubt that the effect of recent changes in government policies is that people are more likely to have to pay for care, whether short-term or long-term, in the rather grey area at the margins of health and social care rather than receiving it free at the point of use on the National Health Service or through local authorities or the social security budget. This does not only apply to residential or nursing home care. All the signs are that charging for social care will increase.

As more and more older people enter that shadowy area between health and social care, there will undoubtedly be much greater pressure for them to capitalise on their assets. The nation of inheritors looks much further off now than it did in the 1980s, and, if there is no change in social and economic policy, few middle-aged 'children' can assume that they will inherit their parents' property unless they have very healthy parents or they ensure that they themselves take over most of their parents' caring needs outside the acute health sector.

What about long-term insurance for health and social care? Few elderly or middle-aged people have thought that long-term health or social care insurance would be necessary. This generation of older people have assumed that the state would provide 'from the cradle to the grave' and few have the resources to start paying for it in their sixties and seventies. It is perhaps ironic that among those most at risk of having inadequate incomes in old age are those who depressed their earning power when they were of working age by substantial front-line caring in a household without other earners and who have no spouse from whom eventually to derive rights to pension benefits.

The future?

Lynda Clarke summarises much of the debate in this book in her final paragraph:

> 'The fundamental issue for public policy is the nature of the partnership between the family and the state that will enable the increasing number of elderly people to live their final years with autonomy and dignity. Care in the community will require substantial state support and intervention in negotiation of the responsibility for care. Informal care cannot be privatised. Care of elderly people cannot be hived off as a family responsibility...The policy agenda should include finance, pensions, social security, housing, employment, as well as the more obvious statutory and voluntary health and personal social services. Only then will the caring capacity of families be supported rather than exploited.'

Sally Baldwin asks whether anything can be done to maintain – or increase – the supply of family care for older people. To be successful, she says, first of all '...policy has to recognise and respond to the heterogeneity of carers...' and then to ease the strain and reduce the financial penalties of care-giving. She summarises the main factors which would help carers. She calls for creation of a truly independent income at a reasonable level and covering both long-term and short-term caring; greater ease of combining paid work and benefit receipt; ease of transition from caring back into paid work; and protection of pension entitlements, particularly in occupational and earnings-related schemes.

But this, she argues, is not enough and may well not be 'a sensible, productive or just policy...Focusing on family carers and their burdens is understandable, and welcome – but no substitute for the development of sound policies for later life...' She concludes that although better support for carers is an essential element for the success of community care, it is not enough, and recommends that every effort should be made to raise the capacity of older people in general to function independently as long as possible. She summarises the need for flexible employment, employment protection, financial security, better housing, more effective health promotion and health care and developing statutory, voluntary and private services in a more coordinated fashion so that they link with family care.

Although family care is a resource to be nurtured, it cannot stand alone, and she argues that 'the primary goal of policy must be to secure the dignity and quality of life of older citizens to ensure that they receive the support they need in the place, and manner, they prefer. The evidence from research,' she concludes, 'is that this would mean reducing dependence on the next generation – not increasing it – in order to preserve the essential qualities of these relationships.'

Alan Walker argues that there is a need for more shared care. He advocates a strategy for involving users and carers in the development, management and operation of services as well as the assessment of need; change in the organisation and operation of formal services so that there is more of a 'care partnership'; an open policy of supporting carers and recognising their needs as equal to those of users; change in professional values and attitudes so that cooperation and partnership with users is regarded 'as a normal activity'; a 'major transformation in training and retraining for service personnel'; a shift in emphasis in the provision of community care services from short-term crisis intervention to a longer-term strategy of prevention; and, finally, increased resources in the mixed economy of care, not only to improve the choice and quality of services but also to ensure user-involvement.

He warns of the danger that the present development of the mixed economy of care might be seen by policy makers purely as a mechanism to ensure 'least cost' efficiency. He notes that the family is the most efficient form of care in these narrow terms but that the family is undergoing considerable change and is already over-providing in any case. He concludes that the adequate resourcing of user involvement and empowerment is necessary to develop a genuine mixed economy of care regulated and coordinated by statutory authorities committed to user empowerment. This, he concludes, would 'help to ensure that the growing care needs of older people into the next century will be met and in ways that increase the well-being of both older users and their family carers.'

Possible consequences

There are a number of scenarios which can be derived from the evidence and discussion presented in this book. The authors have been reluctant to reach firm conclusions about the future of family care for older people, and it remains for us to draw out some of the possible consequences of their findings.

There are clearly many imponderables in attempting to look at the future and it would be foolish to assume that we can do anything other than point to a series of possible outcomes from what we know at the moment. Given the speed of change in the organisation of health and social care alone over the last ten years there is no reason to suppose that we are in for a period of little change. In addition, there are major changes which might ensue in other areas, for example, from a change in government, economic circumstances or a dramatic development in medical research. We do not pretend to be in the business of 'modelling', but in these final paragraphs we draw together the threads of what we know and what the preceding chapters have suggested.

On balance we take the view that the evidence suggests a decline in the supply of family care together with an increase in demand for care from older people, and we suggest that the increase in demand will also have a major impact on the supply side of family care.

We would argue that a straightforward increase in demand can more or less be taken as given, with the projected increase in the numbers of very elderly people with high dependency needs through mental and physical impairment. There is no evidence that there will be any major breakthrough in, for example, the treatment of Alzheimer's Disease which causes so many problems for family carers. The evidence suggests that developments in medical science may well keep more people alive for longer, but that the last years of their lives will still be subject to disability or illness which will require care from others. Health promotion and healthy living may prolong life, but there will still be major problems in promoting long-term independence among very elderly people with chronic degenerative conditions.

We would suggest that all the signs are that the demand for family care will rise for reasons related to a relative decrease in the supply of universally available formal health and social care services. The evidence presented in the preceding chapters has made it clear that few elderly people will have the financial resources to fund their own care needs above a very low level. Even if most older owner-occupiers tap into the capital resources tied up in their property, the relatively low average values of these properties will soon be used up if residential or nursing home care is needed, and there can be little doubt that expensive packages of community care will soon be subjected to much more rigorous means-testing than usually found at present.

It is increasingly recognised that the trend towards 'targeting' care services on those most in need is leading to a decline in the provision of preventative services, even for older people who are only just below the 'eligibility criteria'. Elderly people can no longer assume that they will have access to a cleaning or shopping service, which often brought the extra bonus of checking on their general condition. Family members are increasingly taking on additional responsibilities in providing or arranging care of this kind, if they are available, but, as we have seen in so many research reports, a substantial minority of older people have no immediate family. As these people will always have priority in the 'eligibility' queue if they are dependent enough, older people with any kind of potential family help will be very unlikely to receive this kind of service. The demand for family care will therefore rise among this group.

There are a number of dangers in the withdrawal of preventative services by health and social services. One of the consistent findings in the preceding chapters has been the overwhelming desire for older people to remain independent of their families for as long as possible. It has been apparent in the strong and growing resistance to co-residence with younger members of the family, and is found in many of the research accounts which actually listen to the voices of older people and their carers.

The preceding chapters have shown that co-resident carers give more personal and intensive care than carers who live elsewhere, and yet, with increasing numbers of older people living alone, their demand for care will undoubtedly increase. The extent to which non-resident carers will be able or willing to provide this kind of care in the absence of considerable support from health or social care services cannot be accurately assessed. But in our view, there will be an increasing move towards seeking a residential or nursing home solution both by carers and older people themselves as it emerges that the only alternative is a means-tested community care package which still demands considerable family care input. This solution may well be at the expense of an inheritance family members would otherwise have expected.

There is a strong argument to suggest that the point at which family carers weigh up the alternatives or options about the future of the care they give often comes at a time of crisis. They may well have drifted into caring without recognising how far the initial commitment would impinge upon their lives. All the research evidence suggesting that the majority of elderly people enter residential or nursing home care at a time of crisis or after a fall, illness or a stay in hospital often reflects the understandable behaviour of carers who feel that the price they have to pay for ensuring that an older person remains in the community is simply too great. The pendulum towards community care may well have swung too far in any case, and further pressure on carers without much stronger coordinated support from community services could produce a hardening of attitudes among carers which will be good neither for family relationships nor for the future of community care policies.

The aim of policy-makers over the past thirty years or so has been to keep older people living in the community for as long as possible. It has been recognised that the continuation of a high level of family care is absolutely essential in pursuing this policy. And yet, in spite of a decade of policy statements promising support for carers, as Alan Walker points out, much of the policy development in recent years has been geared to imposing a top-down solution on the future of care provision. Although the thrust of policy has been to increase choice and participation, the move towards real involvement by users and carers in the design and delivery of services has been very slow and patchy.

The changing nature of the family, the changing role and expectations of women, the changing world of work and employment, the increasing recognition that younger people will need to provide financially for their own old age have all been shown in the preceding chapters as vital components of the future propensity of people to care for older family members. The main theme put forward by most of the authors has been the need for flexibility in approach by government, policy-makers and professionals alike, together with a recognition that real partnership with families and carers is needed if care for older people is to be shared. All the signs are that this will become more and more essential if the present policy of community care is to succeed. It would be naive to assume that there are no resource implications, but there is plenty of evidence in this book that a wise use of resources now, for example in housing and technological advance as well as in preventative health and social care services, could help to provide a much firmer foundation for the future. There is also a pressing need for policies which look at the family as a whole and which adopt a strategic approach to the future needs of all the different generations encompassed within the modern family.

Printed in the United Kingdom for HMSO
Dd301255 9/95 C30 G3397 10170